HISTORICAL
ATLAS
OF
ANCIENT
MESOPOTAMIA

HISTORICAL ATLAS OF ANCIENT MESOPOTAMIA

NORMAN BANCROFT HUNT

Checkmark Books™

An imprint of Facts On File, Inc.

HISTORICAL ATLAS OF ANCIENT MESOPOTAMIA

Checkmark Books
An imprint of Facts On File, Inc.
132 West 31st Street
New York, NY 10001

For Library of Congress Cataloging-in-Publication data, please contact
Checkmark Books. Control Number 12803030.
    ISBN 0-8160-05730-3

Checkmark Books are available at special discounts when purchased in bulk quantities for businesses, associations, institutions or sales promotions. Please call our Special Sales Department in New York at:
(212) 967-8800 or (800) 322-8755.

You can find Facts On File on the World Wide Web at:
http://www.factsonfile.com

For Thalamus Publishing
Project editor: Warren Lapworth
Maps and design: Roger Kean
Illustrations: Oliver Frey

Printed and bound in Singapore

10 9 8 7 6 5 4 3 2 1
This book is printed on acid-free paper

PICTURE CREDITS

CORBIS/Paul Almasy: 117, 135, 176, 181; CORBIS/Archivo Iconografico, S.A.: 7, 13, 15 (right), 41, 55, 94, 102, 103 (top), 106, 107, 131; CORBIS/Yann Arthus-Bertrand: 75 (top); CORBIS/Dave Bartruff: 138. 140; CORBIS/Bettman: 26, 34 (left), 49 (bottom), 50, 57, 142; CORBIS/Burstein Collection: 1, 37 (top), 158, 182; CORBIS/Christie's Images: 125; CORBIS/Lloyd Cluff: 145 (top); CORBIS: 2–3, 53, 186; CORBIS/Gianni Dagli Orti: 9 (bottom), 12 (both), 14, 21 (top), 22, 24, 25, 27, 34 (right), 35, 37 (bottom), 38, 39 (top), 42, 43, 44, 49 (top), 54, 56, 58, 66, 68, 70, 75 (bottom), 76, 77, 83, 85, 89, 91, 95, 98, 101 (top), 101 (bottom),103 (bottom), 104, 105 (top),111, 115 (top), 116, 121 (top), 129, 132, 141, 145, 159 (bottom), 173, 179, 183; CORBIS/Françoise de Mulder: 121 (bottom), 123 (bottom), 126; Thalamus Studios/Oliver Frey: 11, 15 (left),17, 21 (both), 29 (top), 30, 32 (both), 33 (both), 45, 47, 72, 86, 88 (both), 96, 99, 105 (bottom), 110, 115 (bottom), 119, 120, 124, 144, 150, 155, 159 (top), 161, 164–5 (all), 166–7 (all), 175, 180; CORBIS/Jose Fusta Raga: 148; CORBIS/Chris Heller: 78, 79; CORBIS/ Hulton-Deutsch Collection: 65, 122; Thalamus/Roger Kean: 36; CORBIS/ Kimbell Art Museum: 22–3, 112; CORBIS/Larry Lee Photography: 149; CORBIS/David Lees: 28, 31, 62, 63, 112–13; CORBIS/Charles & Josette Lenars: 39 (bottom), 123 (top), 177; CORBIS/Diego Lezama Orezzoli: 87 (top); CORBIS/Francis G. Mayer: 40; CORBIS/Jehad Nga: 171; CORBIS/Michael Nicholson: 134; CORBIS/Chris North–Cordaiy Photo Library Ltd.: 67; CORBIS/ Stapleton Collection: 109; Thalamus Publishing: 48, 81, 84, 90, 91 (top), 91 (right); CORBIS/ Underwood & Underwood: 82; CORBIS/Ruggero Vanni: 128; CORBIS/Gian Berto Vanni: 139; CORBIS/Brian A. Vikander: 184; CORBIS/Reza–Webistan: 9 (top); CORBIS/Nik Wheeler: 8, 20, 97, 108, 168, 169; CORBIS/Roger Wood: 87 (bottom), 136–7, 137 (top), 146, 147, 160, 163, 170, 178; CORBIS/Alison Wright: 156–7; CORBIS/Michael S. Yamashita: 29 (below).

Page 1: Fragment from an Assyrian relief sculpture of a royal attendant with two horses, from the seventh century BC

Frontispiece: The two great rivers of Mesopotamia, the Tigris and Euphrates, finally join together to flow into the Persian Gulf. At the time when history began this satellite photograph would have revealed only sea, for the gulf stretched a further 150 miles inland to the point where the rivers now join.

CONTENTS

AN OVERVIEW OF ANCIENT MESOPOTAMIA

Lake Van

Lake Urmia

CASPIAN SEA

Carchemish •

MESOPOTAMIA

Tigris

Nineveh •

Ugarit •

Ashur •

Euphrates

SYRIAN DESERT

Byblos •

Diyala

ZAGROS MOUNTAINS

Karkeh

MEDITERRANEAN SEA

Damascus •

The lakes seen between the two rivers, right, are the result of modern irrigation programs.

Sippar •

Agade ?

Bablyon • • Kish

• Nippur

Tigris

Susa •

Euphrates

Lachish •

Uruk • • Lagash

LOWER EGYPT

Eridu • • Ur

• Heliopolis

SINAI

Memphis

ancient coastline

PERSIAN GULF

UPPER EGYPT

• Thebes

Mesopotamia is "the land between the rivers," specifically between the Euphrates and Tigris in southwestern Asia, corresponding roughly to modern Iraq. Some confusion in terminology results from the fact that the Romans called only the northern parts of the region Mesopotamia, referring to the southern areas as Babylonia; Arab terminology similarly refers to the north as Al-Jazirah and the south as Iraq-Arabi. Geographic conditions reinforce this division: northern areas are dominated by steppes through which the Euphrates and Tigris flow in deep channels, whereas the southern alluvial plain is marshland interspersed with desert.

Throughout the region, the typical climate is hot summers and relatively cold winters. Rainfall occurs in the winter and spring, but is unevenly distributed and concentrated primarily on the northern rim. For this reason, only the northern regions were capable of supporting rain-fed agriculture. The rest of the cultivable area was dependent on the flood plains of the Euphrates, Tigris, and their tributaries, or on the use of irrigation canals, with the central plain between the two rivers and beyond the river valleys inhabited only by nomadic tribesmen—the modern Bedouin.

Climatic conditions have remained relatively stable for at least the last 10,000 years; changes have taken place only in a few marginal areas. We should, therefore, expect to find settled

communities localized at specific sites and evidence of continued occupation over sustained periods; but this is not the case. Instead we find many ancient city ruins scattered in what are now desolate deserts.

The siting of these cities and evidence from hydrographic surveys suggest that both the Euphrates and the Tigris have significantly altered their courses over time, leaving once prosperous cities—particularly in Babylonia—waterless and uninhabitable. It is nevertheless within Greater Mesopotamia that we find the earliest developments of agricultural communities, urban settlements, and the growth of writing and mathematics, and the introduction of coded laws and formally structured societies.

These developments began in about 9000 BC within the foothill regions of the Zagros mountains, which lie within critical areas where rain-fed agriculture could be practiced, and where wild ancestors of plants and animals that could be domesticated were found. Although most of these very early settlements or "tells" now exist only as mounds in the desert, sufficient evidence has emerged for us to know that wild wheat and barley were being cultivated and that dogs and sheep had been domesticated. From excavations at sites such as Jarmo it is clear that the settlements were relatively large and permanent, consisting of mud-brick and stone buildings that had both domestic and public functions.

By 6000 these settlements had been extended into the plains, primarily by digging transverse trenches or canals to divert water from streams into irrigated fields. Again, our knowledge of these developments comes primarily from small isolated sites, such as Hassunah; but we know from these that there was increasing domestication of more varied plant crops, the introduction of pottery and clay figurines, and the establishment of extensive trade. Trade, immigration, conflict, and imitation saw rapid increases in population and wealth, the elaboration of architecture, and the beginnings of temple building, such as that at Eridu. Pictographic writing (later to develop into cuneiform texts) was introduced by the Sumerians about 3500, initially as a means of recording economic transactions.

There is some dispute whether the Sumerians were indigenous or if they had entered Mesopotamia as immigrants via Persia. What is certain is that they refined existing patterns of cultivation, extended the trading routes, and built the first true cities at Ur and Uruk (Warka). They were also responsible for evolving a new social organization in which secular control of the cities passed into the hands of dynastic rulers, who controlled what were essentially city-states.

Babylonians and Assyrians supersede the Sumerians

The fragile alliances between the Sumerian city-states were challenged in 2340 when an immigrant Akkadian official at the court of Kish usurped the throne and established a new capital at Agade. Using the name Sargon (True King), he campaigned for the overthrow of the city-state system and the establishment of centralized government. Through conquests in Persia, Syria, and Asia Minor, Sargon and his successors, in particular his grandson Naram-Sin, created the first Sumerian empire, which they maintained for more than a century.

Internal pressures, coupled with invasions by Gutian hill-tribes from Zagros, resulted in a resurgence of the Sumerian city-states and a period of anarchy, from which the Third

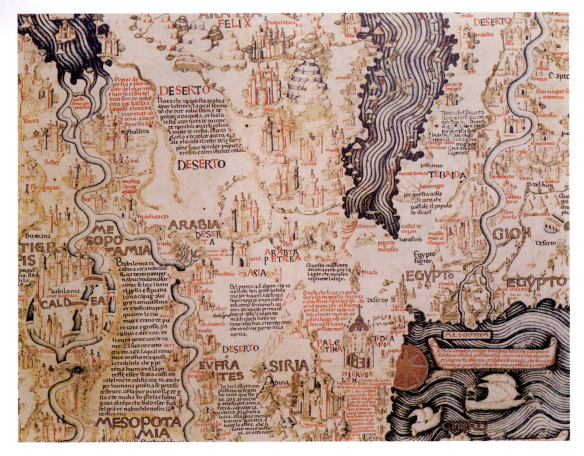

A 15th-century map shows the Middle East and Mesopotamia from a Eurocentric perspective—north and south are reversed from the modern convention, so that the Mediterranean is at the bottom right and the Persian Gulf and Red Sea are at the top.

Above: The Euphrates at Khan El Baghdadi, Iraq creates a sharp contrast between desert and vegetation.

Facing top: The Tigris winds throught the mountains of Turkish Kurdistan.

Facing bottom: An illustration of 1849 depicts the astonishment of Arabs discovering a giant head from ancient Mesopotamia.

Dynasty of Ur eventually emerged as the dominant force. Ur, in turn, fell to invasions by new immigrants, the Elamites (Amorites), in about 2000, followed by the re-establishment of dynasties based on the old kingdoms and city-states and reigniting feuding and conflict between various interests. The main protagonists in these renewed conflicts were Babylon and Mari; a conflict that was finally resolved by the victories of Hammurabi, the Babylonian king, and the establishment of the Babylonian empire in about 1800. Babylon was to remain as a center of political power for nearly six centuries, initially under the control of Hammurabi and his successors and, from 1595 BC, under the Kassites after Hittite invaders sacked Babylon and left it open to Kassite domination.

Shifting fortunes in Mesopotamia meant that by 1200 new forces were at play. Assyria had been the focus of contention between the Hittites and a northern coalition of Indo-Aryan tribes, the Mitanni. Initially, Assyria had been vassal to the Mitanni kings, but Hittite pressure had gradually permitted the Assyrians to gain a degree of independence. With the collapse of the Hittite empire, brought about by pressures from outside the region, the Assyrians were able to assert their dominance, retaining a religious center at Ashur but forming new capitals at Nineveh, Nimrud, and Khorsabad.

Assyria, in an attempt to consolidate its power over the entire Near East, eventually found its resources overstretched. Aramaean groups had occupied many of the former Hittite territories and one of them, the Chaldeans (Neo-Babylonians), had established themselves in southern Babylonia. Already weakened by civil war, the Assyrians were unable to resist a combined Chaldean and Mede assault on Nineveh in 612, despite receiving help from Egypt. Egypt's own attempts at gaining influence in Mesopotamia were subsequently prevented when the Chaldean crown prince, Nebuchadnezzar, defeated the Egyptian army at the Battle of Carchemish in 605.

Alexander's helenization

Following the Assyrian and Egyptian defeats, Mesopotamia was divided between the Chaldeans and the Medes, although the frontier between the two kingdoms is unclear. However, this division left the region vulnerable to Persian (Achaemenid) incursions under Cyrus and the annexation of Mesopotamia as part of the Persian empire in 539, where it remained until the campaigns of Alexander of Macedon in 331.

The break-up of Alexander's own empire following his death in 323 left Mesopotamia under the control of one of his generals, Seleucus Nicator, and marks the beginning of the Hellenistic, or Seleucid, period. Although Hellenistic influence is very apparent, it is nevertheless clear that the situation in Mesopotamia was far from stable. Ptolemy III of Egypt briefly annexed the area in 245, leading to a revolt led by Antiochus and opening the way for Parthian expansion and conflicts with Rome.

Invasions by Roman legions were largely

unsuccessful, and the Romans were defeated by
the Parthians on several occasions. Even
successful Roman campaigns were short-lived
and had little lasting effect. The threat to the
security of the Parthian empire came from
internal dissent rather than outside pressures,
culminating in AD 224 with a revolt led by
Ardashir, prince of Persia and founder of the
Sassanian empire, against his Parthian
overlords. Claiming descent from the original
Achaemenid kings, Ardashir set up a centralized
administration with a state religion,
Zoroastrianism; but conflicts with Rome, and a
series of attacks and counterattacks, led to
shifting control of the region.

By AD 637 Sassanian and Roman influence in
the area had been lost to a Muslim Arab
conquest and conversion to Islam became
general. Mesopotamia was still subject to
sectarian and political disputes between rival
Arab factions, leading to a division between Shi'a
devotees in the south and the Sunni in the north.

CHAPTER 1
THE FIRST FARMERS

The Late Neolithic period in Mesopotamia, dating from about 10,000, saw a gradual shift from subsistence hunting and gathering and a semi-nomadic lifestyle to the establishment of larger and more permanent settlements based on agriculture and the domestication of animals.

Early evidence of agriculture comes from sites such as Tell Abu Hureyra, now submerged beneath Lake Assad, and the prehistoric village of Zawi Chemi Shanidar in northern Iraq. While it is difficult to determine whether true domestication was occurring at this stage, it is apparent that there was deliberate management of existing resources such as the processing of wild grains.

These first villages may have been little more than temporary camps that were set up annually in areas where crops could be harvested as they ripened naturally or which were on the migratory routes of smaller game animals. Remains excavated from refuse dumps and hearths imply that migratory birds were a major feature of the diet and that gazelle were hunted; there are inconclusive suggestions that the herding of wild sheep may have been practiced.

The transition to sedentary life took place in these regions at least by 7000, at a time when Europe was just emerging from the Ice Age. Qal'at Jarmo, near Kirkuk, is the earliest known permanent settlement and has a series of archaeological levels contained within a 21-foot high artificial mound that show continuous occupation over a period of some 3,000 years.

The village consisted of about 25 mud-brick multi-room houses built on stone foundations, together with storage pits for emmer and einkorn wheat and two-row barley that had been grown from seed, as well as bitter vetch, lentil, and pea. It is evident that the people of Jarmo had domesticated goats, sheep, and pigs, and probably also dogs and cattle.

Bountiful rain

In addition to skills in husbandry, the populations of these early settlements were developing pottery and weaving and, possibly, some cult activities. Evidence for the latter is, however, inconclusive. It is based on the fact that some house sites were differentiated from others by size; but an equally plausible explanation could be that the larger buildings simply served a function as communal meeting places. A lack of cult activity is further suggested by the absence of any clear form of social stratification, such as might have been accorded to cult leaders, since there are no burials associated with grave goods that would act as status markers.

Despite advances made in the move from semi-nomadic to sedentary communities, the mobility of the populations of this period remained severely restricted by the necessity to stay within the rain belts to tend their crops. Some evidence points to greater longevity and higher birth rates, though the proof for this is uncertain, as well as that occupation densities were showing marginal increases.

Other sites roughly contemporary with Qal'at Jarmo, such as the early settlements at Tell-es-Sultan at Jericho and Çatal Hüyük in central Turkey, show a similar transition from managed resources to true domestication. It is significant that all lie within the mountain foothill ranges, where there was a critical minimum of 12 inches of annual rainfall, permitting rain-fed agriculture, and where flora and fauna were suitable for domestication.

MEDITERRANEAN SEA

Çatal Hüyük

△ Hacilar

Can Hasan

Rhodes

Cyprus

Khirokitia △

Nile

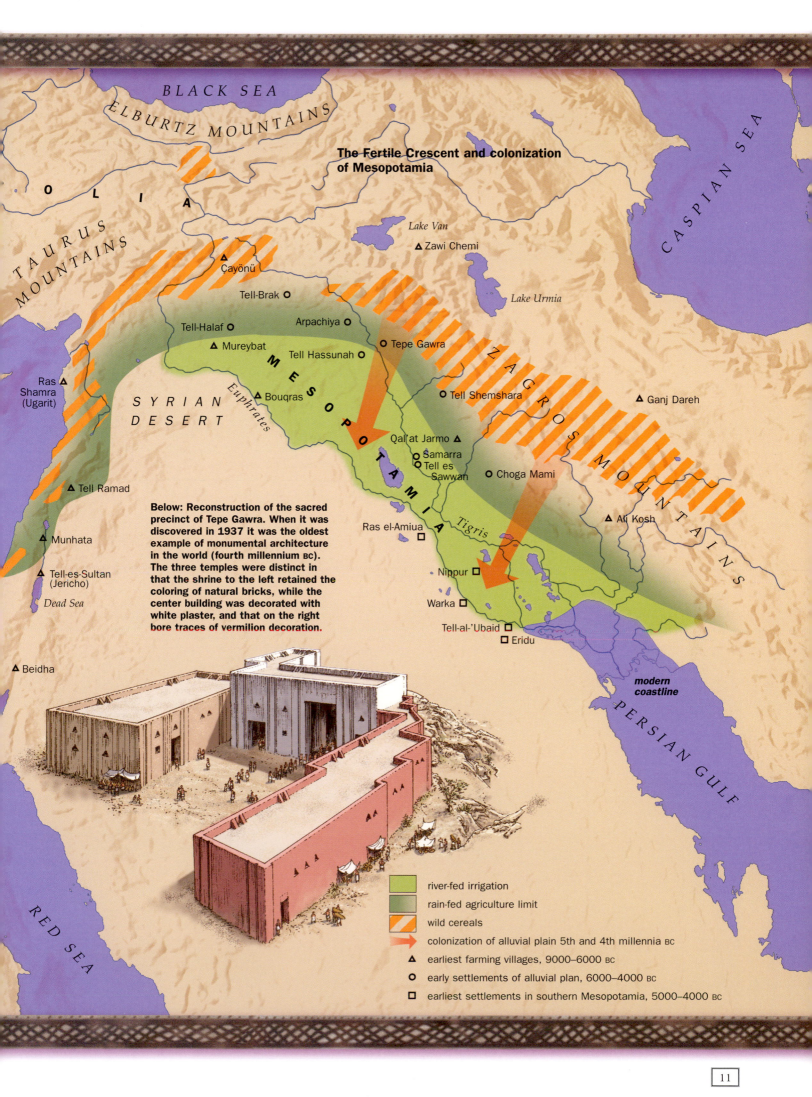

BLACK SEA

ELBURTZ MOUNTAINS

The Fertile Crescent and colonization of Mesopotamia

CASPIAN SEA

TAURUS MOUNTAINS

O L I A

Lake Van

△ Zawi Chemi

Lake Urmia

△ Çayönü

Tell-Brak ○

Tell-Halaf ○   Arpachiya ○

△ Mureybat   Tell Hassunah ○   ○ Tepe Gawra

M E S O P O T A M I A

Ras
Shamra
(Ugarit) △

S Y R I A N
D E S E R T

Euphrates

△ Bouqras

Z A G R O S   M O U N T A I N S

○ Tell Shemshara   △ Ganj Dareh

Qal'at Jarmo △
Samarra
Tell es ○
Sawwan   ○ Choga Mami

△ Tell Ramad

Below: Reconstruction of the sacred precinct of Tepe Gawra. When it was discovered in 1937 it was the oldest example of monumental architecture in the world (fourth millennium BC). The three temples were distinct in that the shrine to the left retained the coloring of natural bricks, while the center building was decorated with white plaster, and that on the right bore traces of vermilion decoration.

△ Ali Kosh

Tigris

Ras el-Amiua ☐

△ Munhata

• Nippur

△ Tell-es-Sultan
(Jericho)

Dead Sea

Warka

Tell-al-'Ubaid ☐
☐ Eridu

△ Beidha

*modern
coastline*

P E R S I A N   G U L F

R E D   S E A

🟩	river-fed irrigation
🟫	rain-fed agriculture limit
🟧	wild cereals
➜	colonization of alluvial plain 5th and 4th millennia BC
△	earliest farming villages, 9000–6000 BC
○	early settlements of alluvial plan, 6000–4000 BC
☐	earliest settlements in southern Mesopotamia, 5000–4000 BC

EXPANDING ONTO THE PLAINS

A major shift in population distribution occurred within the region shortly after 6000, when some northern farmers moved out of the rain belt and onto the Mesopotamian plains. Although earlier sites continued to be occupied, the establishment of new villages is of major significance, since they lay outside the rain-fed areas.

Right: This tomb figurine of c.5800 BC—a geometric abstraction of a woman representing a mother goddess—was found at Tell-es-Sawwan.

Below: A neolithic jar with incised motifs of c.6000 BC from Hassunah.

Movement away from the rain belt can be explained by the development of artificial irrigation, by drawing water off the Tigris and channeling it into fields. The earliest phase of this period is known as Hassunah, after a small site near Mosul. Excavated in AD 1943–44 by Seton Lloyd and Fuad Safar, Hassunah is a low tell (mound) in which a series of successive habitations have been uncovered. The most recent of these are larger and better built than earlier phases, using a similar size, plan, and building materials as modern northern Iraqi villages.

These usually consist of six rooms arranged in two

c.10,000 BC	c.8000	c.7000	c.6500	c.6000	c.6000	c.5200	c.5000
Hunter-gatherers in Syria gather wild cereals	Domestication of barley and wheat in the Fertile Crescent of the Middle East	Permanent settlements are established in Mesopotamia	Pottery is in common use	Northern farmers begin to leave the rain belt and settle on the plains	Cattle are domesticated in the Middle East	Southern plains are populated; beginning of the 'Ubaid period	Mesopotamians dig canals and employ irrigation techniques

blocks around a courtyard, with one block used for living quarters and the other as kitchens and for storage. Large granary storage jars and domed bread ovens are also a feature of these sites. Populations, however, were still relatively small and probably did not exceed about 500 persons in a typical village.

The slightly later sites of Tell-es-Sawwan, near Samarra in the Tigris Valley, and Choga Mami on the eastern rim of the plain, include more rooms and more complicated ground plans, and with populations about double those at Hassunah. Buildings here are made from molded brick with rooms arranged around a central T-space. They may have had a second story supported by buttressed walls, enabling a large ground floor space to be used as a reception area.

There are also suggestions that defensive considerations played a part in the design and layout of Tell-es-Sawwan and Choga Mami, which are both walled villages with ditches and ramparts. Choga Mami has, in addition, a tower guarding one of the entrances. At Tell-Halaf, on the Turkish-Syrian border, there is evidence for the introduction of cobbled streets, the first attempts at building townships, and for some form of civil authority responsible for maintaining shared areas.

The shaping of trade

It is likely that many of these large building complexes were attached to farms or served the needs of local farming communities, since there are indications of the communal growing of linseed (flax) and six-row barley (later to be the staple crop of southern Mesopotamia). Most important in terms of later developments, however, is a large increase in trade and the exchange of goods, particularly of pottery.

This is the earliest indication of what may have been the first widespread Mesopotamian cultural horizon, since Tell-Halaf pottery styles were not confined to local populations but appear in virtually identical form at all Samarran and related sites. Technical analysis of the clays used in pottery and figurines further supports the notion of large-scale trade and exchange,

with some of the regularly used clay sources being as much as 600 miles apart.

Architectural styles underwent some major changes toward the close of this period. Many of the T-shaped houses were converted into granaries and the enclosure walls went out of use. There are also spaces within villages that would have been more readily open to public access, and interestingly most of the decorated pottery and burials are located within these public spaces, rather than restricted to household areas, as they had been previously. The conclusion drawn from these factors is that a redistribution of resources was taking place, linked with the introduction of community rituals and, possibly, an associated formal leadership or chiefdom.

Above: A vase from Tell-Halaf is decorated with a simple painted pattern and dates from c.5000.

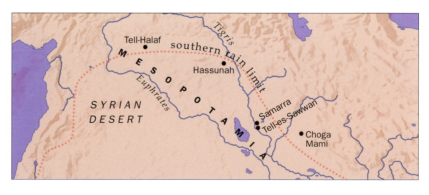

c.5000	c.5000	c.4500	c.4000	c.3800	c.3700	c.3500	c.3500
Eridu is established, deemed the world's first city	Nippur founded. The reign of Mesopotamian kings is recognized by the priesthood	The plow is invented, drawn by cattle	The Elamites establish their capital city of Susa	The wheel is invented and used on cattle-drawn carts	The city of Uruk is founded	End of the 'Ubaid period	Sumerians occupy southern Mesopotamia

THE 'UBAID PERIOD, C.5200–3500 BC

The earliest permanent settlement of the southern plains of Mesopotamia occurred some time before 5000, probably the consequence of non-Semitic peoples moving into the region. This marked the beginning of the 'Ubaid period, named after the site of Tell al-'Ubaid, where distinctive artifacts were first discovered.

T he influence of the 'Ubaid people, who are sometimes referred to as proto-Euphrateans, spread north to gradually replace the earlier Hassunah and Halaf cultures, but exactly who they were and what their relationship was to the preceding cultures remains unknown. It is presumed that they were a mix of foragers and pastoralists who already lived in the region and formed settled communities after intermingling with the new arrivals. Curiously,

Right: 'Ubaid ceramic vessel with pouring spout. Dating from a later period than the vase on the far right, probably c.3500 BC, it is more utilitarian in design.

however, all 'Ubaid villages were built in virgin areas where there is no evidence of previous occupancy. The only exception is Tell Oueli, near Larsa, where a French expedition discovered an earlier Hassunah site.

'Ubaid culture had two phases, named after the sites of Eridu and Hajji Muhammed, which are distinguished primarily through pottery types. Early 'Ubaid pottery is often highly

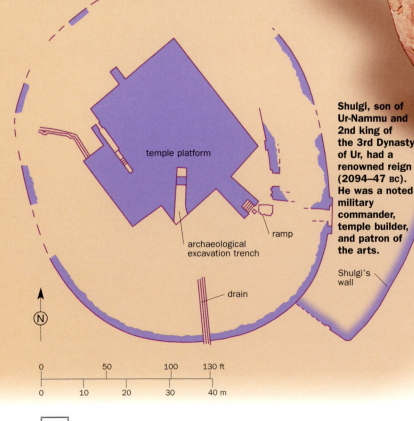

The excavated area at Tell al-'Ubaid, showing the temple of Ninhursag and oval enclosure

temple platform

archaeological excavation trench

ramp

Shulgi, son of Ur-Nammu and 2nd king of the 3rd Dynasty of Ur, had a renowned reign (2094–47 BC). He was a noted military commander, temple builder, and patron of the arts.

Shulgi's wall

drain

N

| 0 | 50 | 100 | 130 ft |
| 0 | 10 | 20 | 30 | 40 m |

decorated, with geometric patterns in brown or black paint, but during the later period pottery became increasingly simple and more utilitarian, even including the manufacture of hard-baked clay sickles.

While pottery gives us identifiable and durable artifacts by which 'Ubaid periods can be ascertained, the most significant contribution that 'Ubaid people made to Mesopotamian development was in the growth of urban settlement. Early settlements were small, generally on a par with those of Hassunah but—

for reasons that are not yet understood—'Ubaid villages continued to grow in size until by the late period they had populations of 5,000 or more.

Beginnings of religion

A typical 'Ubaid village consisted primarily of rectangular mud-brick houses and courtyards separated by alleys, with areas of larger and more elaborate buildings containing storage pits and granaries. A new feature was a central earth mound surmounted by a single-roomed building, which presumably served a ritual function. During successive rebuildings at periodic intervals these so-called temples became more complex.

We can understand these developments from excavations carried out at the temple complex of Eridu (*see also following spread*), since these were repeated at other sites as well. By the close of the 'Ubaid period the earth mound at Eridu had become a raised platform that was reached by a flight of steps. On its summit stood a complex temple, developed from the original single-room building, which contained an altar surrounded by a series of subsidiary rooms. Surrounding the earth mound were elaborate homes, presumed to belong to a social elite, and craft workshops beyond these. Farmers' houses were on the outskirts of the village, with irrigated fields farther out.

Similar complexes were being built further

north, as at the site of Tepe Gawra, where three temples were erected facing a central plaza. The exact relationship between the various 'Ubaid villages is unknown; although it is unlikely that there was any form of centralized authority, there were trade contacts both within and outside the area. Tepe Gawra may itself have been a trading outpost. What is clear during this period is a stratification of society based on some kind of religious or cult worship, with larger villages containing temple complexes that served as ritual centers for smaller outlying rural communities.

Below: An early 'Ubaid pottery vase of c.4500 BC, typically decorated with brown-colored geometric patterning.

An inscription identifies this as the statuette of an official of Uruk called Kurlil, who was responsible for building work on the temple of the Sumerian fertility goddess Ninhursag at Tell al-'Ubaid, where it was found. It dates from c.2500 BC. Figurines like this were commonly set up to pray on behalf of the donor.

Trade between Mesopotamia and Arabia during this period is indicated by finds of 'Ubaid pottery from Ur along the Persian Gulf coast

THE ERIDU GENESIS

The 'Ubaid village of Eridu (or Eridug) became the key city in Mesopotamian mythology, the seat of kings who reigned for many thousands of years. But what the Anunnaki gods created, they deemed to take away, when man and his domesticated animals became troublesome.

To later occupants of Mesopotamia, particularly the Sumerians, Eridu became elevated from its position as an 'Ubaid village site to that of a mythical city. The Sumerian King List, written in 2125, recounts the origin of the world, which was created by the Anunnaki (Four Gods). They brought people and animals into being and oversaw the move from hunting-gathering to pastoralism and farming. Under the leadership of the Anunnaki,

animals were domesticated, cities founded, and kingship was introduced.

According to these tales, kingship descended from heaven and the first cities were given names by Nintur, the Lady of the Stony Ground and Mother of Wildlife. Eridug (Eridu) was the original seat of kingship, the second was Bad-Tibira (Bad-Tabira), the third Larak, the fourth Sippar, and the fifth was Shuruppak.

In the beginning, the Anunnaki were pleased with their creation. The cities flourished, introducing irrigation to their fields and devising economic systems of exchange and redistribution of wealth. The kings built "the cult cities in pure spots and [to] found places for divination in pure spots" and were seen to "perform to perfection the august divine services" (Thorkild Jacobsen, *The Treasures of*

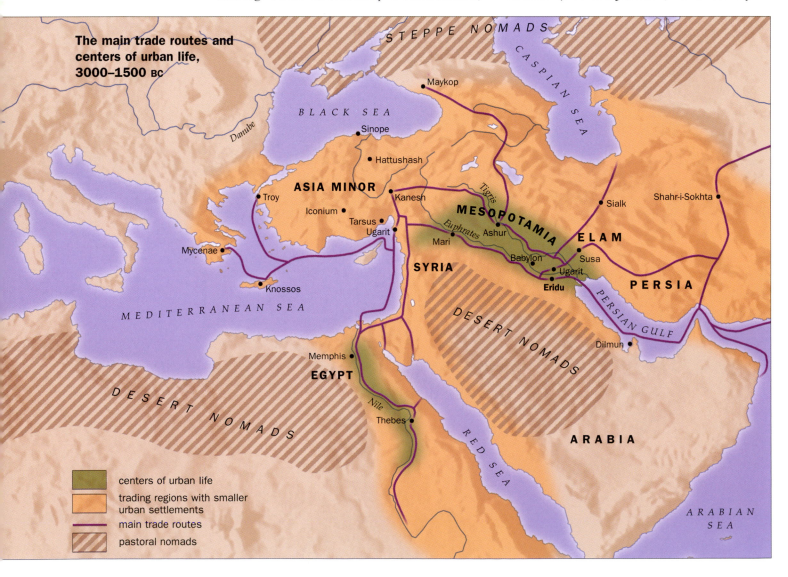

The main trade routes and centers of urban life, 3000–1500 BC

- **centers of urban life**
- **trading regions with smaller urban settlements**
- **main trade routes**
- **pastoral nomads**

Darkness, 1986). So stable and peaceful were these communities that the first king, Alulim, ruled for 28,800 years. His successor, Alalgar, ruled for 36,000 years. Then two unnamed kings ruled for a further 64,800 years.

Savior of man, beast, and god

But as the cities grew in size, so too did the noise made by their teeming multitudes. Finally the Chief God, Enlil (Lord Wind), could no longer stand this disturbance and connived with the other gods to cause a great flood that would destroy mankind. Enki, the God of Water and to whom the temple at Eridu was dedicated, was unable to overturn the ruling of the other gods, but hastened to warn Ziusudra, a pious and obedient man, to "tear down the house, build a ship… aboard ship take the seed of all living things" (*The Treasures of Darkness*). Thus Ziusudra was able to ride out the storm, which raged for seven days and seven nights.

When the storm abated and the flood waters receded, Ziusudra broke open the side of his ship and disembarked the animals he had taken aboard. Enki, renowned for his skills as a counselor and adviser, was able to persuade the other gods not to vent their anger on him for having escaped destruction and to spare Ziusudra's life.

Indeed, Enki's skills were such that he convinced the gods that, but for Ziusudra's actions, all life on earth would have been extinguished, and with no one to tend to the

rituals at the temples, the glory of the gods themselves would have dissipated. Thus, as a reward for having saved all living things, Ziusudra was forgiven and granted immortality.

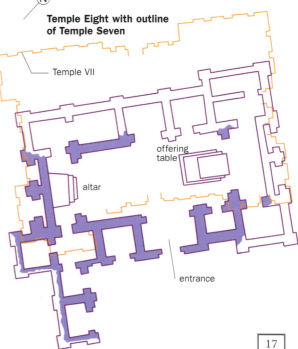

unfinished Ziggurat of Amar-Sin (c.2047–2039 BC)

18-layered temple site (see below for plans levels seven and eight)

The sacred complex of Eridu

Eridu was located by the mound called Abu Shayhrayan. One of the most important prehistoric urban centers in southern Babylonia, Eridu was once located close to the Persian Gulf at the mouth of the Euphrates, but the city's remains are now some distance from the gulf at Abu Shahrain (Abu Shayhrayan).

| 0 | 150 | 300 ft |
| 0 | 50 | 100 m |

N

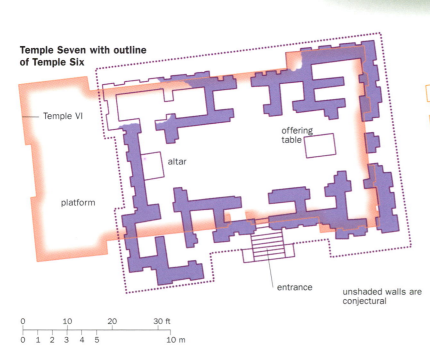

Temple Seven with outline of Temple Six

Temple VI

offering table

altar

platform

entrance

| 0 | 10 | 20 | 30 ft |
| 0 1 2 3 4 5 | | | 10 m |

Temple Eight with outline of Temple Seven

Temple VII

offering table

altar

unshaded walls are conjectural

entrance

CHAPTER 2

SUMERIA, THE EARLY EMPIRES

By 3500 BC the southern regions of Mesopotamia were occupied by a people speaking a language unrelated to any other. Exactly where these people came from is unknown, and their own complex history speaks only of permanent occupation of this region.

They formed large independent city-states, which flourished by 3000 and held control over areas of several hundred square miles. We should not, however, think of them as having a homogenous culture, since records that are available to us hint at constant conflict over access to scarce water resources. Inevitably the larger city-states, such as Ur, began to exercise authority over weaker neighbors.

Finally, in 2340, the intrusion of Semitic-speaking migrants, the Akkadians, led to the fall of the Sumerian city-states and the imposition of Akkadian rule. Sumerian influence was nevertheless to remain dominant, with the Sumerian systems of government, economy, law, and writing being taken over wholesale by the Akkadians and later groups.

Perhaps the most striking contribution made by the Sumerians was the idea of centralized authority and bureaucracy. Power was vested in a monarch, or priest-king, who ruled through a system of administrators, or bureaucrats, who

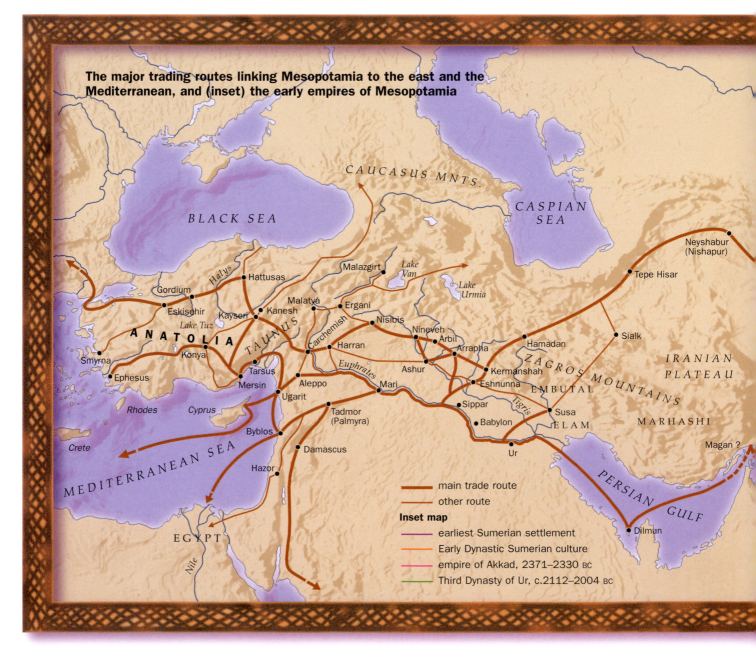

The major trading routes linking Mesopotamia to the east and the Mediterranean, and (inset) the early empires of Mesopotamia

main trade route
other route

Inset map
earliest Sumerian settlement
Early Dynastic Sumerian culture
empire of Akkad, 2371–2330 BC
Third Dynasty of Ur, c.2112–2004 BC

assigned fields and distributed crops, had responsibility for the military, and adminstered justice, adjudicating disputes through a system of laws and courts. They invented writing and kept written records by inscribing business details on baked clay tablets which, in turn, led to the development of higher mathematics, the calendar, and astronomical observation.

Supporting the nobility

Linked with the idea of the monarch was the introduction of hierarchical structures based on social stratification, with the priest-king at its head, supported by the nobility, bureaucrats, and scribes, with a secondary strata of society consisting of craftworkers and farmers, who in turn were assisted by menial laborers with the status of slaves. The relative social position of

individuals was recognized in law and has been preserved in a later Babylonian document, the Code of Hammurabi, in which the seriousness of an offence is directly related to the class of both the perpetrator and the victim. Crimes against the nobility were subject to harsher penalties than crimes against those of lower status.

The Sumerians placed greater emphasis on the redistribution of goods and refined the earlier exchange networks. Farmers had to produce excess crops, which were taken to redistribution centers where scribes arranged for them to be distributed to non-productive members of society; penalties were imposed if they failed to meet their quotas.

In religion, too, the beliefs of the Sumerians were to have a profound effect on later cultures. Sumerian belief was in numerous anthropomorphic deities who controlled the natural forces and ordered the lives of the people, but who regretted the creation of the human race. People were, therefore, given

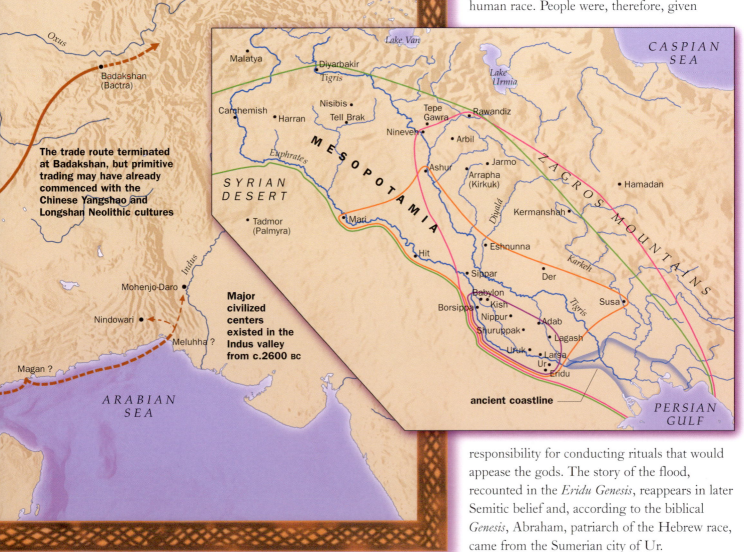

The trade route terminated at Badakshan, but primitive trading may have already commenced with the Chinese Yangshao and Longshan Neolithic cultures

Major civilized centers existed in the Indus valley from c.2600 BC

ancient coastline

responsibility for conducting rituals that would appease the gods. The story of the flood, recounted in the *Eridu Genesis*, reappears in later Semitic belief and, according to the biblical *Genesis*, Abraham, patriarch of the Hebrew race, came from the Sumerian city of Ur.

URUK, THE TRUE GENESIS, C.3700–3500 BC

The Uruk period is marked by rapid population growth and increased prosperity, leading to the establishment of the world's first cities. Two settlements merged to form Uruk city, its ziggurat-style temples influencing worship in other centers.

Right: Detail from a Sumerian vase from Tell al-Warka (Uruk) depicting a scene of offerings made to the goddess Inanna.

The great kingdoms described in the *Eridu Genesis*—the mythical account of origin with its improbably long reigns of early kings—started to become reality with the foundation of Uruk (Tell al-Warka) on the Euphrates in about 3700. By the close of the early Uruk period, in about 3100, the population of the city was between 30,000–50,000 people.

Uruk is known in the Bible as Erech and is located at the modern city of Warka in Iraq. According to legend, it was founded by Meskiaggasher and his successors, although it was a later king, Gilgamesh, who engaged in a power struggle with the rival Sumerian kingdoms of Kish and Ur that was to see Uruk's influence diminished. Gilgamesh was responsible for building the fortified city walls of Uruk and oversaw the erection of the Eanna

Below: Ruins of the ancient Sumerian city of Uruk in southern Iraq.

(House of An) temple complex that was dedicated to the goddess Ishtar (or Inanna): the goddess of love, procreation, and war.

Uruk's significance is in the emergence of the first kingdoms, generally referred to as the Early Dynastic period, and the fact it was the first fully urbanized city-state in Mesopotamia. At this time it was the largest settlement in the world—the first true city—covering an area of approximately 1,200 acres with a city wall extending some six miles. It was also at Uruk that the first writing systems were developed. Literally thousands of clay tablets marked with early pictographic scripts recording the produce of local farms and similar listings have been recovered from the site.

Ur supersedes Uruk

Archaeological investigations carried out by German teams since 1912 suggest that Uruk enclosed two earlier settlements, Kullaba and Eanna, which amalgamated during the early Uruk period. This assertion is borne out by the fact that there are two clearly demarcated religious complexes, or compounds: that of

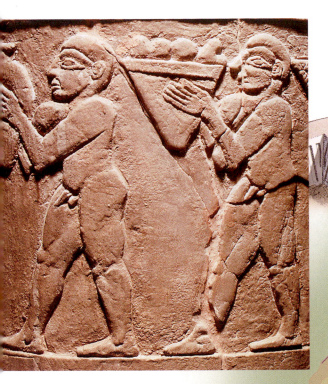

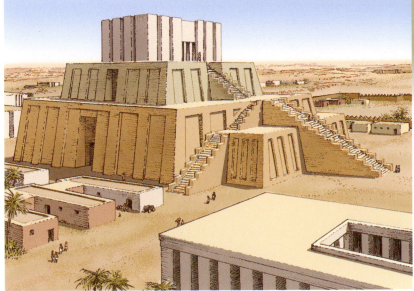

North Gate

remains of city walls

early dynastic houses

Palace of Sinkashid

Bit Resh

Ziggurat

Anu Ziggurat with White Temple

Sanctuary of Eanna

Parthian period ruins

remains of city walls

Mithreum

Irigal

Parthian period ruins

Temple of Gareus

Ur Gate

0   500 yds

0   500 m

Eanna, dedicated to the goddess of love and initiated by Gilgamesh, and the Sanctuary of Anu, which appears to have originally been part of the settlement of Kullaba.

Both of these contain temples on top of stepped pyramids (prototype ziggurats). These are the White Temple in the Sanctuary of Anu, and the Limestone and Pillar Temples in the Sanctuary of Eanna. Both have clay cones with painted tops pressed into the mud-plaster facing of the buildings as decoration. The influence of Uruk on Mesopotamian belief is further supported by the contemporary erection of similar ziggurat-prototype temples at the secondary sites of Tell Aqair and Eridu.

Uruk was a site of major importance until the third millenium BC, when its influence was usurped by Ur. This is testified by the fact that the Eanna Sanctuary was extensively modified by Ur-Nammu, the king of Ur, in about 2600, following the overthrow of Gilgamesh. Although the city was occupied throughout the following two millenia, until the advent of the Parthian kingdoms, its later history is that of a minor center.

THE KING OF KISH, 3000 BC

According to the Sumerian King List, the first city to claim dynastic privilege after the great flood was Kish (Kic). However, its supremacy was far from assured, and rivalry from Lagash and Umma weakened Mesopotamia at a time when Semitic invasions threatened.

Enmebaragesi and his son Agga are the first Kish rulers we know from early inscriptions; it is likely that Kish rivaled Uruk in the early days of its ascendancy. The first dynasty, as recorded in the *Epic of Gilgamesh*, is said to have been founded at Kish and only later passed to the ruling elite at Uruk. Archaeological evidence suggests that the ruling dynasties at Kish and Uruk, together with a similar ruling elite at Mari, were contemporary.

The site of ancient Kish is in the flood plain between the Euphrates and Tigris, about eight miles east of Babylon. It consists of a series of low mounds, or tells, scattered over a wide area, first excavated in the 1920s. Although the excavations are incomplete, they show continuous habitation from the protoliterate period until the climax of Sumerian civilization, when Kish was apparently overthrown by an invasion of Semitic-speaking peoples. It was the birthplace of Sargon of Agade, who was to rebel against the Sumerian dynasties and found the Akkadian empire, and there are remains of a temple built by Nebuchadnezzar and Nabonidus during the later Babylonian period.

Although evidence from Kish is relatively meager, the city apparently played a major role in the formation of the Sumerian dynasties. Power struggles in Sumeria appear to have come to a head about 2500, with Kish briefly exercising hegemony over the entire region. This, however, was challenged by the rulers of Uruk and Ur. Kingship of Sumer initially passed from Kish to Uruk, under the leadership of Enmerkar, Lugalbanda, and Gilgamesh, but was then seized by Mesannepadda of Ur who took the by then legendary title King of Kish to Ur.

Below: Detail of a lion-hunting scene on a a Sumerian stele found at Uruk.

claimed title to the King of Kish but failed to consolidate the region. Lugalzagesi, the Ensi (king-priest) of Umma in 2360–35, attacked and destroyed Lagash, burning its temples to the ground and declaring himself King of Uruk and the Land. These rivalries weakened the Sumerian empire. Even Ur, that had emerged as the strongest force in the region, was unable to retain its hold over Sumeria. The region was left open to dissent, and unable to resist the incursions of the Semitic tribes.

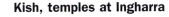

Kish, temples at Ingharra

central courtyard

central courtyard

N

0		90 ft
0		30 m

Kish comprises about 40 tells within an oval measuring some 1¹/₂ by 5 miles. The two most important archaeological mounds are called Uhaimir and Ingharra (the temple plans of the latter are shown here), situated on the eastern side of the ancient city. It is in this area that excavations uncovered extensive remains dating to the early 3rd millennium BC.

Fragmentation

Kish is also important from excavations carried out in its extensive cemetery, which have revealed a complete sequence of pottery from the earliest proto-literate period through to that of Nebuchadnezzar. Characteristic of these are the so-called goddess jars that provide a chronological reference for dating remains at other sites.

Despite the importance of Kish, at the height of its power it shared authority with some 30 other city-states; Ur and Uruk were simply the major rivals. The Palace at Kish, a complex of buildings that seems to have served a royal function, was echoed by a similar construction at Eridu, which was still revered as the city of the first kings. Important innovations were taking place elsewhere, such as the first evidence of poetry at Abu Salabikh.

Other kingdoms, particularly that at Lagash,

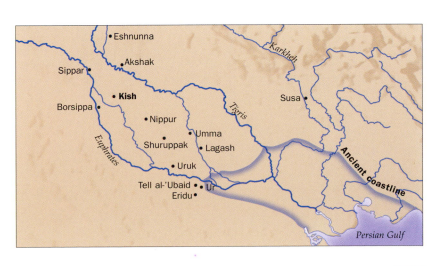

EARLY DYNASTIC SUMERIA, 2900–2400 BC

In the Early Dynastic period, leaders of city-states competed to gain political power over neighbors, but not for ideological change. In terms of cultural identity, the rival city-states were remarkably homogenous: They not only recognized the deities of their enemies, but worshipped them under the same names.

Below: This Sumerian ceramic jar decorated in the "Scarlet Ware" style, with animal motifs, dates from c.3000 BC.

Shared culture allowed the Sumerians to stabilize their economies, social and legal structures, and religious outlook. It was this that, despite political upheavals, enabled the Sumerians to eventually form unified states at the end of the Early Dynastic period and to create a socio-political standard that would remain essentially unchanged throughout the later Sumerian, Babylonian, and Assyrian periods.

Underlying these achievements was the Pre-Dynastic shift from subsistence economies to agriculture and husbandry, which permitted Sumerians to produce food surpluses. Excess food could be kept in city granaries and warehouses for distribution to those engaged in activities other than farming. The professional classes developed skills in architecture, science, mathematics, writing, and law; or they could pursue careers in the service of the temples or military, as manufacturers and traders, or within the diplomatic services. Their skills could be traded back in exchange for support for their families and themselves using state resources.

Beyond the state, skills could be traded for the produce and talents of neighboring cities and farms, leading to an exchange not only of goods and services, but also of ideas and technology. As trade expanded, the political, economic, and intellectual exchange became international and included the import and export of raw materials and finished products.

The sharing of ideas and of state controls led to a degree of standardization, in weights and measures and legal process, for example; but it also enabled agreement to be reached in the areas of politics, economics, trade, and production. Education became more specialized and was essentially training for a specific career, although there remained a tendency for a boy to follow in his father's footsteps.

A versatile pantheon

Underlying all these developments was a belief that destiny was ruled by the gods. Early Dynastic deities remained important in later periods, and although their names sometimes changed, the belief that deities were human in character and part of the human realm remained constant. Their role was to order life on earth, and it is said that they created people so they did not have to work for themselves. This was a reflection of Sumerian social organization, in

c.3200	c.3100	c.3000	c.3000	c.3000	c.2900–2400	c.2900	c.2700
Bronze tools are in use	Sumerians develop cuneiform writing	Babylon is founded	Sumerian city-states dominate	The city of Nineveh has developed around the ancient tell of Kuyunjik	Early Dynastic period of Sumeria	The village of Mari, Syria, has grown to a city	Under their first kings, Elamites of southwest Iran battle the city of Ur

which there were hierarchies of rulers, priests, intellectuals, the military, producers, traders and merchants, and manual workers and slaves, with deities above them all.

The status of an individual deity might vary according to the economic life of a particular area. Thus in the south particular importance was given to the deities of marshland, fishing, and hunting, whereas in the west and east the gods and goddesses of water were eminent. On the Lower Euphrates deities of the orchards were interspersed with those responsible for cow-herding, while in the north the gods of shepherds had greater prominence.

Prior to political unification toward the end of the Early Dynastic period, conflicts between cities were inspired by similar conflicts among the gods. They seem to have shared the same emotions and jealousies, and the need for individual power, as the ruling families of the different cities. Much of Sumerian unification therefore centered on the resolution not only of political differences but of the ritual status claimed by various cities. One of the first acts when entering a defeated city was the destruction of the temple dedicated to its patron deity. When the religious leaders of powerful cities such as Uruk, Ur, Lagash, and Kish reached agreement about the status of the gods, political unity followed.

Left: An Early Dynastic tablet fragment of c.2700 BC—found in the Shara temple at Tell Agrab—depicts scenes from a royal banquet and a hunt.

c.2600	c.2600	c.2600	c.2560–25	c.2500	c.2500	2454–25	2404–375
The legendary Gilgamesh rules Uruk, defeating the kings of Kish	Uruk domination is superseded by Ur	Date of the royal tombs of Ur, excavated by Leonard Woolley in the 20th century	Ur has authority over much of Mesopotamia under its first king, Mesannepadda	The city of Kish briefly rules Sumeria	Ashur city is founded on the site of a Sumerian settlement	Eannatum defeats Umma and begins conquest of Ur, Uruk, and Kish	Entemena restores Lagash supremacy, previously reversed by Umma

SUMERIAN CUNEIFORM AND CYLINDER SEALS

Writing was invented in Mesopotamia by the Sumerians during the late fourth millenium BC, from whence it spread to Egypt, Elam, and the Indus Valley. Its simple block marks elaborated over time and its use spread from commerce to the fields of science and religion.

Facing: One of the clay tablets with cuneiform inscriptions found at Warka (Uruk).

According to the Sumerian epic poem of *Inanna and Enki*, the "one hundred basic elements of civilization" were transferred from Eridu, City of the First Kings, to Uruk. Among these basic elements was writing, considered to be a divine decree from the deities and under the patronage of Enki, God of Wisdom. From its inception, writing was therefore considered a gift of the gods and carried with it both power and knowledge.

In more prosaic terms, true writing developed from earlier forms of mark-making on clay tablets. The earliest were plain cones and discs that served as tokens or counters in economic exchange. Some of these were shaped to represent goods, as in the form of a cow's

Right: This 4,000-year–old Sumerian tablet is the world's oldest known medical handbook. Discovered during excavations by Pennsylvania University it was translated in 1952–3. A portion of the right-hand column reads: "White pear tree, the flower of the 'moon' plant, grind into a powder, dissolve in beer, let the man drink."

head, and further identified by scratched marks of ownership.

By 4300 the tokens had become elaborated into complex tablets and cylinder seals containing a series of marks pressed into the wet clay surface, either to identify ownership or as official certification. This was followed shortly after by the use of pictographic or representational symbols, each representing a complete concept or object.

A versatile form

The process of marking wet clay with a stylus led to refinements after 3000, especially in the simplification of marks to convey abstract rather than representational ideas. The main impetus for change appears to have been the difficulty in inscribing curvilinear pictographs with a straight-edged stylus; but the change had far reaching consequences. A dramatic shift in thinking appears to have occurred, with the realization that a mark could be used to represent a part of an idea and not the totality—by arranging a series of marks in a linear sequence, a word or sentence could be constructed that carried greater meaning than a single symbol. This form of writing is known as *cuneiform*, from the Latin for "wedge-shaped," after the characteristic straight-edged and block-like forms made with the stylus.

As cuneiform developed, it acquired additional complexities. Some marks became phonetic, and words could include a suffix or prefix to give more precise meaning. This, in turn, gave the Sumerians not only an extensive written vocabulary, but also clear grammatical structure. This was so precise that is even possible to determine dialectical differences between cuneiform used at various regional centers.

During the early period, until about 2000, virtually all the extant Sumerian texts are concerned with the economy and its admin-istration. After this date, particularly with the advent of new alphabets, texts begin to deal with more abstract and esoteric matters, and concern diplomacy, religion, and scientific knowledge, a trait that was to persist within southern

Mesopotamia until the second century AD.

The role of the scribe was also undergoing change. From their early status as record-keepers, they became more specialized and underwent training with an *edubba* (master scribe) that could take many years to perfect, after which they might occupy positions as temple administrators and prominent members of royal households. They were at the forefront of the Sumerian search for knowledge and began to create libraries in which this knowledge could be stored and made available to other scholars, and were responsible for developing new theories in the fields of mathematics, medicine, and law.

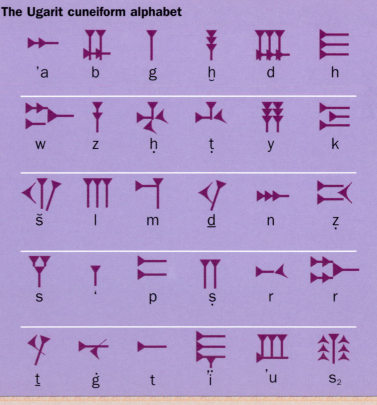

The Ugarit cuneiform alphabet

ʾa	b	g	ẖ	d	h
w	z	ḥ	ṭ	y	k
š	l	m	ḏ	n	z̧
s	ʿ	p	ṣ	r	r
ṯ	ġ	t	ʾi	ʾu	s₂

The earliest forms of cuneiform writing were pictographic, representations of familiar objects, such as a fish, an ox-head, and a bird—shown above in the first column. In time cuneiform became abstract representations of the pictographs (second column), the symbols were commonly rotated (third column), and eventually further abstracted (right column).

Cuneiform writing was developed by the Sumerians shortly before 3100 BC, although some scholars trace its origins back to the beginnings of agriculture, c.8000 BC. The Sumerian method of writing had a long and useful history through Babylonia (example right), Assyria, the Elamites, Kassites, Hittites, Mitanni, Hurrians, and Persians, developing into a complex system of phonetics before yielding to the alphabet c.13th century BC. At this time in the Syrian mercantile

TCH
SH

kingdom of Ugarit a 30–32 character cuneiform alphabet (shown above) was developed, that was later adapted by the Phonencians and then the Greeks and Romans.

THE SUPREMACY OF UR, 2750 BC

The rise of independent city-states in Mesopotamia led to increased competition between the dynastic families that controlled trade and commerce. Ur broke ahead of Uruk and ruled with three dynasties of kings, its prosperity and influence belying its agrarian foundation.

Eridu claimed to be the birthplace of the kings, but had lost importance to Kish, which claimed the origin of the first dynasties. This was challenged by Lagash, Uruk, and Ur, as well as by the kingdom of Mari in modern Syria. In the course of these power struggles Ur rose to prominence in about 2750, although at this period Uruk was still exerting considerable influence.

Under its first king, Mesannepadda (r.2560–25), Ur claimed authority over most of Mesopotamia, an expansionist policy that was continued under his son and successor, Aannepadda. Both Kish and Lagash were defeated and the role of their kings diminished. Uruk's influence had been questioned even earlier, in 2600, when Ur had imposed its rule.

Ur (Tall al-Muqayyar) lies about186 miles southeast of modern Baghdad on a bend of the original course of the Euphrates. Excavations conducted by Leonard Woolley between 1922–34, under the auspices of the British Museum and the University of Pennsylvania, revealed continuous occupation of this site from the Al-'Ubaid period until it was defeated by the Elamites in 1950 BC.

Even after that date its religious buildings acted as a focus for later rulers; both Nebuchadnezzar and Nabonidus rebuilt parts of Ur in the sixth century BC. Ur is mentioned in the Bible, where it is the legendary birthplace of Abraham and known as Ur of the Chaldees, a reference to the Chaldean invasions of the city that took place about 900.

At the height of its power under Mesannepadda, Ur controlled much of southern Mesopotamia. Merchants from Ur traded as far as the Indian Ocean and imported precious goods and materials for the ruling elite during this first dynastic period.

It appears, however, that its influence was strongly resisted, particularly in the northern regions where other powerful dynasties held sway. Raiders frequently attacked and laid siege to Sumerian cities, until eventually a non-Sumerian Semitic-speaking tribal leader, Sargon of Agade, overthrew Ur in about 2340.

Akkadian rule

Sargon's incursions brought the first dynasty of Ur to an end and signaled the beginning of the Akkadian period. Sargon united the cities of Sumer and Akkad, and Ur lost its significance when the royal court was moved to Akkad (later renamed Babylon). Although practically nothing is known about what happened at Ur under the Akkadians, it is apparent that a second dynasty of kings remained in place but with their authority considerably weakened. They had little direct impact on contemporary developments, including the blending of Sumerian and Akkadian elements.

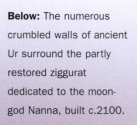

Below: The numerous crumbled walls of ancient Ur surround the partly restored ziggurat dedicated to the moon-god Nanna, built c.2100.

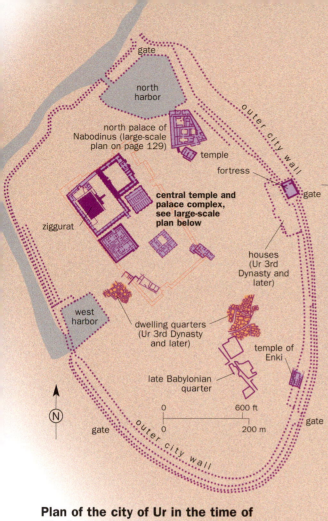

gate

north harbor

north palace of Nabodinus (large-scale plan on page 129)

temple

fortress

central temple and palace complex, see large-scale plan below

gate

ziggurat

houses (Ur 3rd Dynasty and later)

west harbor

dwelling quarters (Ur 3rd Dynasty and later)

temple of Enki

late Babylonian quarter

outer city wall

0		600 ft
0	200 m	

N

gate

gate

outer city wall

gate

Plan of the city of Ur in the time of Abraham, 2100–1900 BC, with a detailed plan of the central palace and temple complex, right.

Left: Reconstruction of the Ziggurat of Nanna and, **below,** the northeast facing staircase today after reconstruction.

shrine of Nanna

gate

court of Nanna

gate

gate

Ziggurat of Nanna

E-Temen-ni-Gur of Ur-Nammu

E-Dub-Lal-Mah

E-Nun-Mah

Giparu of Amar-Sin

gate

later Temenos Wall of Nebuchadnezzar

gate

E-Hursag palace of Ur-Nammu & Shulgi

gate

Dungi temple of Nimin-Tabba

N

0	50	100	150 ft
0	25		50 m

Royal tombs

The royal tombs are shown in more detail on page 36

gate

The rule of Sargon and his successors was also a turbulent one, subject to constant incursions and invasions. A new leader at Ur, Ur-Nammu (r.2113–95), ousted the Akkadians and started the Third Dynasty in about 2100, heralding a golden age. Most of the religious buildings at Ur date from Ur-Nammu's reign, including its famous ziggurat dedicated to the moon god Nanna. The region rose to new prosperity and enjoyed a prolonged period of relative peace. Ur-Nammu wrote a new code of laws, there was an agricultural revival, and considerable rebuilding took place in towns and cities.

The third dynasty flourished until the invasions of the nomadic Elamites (referred to as Amorites in the Old Testament), after which it went into a decline from which it never recovered. We can surmise that other factors contributed to Ur's downfall. One of the most significant was a change in the course of the Euphrates that left Ur without the agricultural base on which its prosperity was dependent. Today, the Euphrates passes about nine miles north of the ancient city.

TEMPLES AND ROYAL ESTATES

The relationship between kings and priests during the Sumerian period is not fully understood, their roles blurring and changing with time. Rulers depended upon the priests' approval, but central to both was the temple, a symbol of the city, its prosperity, and its patron deity.

It appears that little distinction was made between the monarchy and the clergy during the early period, when a priest-king had religious and secular roles; however, as Sumerian civilization developed, some divergence took place. In late Sumeria there was apparent tension: kings sought a divine status through which they claimed political and military authority, yet in order to exercise these rights they required sanction from the priests. To understand this more fully, it is necessary to look at the role of the temple in Sumeria.

The focal point of each city was a temple devoted to a patron deity, who was believed to frequent it regularly. In the late Sumerian periods the temple became a symbol of the city's wealth. It consisted of a mud-brick building raised on a platform or plinth, and typically had a central sanctuary or shrine, the *cella*, flanked

Below: Reconstruction of the Oval Temple of Khafaji in northern Babylonia, which dates from the Early Dynastic Period, 3000–2340 BC

by a series of rooms.

There was an altar and offering table behind which stood a statue of the city's patron deity. Surrounding this was a protective wall, often oval in plan, ornamented with alternating buttresses and recesses. Temples became more elaborate during the protoliterate period. Interior walls were often decorated with patterns made by terracotta mosaic cones painted in brilliant colors or covered in bronze sheaths; others bore wall-paintings depicting mythological scenes.

Most, if not all, Sumerian art served a religious purpose. Sculpture was generally used as adornment in or as ritual equipment for temples, and commemorative art was usually produced in conjunction with temple dedications.

The *cella*'s adjoining rooms served as residences for the temple's priests, priestesses, officials, musicians, singers, eunuchs, and *hierodules* (slaves dedicated to the temple deity). These people performed daily public rituals, food sacrifices, and libations, and functioned in both the ritual and economic spheres.

The temple administrators owned as much as one-third of the city's land, which they loaned

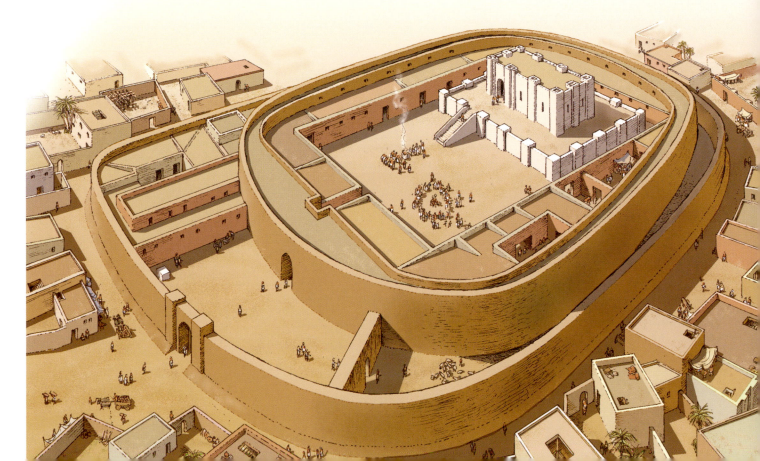

or leased in return for a share of the harvest. They ritually owned rights in all property in the name of the deity, from which they received regular offerings kept in a temple storehouse. There were workshops for bakers, potters, weavers, and jewelers, and pens for sheep, goats, oxen, and donkeys within the temple precincts.

A gray area

It was incumbent on the king to dedicate new temples, as a sign of piety and a display of his sacred origins. New temples were erected over earlier ones, which became incorporated into the structure of the mound on which the temple was erected. The platform became enlarged and elaborate, and began to acquire symbolic meaning. The temple platform or ziggurat at Ur, for instance, measured approximately 150 by 200 feet and was 80 feet high, its terraces planted with trees as a representation of a sacred mountain.

The king had an intermediate position between the gods and the priests, since he was both an agent of the deities (and might claim divine origin), yet was dependent on the priests for the validation of his position. This created tension between the palace and the temple, setting the luxurious residence of the king, with its annexes, administrative staff, and landed property, against the ritual and economic functions of the temple priests and stewards. The king would often appoint members of the royal household to important temple positions, and palace lands were sometimes assigned to priests, blurring the division.

Other private lands were owned by the *lugals* (great men). Originally titled landowners, some of these became so powerful that they usurped the throne and placed themselves and members of their families in ruling positions, until eventually the title *lugal* became closely associated with that of the king.

THE EPIC OF GILGAMESH

The Epic of Gilgamesh is perhaps the greatest literary tradition known to us from Mesopotamia. It is the oldest written epic poem to have survived, and can lay claim to being the world's oldest recorded story.

Although it is known from several versions at different periods, the most complete telling of the *Epic of Gilgamesh* was discovered among the ruins of the Library at Nineveh, built by the Assyrian king Ashurbanipal in the seventh century BC. This consists of 12 stone tablets inscribed with some 3,000 lines of cuneiform characters that describe the life and adventures of Gilgamesh.

Gilgamesh was both a historical and a legendary figure. In his historical role he ruled Uruk in about 2600, and is credited with establishing Uruk as a model city and for bringing civilization to the previous untamed world. As a legendary figure he has his counterpart in Enkidu, who was created by divine decree to be Lord of the Wilderness, whom Gilgamesh overthrew in single combat. Thereafter Gilgamesh and Enkidu were inseparable.

The epic relates the story of their adventures together, in which Enkidu is led by the warlike and imperious Gilgamesh on a fantastic journey to the distant Land of the Forest of Cedars.

"I am Gilgamesh, I killed the Guardian! I destroyed Humbaba who lived in the Cedar Forest, I slew lions in the mountain passes. I grappled with the Bull that came down from heaven, and killed him." From statues, like this one on the right from the palace of Sargon II, to wall reliefs and cylinder seals, Gilgamesh is pictorially associated with lions and bulls.

They survive many difficulties and overcome various obstacles placed in their way, symbolic restatement of Uruk's rise to power and its expansion after the first kings had "descended from heaven" and become established at Eridu, from where the kingship passed to Uruk.

The difficulties they encounter are nevertheless those of fantasy. On arrival at the Forest of Cedars they confront and defeat its guardian, Humbaba, a giant. Returning to

Uruk, they discover the city threatened by a divine bull, sent by Inanna (Lady of Heaven), the Goddess of Fertility. Inanna holds the power of life and death, and the engagement of Gilgamesh and Enkidu with the Heavenly Bull symbolizes this most fundamental of oppositions. Their success is sufficient to prevent the destruction of Uruk, but also serves as a reminder to the gods that the people they created should not become too powerful.

Everlasting and after-life

The gods decide that Enkidu must die, and after his sudden death the poem begins a new phase. Gilgamesh is now obsessed by fear of death and is driven to despair. The epic recounts his search for eternal life bestowed by a plant he learns about from his ancestor Uta-napishtim. Uta-napishtim's account of the story of the Great Flood, from which he claims to be the sole survivor, is the climax of the *Epic of Gilgamesh*.

This parallels the story of Ziusudra from a stone tablet at Nippur (*see page 17*). In order to prevent the complete destruction of the Sumerian world, Ziusudra built a boat on which he embarked animals of all kinds to protect them from the wrath of the gods. The Gilgamesh episode probably derives from an Akkadian text known as the *Epic of Atrahasis*, which passed into Babylonian epics and from them became the basis of the biblical flood and the story of Noah.

Gilgamesh's search for the plant is successful, but he leaves it unguarded and it is carried off by a serpent. Thereafter he has to assume his human (mortal) form, and in desperation turns to the ghost of Enkidu for consolation. Enkidu's ghost, however, tells him that the dead should not expect to be revered by the living and reminds him that humans "become dust" when they die. He advises Gilgamesh to

listen to the wise innkeeper, Siduri, who tells him that "when the gods created men, they marked out death as their fate."

Above: Clay mask of Humbaba, the giant of the Forest of Cedars in the *Epic of Gilgamesh*, from Sippar, 1800–1600 BC. The mask is formed from a single coiled intestine and would have been used in divination. One method of predicting the future in ancient Mesopotamia was through the examination of a sacrificed animal's internal organs, and formed like this as a representation of Humbaba's face, was an omen meaning "revolution."

SUMERIAN DEITIES

The Sumerian pantheon presents us with a bewildering array of anthropomorphic gods, who share the joys and frailities of human emotional and spiritual life. Sometimes compassionate, they could also vent their anger in the most terrible ways, and seem to be characterized primarily by unpredictability.

The Sumerians had major deities who brought the world into being and controlled natural events, deities of the city-states and their ruling elites, deities of craftworkers, farmers, traders, and travelers, and minor deities of the household and hearth. The stories of the gods were recorded and continuously updated by royal scribes, who created a vast literature of god lists, such as that from Fara, of prayers, poems, and narratives. These have come down to us in fragmentary form, but sufficient remains to decipher the principal tenets of Sumerian belief.

Central to belief was that the gods did not

Right: A detail from a stele found by Sir Leonard Woolley in 1929 at Ur depicts Nanna the moon god seated on his throne. The stele contains a pictorial record of the building of the ziggurat by King Ur-Engur (c.2300) and is considered to be one of the most important finds from the Sumerian period.

2360–35	2340	2279	2254–17	2254–30	2230–109	2217–193	2141–22
Lugalzagesi is Ensi (king-priest) of Umma and takes Sumerian power	Sargon of Agade overthrows Ur; beginning of Akkadian empire	Sargon is succeeded by sons Rimush and Manishtushu	Naram-Sin attempts to maintain Akkadian power	Babylon first mentioned in Sumerian texts, during reign of Shar-kali-sharra	Reign of the Gutian kings	Shar-kali-sharra succeeds his father but cedes Akkadian territory	Gudea of Lagash begins to reassert Sumerian civilization

live in a world separate from that occupied by humans. The world originated in chaos at some distant point in time, and was later personified as the great goddess Nammu who, according to the Sumerian epic tale of Enki and Ninmah, "gave birth to the numberless gods."

Order was created by the division of chaos into the forces of the sky (An), the father of the gods, and those of the earth (Ki). Both sky and earth can therefore be thought of as divinities with human attributes. Mediation between these forces was through the agency of Enlil (Lord Wind), the son of An and Ki. Enlil possessed the Tablet of Destiny, which controlled the fate of the people.

Assisting the major gods and goddesses were a host of powerful deities. Enki (Lord Earth) controlled fresh water and the flow of the Euphrates and Tigris on which survival depended. Nanna (Moon God) controlled the months and seasons; he was the son of Enlil and his wife, Ninlil. Utu (Sun God) governed the days and was the dispenser of justice. Ninurta was protector of agriculture and master of storms. Inanna (Lady of Heaven) was the fertility goddess and patron of store-houses.

A step toward godhood

The order that the gods made out of chaos was intended to be harmonious. However, the gods soon realized that harmony could only be maintained through labor and by offerings that reflected their status. They decided to create people whose status would be beneath that of the gods, and whose labors would be dedicated to maintaining the gods' positions. They were later to regret this decision and send a series of disasters, including a great flood, as punishment for human indiscretion.

Over time, some of these privileged people came to occupy exalted positions of their own as priest-rulers and eventually as kings. Some members of the elite were recognized as minor deities themselves, exercising their rule as a divine right and gaining immortality. For ordinary people death carried neither reward nor punishment; they simply became dust.

Much of Sumerian religion was focused on divination that attempted to predict what the gods' intentions might be. The regularity of the natural world, the recurring seasons, and movements of heavenly bodies implied that these held the key to the secret of order and thus provided insight to the thinking of the gods. The scribes, by imposing similar order in their record keeping, were therefore engaged in a sacred activity. Observation of the movements of the sun, moon, and stars led to astrology and the acquisition of astronomical knowledge, which in turn required complex mathematical records.

Left and right: Sumerian statutettes of the god Abu and his consort. They are part of a colletion of figurines made from gypsum marble, with shell and black limetone inlays, that were buried beside the altar of the Abu temple at Eshnunna (Tell Asmar). Dating from the 3rd Dynasty of Ur, the figures are now though to represent a priest and his wife rather than the god they worshipped. Beside the so called 'square temple' dedicated to Abu, excavations also uncovered the earliest northern palace of the period.

2133–13	2125	2112	2094	c.2050	2025–05	2017–1985	c.2000
Utuhegal of Uruk campaigns against the Gutian king Tirigan	The most complete version of the Sumerian King List is compiled	Ur-Nammu begins the third dynasty of Ur	Shulgi, son of Ur-Nammu, begins a peaceful reign	Ur-Nammu's codes of law are recorded	Naplanum founds a dynasty at Larsa	Ishbi-Erra reigns over Isin	Invading Elamites besiege Mesopotamian cities

THE ROYAL TOMBS OF UR

One of the most exciting stories in Sumerian archaeology began in September 1922, when Leonard Woolley boarded a steamship for Basra. Among the sites he discovered at Ur and Tell al-'Ubaid were a series of tombs, raided by grave-robbers save for the resting place of the divine Queen Pu-Abi.

From Basra Sir Leonard Woolley traveled by car across the desert to arrive at Ur on November 2, 1922, pitching his expedition tents in the shadow of Ur's great ziggurat. He first dug two large trenches near the ziggurat. Trench A showed evidence of burials and jewellery; trench B exposed a large wall and ancient ruins. It was too hot to continue excavations, so he left and returned in the fall of 1923 to continue the dig at Ur and begin excavation at the nearby settlement of Tell al-'Ubaid.

During successive visits Woolley excavated many major buildings at Ur and discovered much about early life in ancient Mesopotamia. At this time he felt his digging crew was too inexperienced to commence further work on trench A. It was not until the fall of 1926 that he permitted work in this area

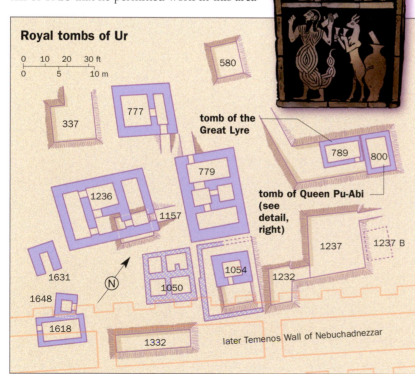

and uncovered some 600 burials containing clay pots, combs, weapons, and jewelry. He found another 300 graves in the following year, and four were very different from the rest, constructed as large multi-roomed tombs rather than burial pits. When he finished his explorations in 1934, Woolley had found nearly 1,850 burials, 16 of which he designated Royal Tombs and most of which he dated to about 2600.

Woolley realized that he had made an important discovery in the Royal Tombs, but was nevertheless disappointed. The tombs had been visited by grave-robbers and their artifacts had apparently been stolen or destroyed. His frustration is palpable when he records findings of "fragments of what may have originally been a headdress."

As Woolley's excavations proceeded he became more convinced that what he had discovered was not only important, but quite extraordinary. In one tomb he found 74 bodies, 68 of them women, arranged in what was a clearly deliberate funerary procession. Elsewhere he found gold ribbon headdresses and gold vessels. And these were only the fragments left after the robbers had taken their lot and sold them in illicit markets in Baghdad and elsewhere. It is difficult to even guess at what these tombs may have held in their original state.

Secrets revealed

Other tombs began to reveal their secrets. Gold and bead pendants, lapis lazuli necklaces, a wooden harp and lyre—crushed but

Royal tombs of Ur

0 10 20 30 ft
0 5 10 m

580
777
337
tomb of the Great Lyre
789
800
779
1236
tomb of Queen Pu-Abi (see detail, right)
1157
1237
1237 B
1631
1054
1232
1648
1050
1618
1332
later Temenos Wall of Nebuchadnezzar

The 16 tombs Woolley uncovered dating to the Early Dynastic IIIA period (c.2600–2500 BC) distinguished by their wealth were dubbed the "royal tombs." The magnificent lyre found in tomb 789 has a sounding board (pictured above) made of shell-decorated plaques. The top panel depicts a common scene in Mesopotamian art, a master of animals—a heroic figure grasping a rearing human-headed bull in each arm, probably representing the protective deity Lahmu ("Hairy"). Below, a hyena and a lion in human postures offer food and drink, animal parts and a large jar. Below them an ass plays a lyre, while a bear steadies the instrument and a seated animal rattles a sistrum. In the bottom register a scorpion-man holds objects in his hands and a gazelle carries two beakers. Mesopotamian representations of animals acting as human beings are rare and the meaning of these scenes remains a mystery.

recognizable—encrusted with gold, silver, and precious jewels. In another tomb were the remains of a richly decorated royal sled, together with the preserved remains of the oxen that had drawn it and the grooms who had attended them. Elsewhere he found an elaborate headdress that had disintegrated, but which with infinite patience he was able to reconstruct as the famous Standard of Ur.

And finally the most extravagant tomb of all, that of Queen Pu-Abi. Woolley knew this was his most significant find: a royal tomb that had escaped the attentions of looters, together with a cylinder seal with her name written on it in Sumerian cuneiform. He immediately telegraphed the University of Pennsylvania, writing in Latin in case it was intercepted, to say that he had "found the intact tomb, stone built and vaulted with bricks, of Queen Puabi."

Queen Pu-Abi's tomb was remarkable. Alongside her body were those of royal attendants, who had taken poison so that they would be subdued when the tomb was sealed. By this act they ensured that they would serve their mistress even after her death, and attested to the fact that royal personages at this period had achieved divine status. Queen Pu-Abi's body was covered with beads of precious metal, her fingers decorated with rings. There was a floral crown and evidence of woven

Tomb Chamber
In the unplundered tomb chamber of Queen Pu-Abi, Woolley found the queen laid out on a bier, with the bodies of two personal attendants and skull fragments of a third. Many of the chamber's content are on display in the University of Pennsylvania Museum, including the queen's headdress and cylinder seal.

Detail of Tomb 800

tomb chamber

0   3   6 ft
0   1   2 m

Wardrobe Chest / Grave Goods
The chest, possibly a wardrobe, had a shell and lapis-lazuli inlaid border (badly decayed). It was surrounded by grave goods, including a gaming board, and stone, silver, and gold vessels and plates.

chest

Sled (chariot)
Two oxen, the bodies of their grooms, a wooden sled, and other objects lay at the bottom of the entrance ramp.

Queen Pu-Abi's Attendants
The bodies of 13 young women were laid out in the "death pit" outside the queen's tomb. One held a harp which, according to Woolley's description, she held as if she played it until the moment of her death.

dromos

pit

Dromos
Five male bodies are laid in the entryway ramp, accompanied by ceramic vessels. Woolley believed the oval depression ("pit") above their heads represented traces of ceremonial activity.

Above left: Headdress of Queen Pu-Abi.

animal figures. The discovery of Queen Pu-Abi's tomb ranks alongside that of Tutankhamun's in Egypt.

Below: Gold dagger and sheath found in the "royal tombs" at Ur.

SUMERIAN HOME LIFE

The social class into which one was born, or to which one was elevated by royal decree, largely defined Sumerian lifestyle. While standards of cleanliness and luxury were high for the elite, living conditions were rudimentary for the average citizen.

The aristocratic class was composed primarily of wealthy landowners, but also included priests, counselors, and military leaders and advisers appointed by the king. The much larger working class included professionals such as architects, scribes, merchants, and farmers, some of whom were quite wealthy, with a lower strata of hired workers and laborers. Beneath these two groups of citizens was a considerable population of slaves, consisting of prisoners of war and indebted families. Some estimates place the slave populations as high as 40 percent in major cities.

For the aristocracy life was luxurious. They lived in two-story brick-built houses with several rooms and spacious courtyards planted with exotic flowers and fruits. There were separate bathrooms with their own plumbing, where slaves poured warm water over the bather and anointed their body with precious oils. Slaves also performed most of the menial tasks in a wealthy family, but management of them was the responsibility of the women of the household.

Women of the upper classes enjoyed considerable freedom, including the right to own property and have an income separate from their husbands', but major decisions—including the arrangement of marriages for sons and daughters—were made by men. Boys attended school, while girls were educated at home. Some of the wealthier families even employed their own musicians and singers to provide entertainment.

For many of the aristrocrats, daily life was a round of organizing and planning their business ventures, tending to religious rites, and entertaining guests and visiting dignitaries. At times of crisis, they would be expected to serve as military officials and provide produce and manpower from their estates.

Town planning

The living standards of the less wealthy free citizens were quite different. Their single-story mud and brick houses were arranged along narrow unpaved roads or alleyways that averaged about six feet in width. Even in the poorer homes a separate area was kept aside to serve as a kitchen, with mud-brick ovens placed outside the rear of the building. These houses generally had no plumbing, so occupants bathed in the river and most household waste was simply deposited in the alleyways.

Municipal workers were employed to keep these communal areas tidy, which for the most part meant spreading a layer of ash and sand over the waste. Over a period of time the accumulated waste, ash, and sand increased the height of the roads, so steps down to the houses on either side were needed.

The layout of a town usually centered on administrative and religious buildings, which in larger cities might include a massive ziggurat dedicated to a patron deity. During the later part

Below: Terracotta relief of a carpenter at work, c.early 2nd millennium BC. Mesopotamia was not rich in trees suitable for woodworking and so most wood was probably imported from Phoenicia (Lebanon), with cedar and tamarisk being the best for religious figure carving.

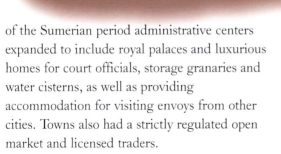

of the Sumerian period administrative centers expanded to include royal palaces and luxurious homes for court officials, storage granaries and water cisterns, as well as providing accommodation for visiting envoys from other cities. Towns also had a strictly regulated open market and licensed traders.

Many towns were surrounded by high protective walls with narrow entrance gates, while beyond the town precincts were irrigated fields bisected by numerous canals that controlled the floodwaters of the Euphrates and Tigris. Farmers either owned or leased fields in which to plant their crops, and were responsible for ensuring that the canals were kept free of rushes and weeds. Court officials were appointed to oversee the management of canals, to weigh produce and issue receipts for cereals placed in the communal granaries, and to generally control affairs of state, as well as having jurisdiction over disputes and the authority to determine appropriate punishment.

Above: From the same period as the carpenter facing, this terracotta relief depicts a young woman playing a lyre.

Right: The lack of a beard on this male figurine means it does not depict a priest, while the elegant clothing suggests a member of the wealthy administrative or land-owning class.

THE SUMERIAN KING LIST

The Sumerian King List details the lengths of reign of the various rulers of Sumer. After fanciful rules of thousands of years, the postdiluvian section of the list gives historically accurate details of the shifting seat of power.

The King List is far from complete, it does not for instance mention the city of Lagash, where Ur-Ningirsu (**above**) ruled between 2122–2118 in the recovery period after the Gutian kings. One of the best finds at Mari is this statue (**facing top**) of King Iku-Shamagan, c.3000 BC.

There are several versions of the Sumerian King List, most of them copied from an early original and modified so that later rulers could be added, as is the case with a list compiled during the reign of Damiqilishu of Isin (about 1800 BC). The most complete list, and the one generally referred to, was inscribed on a clay tablet found in the temple library at the city of Nippur. The scribe who wrote states that it was completed during the reign of Utukhegal of Uruk, thus dating it to c.2125.

The lists are part fact and part fantasy. Although they claim to be accurate records of kingship "from the beginning of history," some of the kings had improbably long reigns and others whom we know from archaeological evidence are omitted. The list is nevertheless a valuable insight into Sumerian politics and the relationships between the city-states of Sumer.

There are two distinct parts to the list, one dealing with the time before the Great Flood, and a second section listing the postdiluvian period. In the former era, the role of the king as a divine representative is established, since this tells us that kingship "descended from heaven" and was inaugurated at Eridug (Eridu), where Alulim was king for 28,800 years. Following a succession of kings with long reigns, Eridug fell and the kingship was taken to Bad-tibira, where Enmenluana ruled for 43,200 years. The three listed kings of Bad-tibara ruled for 108,000 years until the city fell to Larag (Larak), then to Zimbir (Sippar), and finally to Curuppak (Shuruppak).

Then "the flood swept over" and Kic (Kish) became the new seat of government, with numerous kings reigning for periods of 400 to 1,500 years. When Kic was defeated, kingship passed first to Eanna and then to Uruk where, until the time of Gilgamesh, the kings continued to have reigns of a millennium or more (it is worth noting that Eanna was in all probability only another name for Eerech-Uruk). After Gilgamesh the King List and the archaeological record begin to agree and the reigns can be dated with greater historical accuracy. The list gives us a total of 134 kings for the postdiluvian period, with 11 different cities from which kingship was exercised.

Seesawing balance of power

The King List demonstrates how power shifted from one city-state to another: "Erech [Uruk] was defeated, its kingship was carried to Ur…. Ur was defeated, its kingship was carried to Awan…. Awan was defeated, its kingship was carried to Kic [Kish]…. Kic was defeated, its kingship was carried to Hamazi."

From Hamazi the kingship returned to Uruk and Ur, then to Adab and Mari, then reverted to Kish. The kingship then went successively to Akshak and back to Kish and Uruk. Uruk fell to the invading hordes of Sargon of Agade, bringing in the period of Akkadian rule, until Naram-Sin (whose name is disputed in the King List) began to reassert the power of Uruk.

New invasions from King Gudea ended the hegemony of Uruk for "91 years and 40 days," until Utuhegal briefly restored Uruk's rule before losing this to Ur-Nammu of Ur. In the King List from Isin, written at a later date, Ur is defeated and power passes to Ishbi-Berra and his successors for the next 200 years.

Comparison has been made between the Sumerian King List and the biblical account of the patriarchs from the *Book of Genesis*. This ongoing debate suggests that the biblical description may have originated from the Sumerian records, although others claim that the biblical record is more complete. It is clear, however, that some chronological correlation exists between the King List and the *Book of Genesis*.

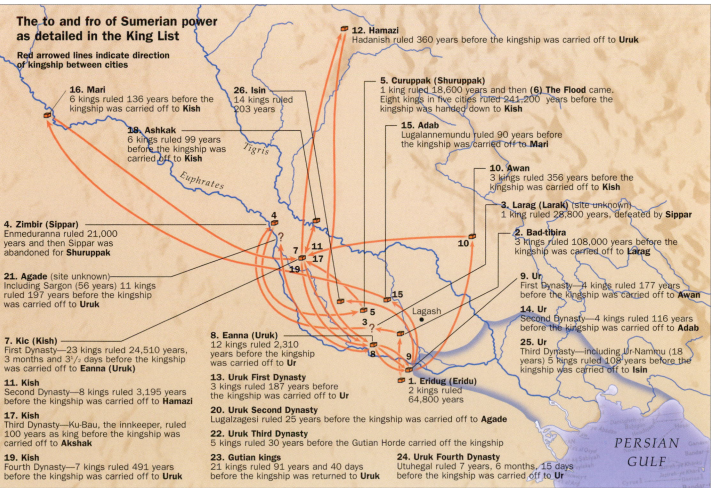

The to and fro of Sumerian power as detailed in the King List

Red arrowed lines indicate direction of kingship between cities

12. Hamazi
Hadanish ruled 360 years before the kingship was carried off to **Uruk**

16. Mari
6 kings ruled 136 years before the kingship was carried off to **Kish**

26. Isin
14 kings ruled 203 years

18. Ashkak
6 kings ruled 99 years before the kingship was carried off to **Kish**

5. Curuppak (Shuruppak)
1 king ruled 18,600 years and then **(6) The Flood** came. Eight kings in five cities ruled 241,200 years before the kingship was handed down to **Kish**

15. Adab
Lugalannemundu ruled 90 years before the kingship was carried off to **Mari**

10. Awan
3 kings ruled 356 years before the kingship was carried off to **Kish**

3. Larag (Larak) (site unknown)
1 king ruled 28,800 years, defeated by **Sippar**

4. Zimbir (Sippar)
Enmeduranna ruled 21,000 years and then Sippar was abandoned for **Shuruppak**

2. Bad-tibira
3 kings ruled 108,000 years before the kingship was carried off to **Larag**

21. Agade (site unknown)
Including Sargon (56 years) 11 kings ruled 197 years before the kingship was carried off to **Uruk**

9. Ur
First Dynasty—4 kings ruled 177 years before the kingship was carried off to **Awan**

14. Ur
Second Dynasty—4 kings ruled 116 years before the kingship was carried off to **Adab**

7. Kic (Kish)
First Dynasty—23 kings ruled 24,510 years, 3 months and 3½ days before the kingship was carried off to **Eanna (Uruk)**

8. Eanna (Uruk)
12 kings ruled 2,310 years before the kingship was carried off to **Ur**

25. Ur
Third Dynasty—including Ur-Nammu (18 years) 5 kings ruled 108 years before the kingship was carried off to **Isin**

11. Kish
Second Dynasty—8 kings ruled 3,195 years before the kingship was carried off to **Hamazi**

13. Uruk First Dynasty
3 kings ruled 187 years before the kingship was carried off to **Ur**

17. Kish
Third Dynasty—Ku-Bau, the innkeeper, ruled 100 years as king before the kingship was carried off to **Akshak**

20. Uruk Second Dynasty
Lugalzagesi ruled 25 years before the kingship was carried off to **Agade**

1. Eridug (Eridu)
2 kings ruled 64,800 years

19. Kish
Fourth Dynasty—7 kings ruled 491 years before the kingship was carried off to **Uruk**

22. Uruk Third Dynasty
5 kings ruled 30 years before the Gutian Horde carried off the kingship

23. Gutian kings
21 kings ruled 91 years and 40 days before the kingship was returned to **Uruk**

24. Uruk Fourth Dynasty
Utuhegal ruled 7 years, 6 months, 15 days before the kingship was carried off to **Ur**

Tigris

Euphrates

Lagash

PERSIAN GULF

UNIFICATION OF THE CITY-STATES

The date for the unification of Mesopotamia is open to speculation. The Sumerian King List credits Sargon (r.2335–2279), who created the combined state of Sumer in the south and Akkad in the north. More recent work suggests that Sumerian unification may have begun at an earlier date.

Above: Detail from Eannatum's stele of victory celebrated the conquests of Lagash over Umma, Ur, Uruk, and Kish.

Prior to Sargon, Sumeria was divided into 12 city-states: Adab, Akshak, Bad-tibira, Uruk (Erech), Kish, Lagash, Larak, Larsa, Nippur, Sippar, Umma, and Ur. The traditional view is that these engaged in constant internecine warfare. Resources were few in these desert regions, which led to intense competition

for land and water. Irrigation schemes that rendered desert areas fertile expanded a city's territorial claims and caused disputes over borders and rights of way. It is also claimed that local patriotism led to feuding, since each city had its own patron deity.

While there can be little doubt that warfare was endemic and that any political unity was fragile, it is important to remember that the Sumerians were culturally united. They spoke the same language (which was different from the Semitic languages of the north) and, despite regional shifts in importance, believed in the same gods.

As early as 2600, during the Early Dynastic

period, Gilgamesh of Uruk had defeated the kings of Kish during an intense period of rivalry between Uruk, Kish, and Ur, and established sovereignty over these important city-states. In 2585 Mesannepadda of Ur (r.2560–2525) defeated Agga of Kish and adopted a title (appelation unkonwn) that indicated he now claimed sovereignty over all of Sumer; although by 2500 the balance of power had shifted back to Kish.

Other city-states were involved in these constant changes of political authority. Eannatum (r.2454–25), grandson of Ur-Nina of Lagash, defeated Umma and embarked on a war of conquest against Ur, Uruk, and Kish, only to be overthrown soon after by Umma's forces. Fortunes were reversed again when Eannatum's nephew Entemena (r.2404–2375) defeated Umma.

It is significant that, once more, Eannatum and Entemena claimed titles that designated dominion over all of Sumeria, not only over those city-states that records tell us they had conquered by force of arms. Lagash lost its dominant position in 2350 when it was in turn conquered by Lugalzagesi (r.2360–35), who was originally from Umma.

Cultural equilibrium

The balance of power was continually shifting from one dynasty to another, and with that the center of power moved between city-states, but there is little to suggest that there were any cultural or ideological shifts. We do not, for instance, see the wholesale displacement of city-state deities, which remained as they were even under the control of a different dynasty, and it is unlikely that local populations saw change that significantly altered their daily lives.

Sargon's eruption on the scene was somewhat different, since he was not a member of one of the Sumerian dynastic families but came from a northern Semitic tribe. He was from humble origins, but had achieved a position of authority in the royal court at Kish and had befriended Lugalzagesi.

Although Sargon declared himself independent of the Sumerian dynasts and established his own capital at Agade, he did not intervene to prevent Lugalzagesi's schemes to dominate Sumeria. However, once Lugalzagesi had achieved this, Sargon sent his Akkadian forces south to conquer the major Sumerian cities (*see pages 46–49*). Sargon appointed his own officials to govern the cities and broke the power of local temple complexes by redistributing their lands and wealth among his own followers. His accomplishment was to join Akkad with Sumer.

Bottom: Detail from the Stele of the Vultures, an important piece of archaeological evidence on the subject of war in ancient Mesopotamia. The commemoration of Eannatum's victory over Umma provides evidence on weaponry, armor, and army formulation—a Macedonian-style phalanx is clearly shown.

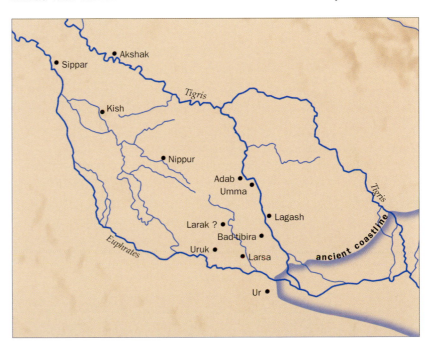

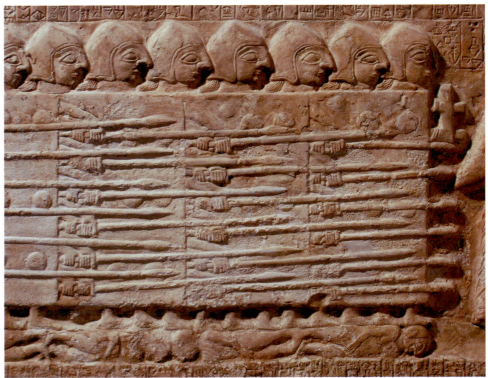

THE KINGDOM OF MARI

Mari (modern Tel Al-Hariri) is located on the west bank of the Euphrates in present-day Syria. A key trade center, it was a miltary base for the Akkadian empire and grew to great size by the time of its destruction by Babylonians.

Although the Kings of Mari are well known from Sumerian texts, the location of the city remained a mystery until it was accidentally discovered by Arab grave-diggers in AD 1933. Subsequent excavations under the direction of French archaeologist André Parrot revealed a series of mud-brick walls and statues. Most importantly, an inscription clearly identified the site and named one of the city's rulers as King Lamgi Mari.

The city was in a strategic position on the trade route between Syria and Mesopotamia c.1800 BC, when its influence extended about 310 miles from the frontier of Babylon, up the Euphrates, to the Syrian border. This effectively gave Mari control over all trade, both overland and along rivers, between Mesopotamia, western Iran, and the Syrian steppes.

Mari maintained a strong military presence to protect its trade interests, but was also a center of art and culture. Although art was predominantly Sumerian, much was modified and shows an amalgam of styles that reflects the different groups that traded here and traveled through the area.

Parrot continued his extensive studies until 1974, and this was continued after 1978 under French anthropologist Jean-Claude Margueron. Their work established that the original village site had grown into a substantial city by about 2900 BC, with a palace and temple complex dedicated to Dagan, god of storms, constructed over the next 200–300 years. Dagan was to become the state deity under the third dynasty of Ur and Mari was to remain as an important center of the cult.

Sargon of Agade used Mari as a base during his expansionist wars against the Sumerians, which saw the rise of the Akkadian empire (2340–1900). He built a second temple and introduced a cult dedicated to the sun god, Shamash, who was related to the Sumerian deity Utu, god of authority and knowledge. When Sargon's power waned, Mari was settled by the Elamites (biblical Amorites), speaking a language that was ancestral to Hebrew and different from that spoken in other parts of Sumer.

Right: Terracotta wall mosaic from Mari depicting warriors on a chariot trampling an enemy to death.

Plan of the royal palace of Mari (Tell Hariri) at the time of King Zimri-Lim

A royal apartments
B kitchens (with brick oven)
C library with 20,000 tablets
D archive with 1,600 tablets
E first throne room
F second throne room
G slave quarters
H store rooms
J palace temple
K sacred high terrace
L temple of Dagan
M temple of Ninhursag
N temple of Shamash

Razed yet preserved

By the time of Mari's last king, Zimri-Lin, the palace complex had grown to 260 rooms on two levels, and included a harem, banqueting halls, a library, royal quarters, and residential areas for court officials. It is apparent that the entire administration of Mari was located within the palace complex at this period. A new temple was also erected over the remains of an earlier one, this time rededicated to Ishtar.

The statues and inscriptions at Mari attest to a long line of exalted kings, but from various cultural backgrounds. All of them took over Sumerian ideas and beliefs, which they modified with their own idea. Zimri-Lin only ruled for about 20 years, before being defeated by Hammurabi of Babylon in 1761.

Hammurabi destroyed Mari, tearing down its walls and burning the palace and temple complexes. Curiously, Hammurabi's acts of destruction were a boon for archaeologists. The palace walls collapsed inward and were covered

by desert sand, leaving behind the most complete evidence of Mesopotamian architecture, since the burning of the city had served to bake and preserve its mud-bricks.

The conflagration hardened and prevented deterioration of clay tablets contained in the library and archive. The archive, explored before the library, revealed 1,600 tablets, giving a virtually complete account of Zimri-Lin's finances. However, this much celebrated find paled into insignificance when the library was excavated, for this housed 20,000 cuneiform tablets containing detailed reports, letters, and diplomatic correspondence from Mesopotamia and the surrounding area.

Above: A circular seal impression with four entwined figures from Mari, dating from about the rule of Zimri-Lin.

CHAPTER 3

SARGON AND THE EMPIRE OF AKKAD

Sargon of Akkad (r.2335–279) was the world's first empire builder, conquering all of southern Mesopotamia and parts of Anatolia, Syria, and Elam (Iran). Curiously, given his importance in Mesopotamian developments, no historical records can be accurately identified. Instead, Sargon reaches us as a mystical figure, famous through legends and tales of his extraordinary triumphs.

According to these tales his mother was a "changeling" who bore him in secret—possibly because he was the result of an illicit affair with a high priest. She placed him in a rush basket sealed with bitumen, which she set afloat in the Euphrates. He was found by Akki, "drawer of water," who, with his wife, adopted Sargon as their son and trained him for the profession of gardener. Sargon was, however, favored by the goddess Ishtar (equivalent to the Sumerian deity Inanna) and destined to achieve great deeds. He rose to the prestigious position of cup-bearer to King Ur-Zababa of Kish, from whom he declared his independence to found the new capital of Agade and began creating an empire of his own.

The Akkadian legends tell us that he fought 34 battles in southern Mesopotamia, where he captured King Lugalzagesi of Uruk and led him in chains to the temple at Nippur. He defeated the kings of Lagash, conquered Mari, Ebla, and the cedar forests (Lebanon), and fought successful battles in Elam and the Zagros mountains.

In Ur, Sargon had one of his daughters, Enheduanna, installed as the priestess of the moon god, Nanna. Flushed with success, Sargon renamed himself Sharrukin, the "Rightful" or "True King," referring to his domination of the region over the rulers of former city-states who had occupied hereditary positions. At various points he adopted the titles of King of the Land, King of Kish, and King of Sumer and Akkad. At the height of his power Sargon claimed to control more than 65 cities, with the "sons of Sargon" installed as *ensi* (governors) of different regions and supported by garrisons of the Akkadian army.

Exaggerated success

It is unclear just how unified Sargon's empire was. It is most likely that the Akkadians established themselves as overseers of important trading cities and that much autonomy remained within the Sumerian regions. In fact cultural borrowing appears to have been from Sumerian to Akkadian rather than the imposition of Akkadian beliefs on a conquered state. It is also probable that Akkadian influences were apparent long before Sargon's rule—the Sumerian King List, for example, provides a series of kings with Akkadian names during the first dynasty at Kish.

It is certain, too, that Sargon's military successes have been embellished over the years by the various scribes who recorded and re-recorded them, partly in an attempt to justify the greatness of their own empires. Both the Babylonians and the Assyrians were later to name kings after Sargon of Akkad, and it is mainly from their records that the legacy of Sargon has reached us.

There is no physical evidence from which judgment can be made. Unlike the Sumerian kings, whose palaces and

Mesopotamia during the time of Sargon the Great, 2350–2100 BC

CASPIAN SEA

Murat

Lake Van

Hurrians

Lake Urmia

BARTU

• Tell Brak

ZAGROS MOUNTAINS

• Nineveh

ASSYRIA

Ashur ▪

Hamazi

Tigris

Gutians

Kassites

Elamites

Lullubi

Mari ▪

M E S O P O T A M I A

Diyala

Hit •

Euphrates

• Eshnunna

• Der

Awan

Sippar ▪

▪ Akshak

Agade ? ▪
Babylon ▪   ▪ Kish
Borsippa

AKKAD

EMBUTAL

Susa •

ELAM

• Nippur

Adab ▪

▪ Shuruppak

SUMER

Bad-tibira ▪   Lagash ▪

Uruk ▪   SUMER

Ur ▪
Eridu •

Amorites

MARHASHI

A Babylonian cylinder seal of Ur-Nammu, depicts a goddess leading a worshipper before the deified king, who first codified the law (*see pages 56–57*).

Legend:

▨ empire of Sargon of Agade, c.2280

▨ region possibly under Sargon's control

→ Sargon's legendary naval conquest of Dilmun

— kingdom of Lugalzagesi, c.2350

▪ city named in the Sumerian King List, c.2100

Legend tells that Sargon the Great led an invasion fleet against Dilmun, which—if true—would have been the first naval campain in history.

PERSIAN GULF

DILMUM

temples provide testimony to their status and achievement, Sargon's capital at Agade has never been identified. The legends tell us it was destroyed at the end of the Akkadian period, and it is assumed that the ruins lie somewhere on the Euphrates between Sippar and Kish. Tantalizingly, but perhaps appropriately, the legend of Sargon recorded in an ancient text begins with "Sargon, the mighty king, king of Agade, am I" but remains inconclusive: the lower portion of the tablet on which it is written has been lost.

SARGON CONQUERS THE CITY-STATES, 2340 BC

The influence of the Akkadian period on the development of Mesopotamia is disproportionate to the brief length of its power. A hereditary chain weakened with each link, its enduring legacy was sharpened administrative, military, and legal practices.

Right: This stele illustrates the victory over the Gutians by Naram-Sin. He is depicted climbing a mountain at the head of his troops, trampling on the bodies of his enemies, while paying homage to the sun for his victory. The king's helmet bears the horns emblematic of divine power.

Just five Akkadian kings ruled for a total of 150 years, yet their ideas profoundly changed the language, art, religion, and culture of Mesopotamia, and led to reforms in military tactics and law that persisted for a further 2,000 years, through the Babylonian and Assyrian periods, until the incursions of the Achaemenids from Persia in 539.

Though shrouded in mystery and legend, Sargon's prowess as a military tactician and politician cannot be denied. He appears in history at a time when the Sumerian city-states of southern Mesopotamia were already in the process of unification under Lugalzagesi of Uruk. Sargon's defeat of Lugalzagesi extended this to the north and beyond the borders of Sumeria, ending the independence of city-states and bringing in a new age of empire.

Although Sargon disputed the idea of hereditary leadership and familial control, he nevertheless installed his daughter as the high priestess in Ur and was succeeded by two sons, Rimush and Manishtushu. Manishtushu was succeeded by his son Naram-Sin, who was followed in turn by his own son, Shar-kali-sharra, the last of the Akkadian kings. Their rule was justified by the claim that it had divine sanction and descended from the goddess Ishtar. This new political ideology was emphasized through the arts, with the introduction of life-size heroic sculptures of the kings and monumental victory stelae.

As part of the process of unification, the Akkadians standardized weights and measures and insisted on the use of the Semitic (Old Akkadian) language in all administrative and official documents. The establishment of a political capital at the port city of Agade and a renewed focus on the religious capital at the holy city of Nippur, that saw it become a cult center for the entire region, further undermined the autonomy of the former city-states.

Losing hold

The Sumerian city-states did not readily accept Akkadian rule, and during Sargon's reign there were a number of local protests. These were quickly subdued, but on Sargon's death several of the cities, led by Ur and Lagash, staged an open rebellion that his son, Rimush, had difficulty in repressing and which had repercussions throughout the Akkadian empire. Despite Rimush's eventual success, it is clear that the Sumerians felt themselves to be a subjugated group and never fully accepted Akkadian domination.

Naram-Sin, who came to the throne in 2254, engaged in a series of extensive military campaigns in an attempt to consolidate Akkadian hegemony. He named himself King of the Four Regions—that is, king to the furthest boundaries of the civilized world—and adopted the title God of Akkad. Judicial documents of the period found at Nippur are signed on oath to Naram-Sin, using a formula that identifies him as a deity.

Despite his apparent deification, Naram-Sin was unable to rely on the full allegiance of southern Mesopotamian towns. At the same time there were incursions along the borders of the Akkadian empire from semi-nomadic tribes such as the Elamites, Guti, and the Lullubi. When Naram-Sin died in 2217, his son Shar-kali-sharra proved to be a weaker leader and, under increasing pressure from the Elamites and Guti, was forced to cede territory and withdraw to the capital.

The Guti however were unable to consolidate their gains, opening the way for a resurgence of Sumerian power led by Gudea, King of Lagash, that was soon followed by a revolt at Uruk. This reversal was, however, short-lived. Eventually Ur-Nammu besieged and defeated Uruk, restoring the city of Ur and putting control over the Sumerian area in the hands of Ur's Third Dynasty.

Above: This bronze head dating from c.2250 BC is thought to represent either Sargon the Great or Naram-Sin.

Right: A clay tablet with an outline map of the world has text relating to the conquests of Sargon. It was not contemporary and dates from the Babylonian era, c.600 BC.

NIPPUR, THE UNTOUCHABLE CITY

When Sargon turned to the priests at Nippur to legitimize his status as the king of Sumer and Akkad, he was following in a revered tradition that had been established in the prehistoric Al-Ubaid period (5200 BC) and would last until the medieval Islamic era (AD 800).

Below: A photograph taken in 1952 shows members of the Universities of Chicago and Pennsylvania digging in Nippur. The excavations uncovered 20 superimposed levels covering a period of 1,900 years through a depth of 60 feet.

Recognition of kings in Nippur (Nuffar) at the Temple of Enlil, chief god of the Mesopotamian pantheon, was a prerequisite to rule that Sargon apparently felt unable to challenge. The earliest records indicate that Nippur was considered to be primarily a holy city rather than a political one, and it was this sacred character that enabled it to survive the rise and fall of the various Mesopotamian dynasties and empires.

Located about 93 miles southeast of Baghdad, between Baghdad and Basra, Nippur today consists of a vast mound, or tell, 65 feet high and a mile long, bisected by an ancient course of the Euphrates known as the Shatt al Nil. Excavations carried out since 1889 by the University of Philadelphia and those currently underway under the auspices of the University of Chicago suggest that as much as one quarter of the Nippur site was dedicated to temples and other religious buildings. Recovered artifacts indicate that the city was prosperous, partly through the presentation of valuable gifts by various kings and noblemen at their investiture, and from their later sponsorship of elaborate building programs for temples, public buildings, and canals.

Nippur was also strategically important, located on the border between the Sumerian groups of the south and those of Akkad in the north. Some of the texts recovered from the site

have contemporaneous inscriptions in both Sumerian and Akkadian, and it is possible that city officials functioned as impartial arbiters between these warring states. Its status as an economic exchange center between the kingdoms is attested to by the texts recovered here, divided almost equally between matters of religious and commercial concern.

A preserved timeline

Despite its importance in the inauguration of new kings, Nippur's administration appears to have been focussed along hereditary family lines, under the supervision of an appointed governor. Even outsiders who were brought in to act in official positions seem to have been under the sponsorship of these families, and changes in governorship had little impact on lines of succession. We know, for example, that members of the Sumerian Ur-me-me family were administrators of the Inanna temple during the Akkadian period and retained this position throughout the following period of control by the Third Dynasty of Ur and into the later Isin period about 1900.

It was nevertheless Nippur's status as a holy city that protected it from the wanton destruction that often befell royal cities in the area whenever there was a shift in political allegiance. In this respect it should be borne in mind that Enlil's status as the "father" of the gods also placed him in a parental relationship to the kings, who, as divine personages, were thought of as Enlil's sons and as his representatives in the conduct of human affairs. Even in the later Achaemenid Persian period, when the god Marduk gained prominence, Enlil continued to be important and Nippur remained as a place of veneration and pilgrimage.

On the rare occasions that Nippur was put under siege, as when the Elamites challenged Ur's supremacy in 2000, it was quickly rebuilt and the temples restored. The long uninterrupted sequences that can be determined at Nippur has enabled archaeologists to use artifacts and other records from the site as a standard by which to judge remains from elsewhere. This is particularly true when attempting to date pottery sequences and changes in architectural style and construction.

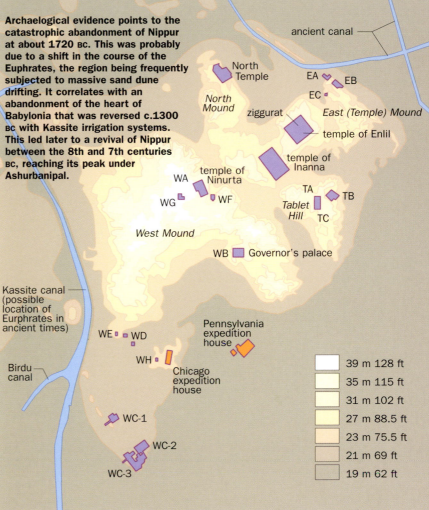

The archaeology of Nippur

Archaelogical evidence points to the catastrophic abandonment of Nippur at about 1720 BC. This was probably due to a shift in the course of the Euphrates, the region being frequently subjected to massive sand dune drifting. It correlates with an abandonment of the heart of Babylonia that was reversed c.1300 BC with Kassite irrigation systems. This led later to a revival of Nippur between the 8th and 7th centuries BC, reaching its peak under Ashurbanipal.

☐	39 m 128 ft
☐	35 m 115 ft
☐	31 m 102 ft
☐	27 m 88.5 ft
☐	23 m 75.5 ft
☐	21 m 69 ft
☐	19 m 62 ft

Tablet Hill
So called because archaeologists on the 1948–52 expedition found a concentration of important tablets there. This led to the belief that all or most of the scribes at Nippur had lived in this part of the site. However, later excavations revealed even more texts in the southern end of the West Mound. More recent excavations have uncovered tablets in almost every part of the site. Work in the trenches TA and TB uncovered houses containing pottery from 2300–500 BC, the Akkadian to Achaemenid periods, which became a standard of reference for all of Mesopotamia. Another trench exposed the North Temple and then the temple of Inanna, goddess of love and war. In 1953–62 archaeologists revealed 17 rebuildings one on the other dating from 3200 BC–AD 100.

West Mound
In the 1970s a new expedition, expecting to find houses dating back to the Kassite period under an earlier revealed Parthian villa (c.AD 100), discovered another sequence of superimposed temples (WA) dating from as early as 2100 BC (Ur third period). At the mound's southern end (WB) a Kassite building was found dating from c.1250 BC. Tablets identified it as the governor's palace. Immediately under the palace was an older house (c.1750 BC) owned by a family of bakers. Texts revealed that they were under contract to the city administrators to bake bread for the for Nippur's administration, temples, and the public.

City wall
In the later 1970s Trenches WC-1 and WC-2 uncovered remains of the city, measuring 46 feet thick. This excavation was also able to date the ancient canal to the west to the Kassite period and it lay approximately where the Euphrates is located on the Kassite map of Nippur found by the University of Pennsylvania. At the same time, the city walls to the east of the ziggurat (EA, EB, EC) were investigated.

THE GUTIAN PERIOD, 2230–2109 BC

Akkadian texts referring to the reigns of their kings and their exploits record numerous campaigns against a people known as the Guti, who appear to have been barbarian raiders from the Hamadan region in the central Zagros mountains of present-day Iran.

Little is known about who the Guti were. The King Lists name 20 (sometimes 21) Gutian kings who ruled in Sumer and Akkad between 2230 and 2109, but they left few traces of their occupancy other than the occasional dedication. The Akkadians were initially dismissive of these mountain warriors, describing them as "not classed among people—not reckoned as part of the land—Gutian people who know no inhibitions. With human instinct but canine intelligence and monkeys' features."

Yet despite this indifference and prejudice, the Guti were largely responsible for the overthrow of the Akkadian empire and forced the last Akkadian king, Shar-kali-sharra, into exile at their capital of Agade. Eventually Agade fell to the Guti as well, who thereafter appear to have adopted Mesopotamian culture and used Akkadian personal names.

While they occupied a few strategic locations, such as Nippur, the Guti never sought to maintain overall control of the region. Throughout this period there were numerous shifting alliances as the Guti favored first one city and then another, dismissing and reinstating the Akkadian governors at will, during which petty kingdoms sought to assert themselves. Even the reigns of Gutian kings seem fragile and subject to constant shifts in allegiance. The longest reign, that of Sium, was only seven years, while the average reign was a mere two to three years.

Under the apparent lack of focused leadership, Mesopotamia fell into a period of anarchy and decline, permitting the Elamites to invade many of the rural areas. Of the Sumerian city-states only Lagash seems to have reasserted any authority, although it is probable that this was as a result of alliances with the Guti: Ur-Bau of Lagash was known to be pro-Gutian, as was his son-in-law Namhanni, who seized Umma for the Gutians but was eventually executed by Ur-Nammu as a traitor of Sumer.

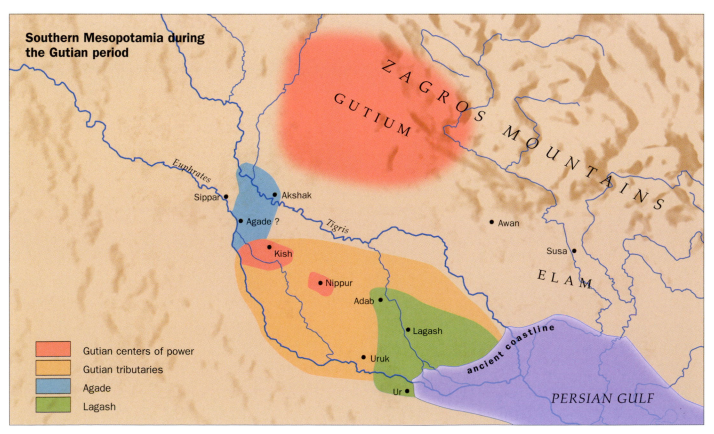

Southern Mesopotamia during the Gutian period

ZAGROS MOUNTAINS

GUTIUM

Euphrates

Sippar

Akshak

Agade ?

Tigris

Kish

Awan

Nippur

Adab

Susa

Lagash

ELAM

Uruk

ancient coastline

Ur

PERSIAN GULF

- Gutian centers of power
- Gutian tributaries
- Agade
- Lagash

Even Gudea, who oversaw the domination of Ur by Lagash and was then to instigate a new Sumerian empire, was known for his pro-Gutian views and assisted them in campaigns against other Sumerian leaders.

A humbled monarch

While little cultural, economic, or political advance was made during Gutian rule, they played a major role in shaping future events. Their loss of control of the countryside enabled the Elamites to install new kings at Babylon, who were to initiate the Babylonian period of Mesopotamian history. Gutian failure to exert effective political control over the city-states enabled the Sumerians to regroup and form new alliances of their own.

Utuhegal of Uruk finally brought Gutian power to an end. Immediately prior to this, the internal squabbling of the Gutian leadership had led to the election of a new king, Tirigan, who had been in power for only 40 days when Utuhegal's army marched out to confront him at the battle of Ennigi. Tirigan was defeated and fled the scene to evade capture, but was hunted down and brought before Utuhegal, who delivered the humiliating symbolic act of putting his foot upon Tirigan's neck.

Utuhegal, who was an experienced statesman as well as a skilled commander, restored some semblance of order and stability to Mesopotamia, but was "carried off by the river" before he could reunify the Sumerian states. The most likely explanation, alluded to in some texts, is that he was assassinated by enemies within the court.

Above: The barren landscape of the Zagros mountains seen from a low-earth-orbit satellite. The view is looking southeast across the southern part of the range toward the Strait of Hormuz, with the island of Qeshm visible at the top of the photograph.

SUMERIAN RESURGENCE

Although the Akkadians dominated Sumeria, the reigns of Sargon and his son and successor Rimush were marked by constant minor uprisings within Sumer and from neighboring regions. Invading Gutians relied on Sumerians to administrate, making rebellion inevitable.

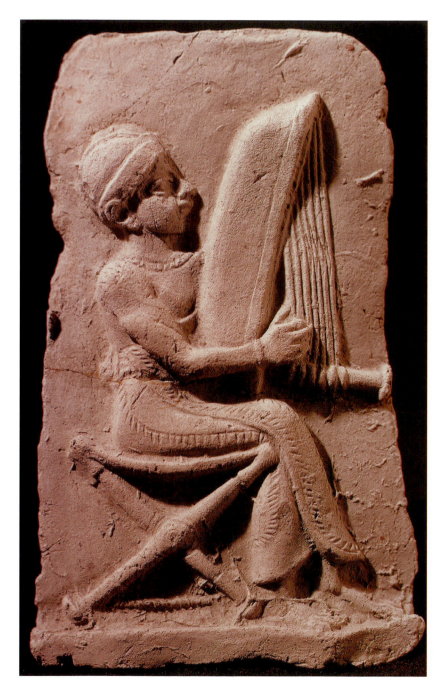

Sargon and Rimush faced revolts and rebellions from Ur, Umma, Adab, Lagash, Der, Kazallu, Elam, and Barahshi. When Manishtushu (r.2269–55) came to the throne—variously described as the twin or elder brother of Rimush—he was opposed by a coalition of 32 rebel kings led by Uruk.

Despite active opposition to Akkadian rule, their policy was generally one of conciliation. A number of Sumerians held high government positions in the Akkadian courts, and the Akkadians took over many Sumerian rites and customs. It was nevertheless necessary for Naram-Sin (r.2254–17), son of Manishtushu and grandson of Sargon, to re-establish Akkadian sovereignty by forcibly putting down a powerful coalition of rebel kings who had been incited by Uruk and Kish. Inscriptions detail how the defeated rebels were brought in shackles before Naram-Sin to receive punishment. The Sargon dynasty ended with the rule of Shar-kali-sharri (r.2217–2193), during which Sumer exploded in revolt and faced into civil war.

As we have seen, internal weakness, rebellions, and foreign attacks left the Akkadian empire vulnerable to invasion by the Gutians, which led to the dismantling of the Akkadian empire. Although two Akkadian rulers, Dudu (r.2189–69) and Shu-Turul (r.2168–54), managed to retain some authority at Agade, most of Sumeria was thrown into a period of anarchy and political chaos. Inscriptions referring to these "dark ages" of Sumeria claim that the Akkadian downfall was retribution for Naram-Sin's desecration of the temple of Enlil at Nippur, and that eight Sumerian deities had laid a curse on Agade, that it would remain forever desolate and uninhabited.

A precarious return

The Gutians had little political or economic infrastructure of their own, and once again we

c.2000	c.2000	c.1900	c.1900	1932–06	1868–57	1834	c.1800
Texts begin to detail science, diplomacy, and religion, as well as administration	Domesticated horses are employed	Elamites from Persia control much of Mesopotamia	A dynasty is established at Babylon city by Sumu-Abum	Gungunum of Larsa seizes control of Ur from Isin	Lipit-Ishtar is king of Isin and writes codified laws	Silli-Adad of Larsa is replaced by Warad-Sin, son of Elamite Kutur-Mabuk	The city of Mari is a key point on the trading route between Syria and Mesopotamia

see Sumerians being appointed as local governors and given important government positions, although many seem to have been awarded in a fickle manner as momentary favors. *Ensis* were placed in and removed from authority with remarkable rapidity, preventing resurgence of Sumerian unity, even though the gods and culture of the Sumerians were incorporated into the Gutian system.

The Gutians favored Lagash, perhaps because of its compliance to their wishes, and it was here that Gudea (r.2141–22) began to assert some semblance of authority. He attempted to re-establish the classical Sumerian civilization, although he and his son, Ur-Ningirsu (r.2122–2118), remained vassal kings, ultimately under the sway of the Gutians.

Gudea was responsible for extensive temple-building, indicating that little had changed in the Sumerian belief system under either the Akkadians or the Gutians. The records are mute on this point, but it is likely that there was some Sumerian independence during these periods.

Utuhegal (r.2133–13), ruling at Uruk, initiated a long campaign against the Gutian king Tirigan (*see page 53*). Utuhegal's brother Ur-Nammu (r.2113–2095) took the kingship back to Ur after defeating Nippur, Adab, and Larsa, and usurping the throne at Uruk. Ur-Nammu claimed ownership of all Sumeria and presented himself as a benevolent reformer. He established the Third Dynasty of Ur in 2112 and was succeeded by his son Shulgi (r.2094–47), who ushered in a period of relative peace and presided over a Sumerian renaissance. Under Shulgi much of the power formerly held by the temples was given over to the royal courts. The new Sumerian empire, however, failed to hold after Shulgi's death.

Facing: The revival of Sumerian culture is evidenced by many statuettes depicting artists such as this Isin-Larsa relief of a harpist or the singer Ur-Nina, **left**, both of which date from c.2000 BC.

c.1800	c.1800	1792	1780	1764	1763	1761	c.1750
Kassites settle in the Hamadan-Kermanshah district of Iran	Assyrian rulers Ishmi-Dagan and Shamshi-Adad I unite Ashur, Nineveh, and Arbel	Rim-Sin conquers Isin and controls central and southern Mesopotamia	Shamshi-Adad dies and control of his coalition of states passes to Hammurabi	Elamite armies are defeated by Hammurabi of Babylon	Hammurabi defeats Larsa and places his son Samsu-Iluna in place of Rim-Sin	Zimri-Lin of Mari is defeated by Hammurabi of Babylon	The Hittite capital of Hattusas, at Boghazköy, Turkey, is established

UR-NAMMU'S LEGAL CODE

Ur-Nammu was the founder of the third dynasty of Ur and was renowned as a successful military commander and social reformer. He created the earliest written code of law in existence, predating the more famous laws of Hammurabi by three centuries.

Ur-Nammu had been appointed as a military governor by Utuhegal of Uruk (r.2133–13), but seized power on the death of the king. He attacked and killed Namhani, brother-in-law of Ur-Bau of Lagash, then also seized power at Ur. At the height of his reign he ruled all of Sumer and much of Assyria and Elam. Ur-Nammu wrote a set of laws during the reign of his son Shulgi (r.2094–47), intended to "free the land from thieves, robbers, and rebels."

The code of a prologue and seven decipherable laws was probably originally inscribed on a stone stela, but exists now only as a copy on a poorly preserved clay tablet. The tablet is divided into eight columns, four on each side, each column containing about 45 small ruled spaces. On it Ur-Nammu is described as a divine king, who was appointed by the gods to be their earthly representative and rule over Sumer and Ur.

The code of law outlines a policy of tolerance and equality and makes no distinctions for wealth or status. It is far more liberal that Hammurabi's policy of an "eye for an eye" and

Right: Carved stone relief of a soldier with his prisoner inset into a wall, c.2300 BC. Ur-Nammu's legal code ushered in a new humanitarianism, but its effects were probably not felt by prisoners of war.

tends to specify payments of fines for transgressions of the law, rather than corporal punishment; even crimes of assault and rape were reduced to payment for injury. Its laws deal with accusations of witchcraft, which was proven through a trial by water, and the return of a slave to his master. It also established a regulated system of weights and measures. Ur-Nammu states that the law was intended to ensure that "the orphan did not fall a prey to the wealthy," "the widow did not fall a prey to the powerful," and that "the man of one shekel did not fall a prey to the man of one mina [60 shekels]."

Matters of record

The manner in which Ur-Nammu's laws were put into practice is evident from records pertaining to the reign of Shulgi. There are over 300 court records, known as *ditillas* (completed lawsuits), detailing legal procedures and social and economic organization. The king was held responsible for law and justice, but in practice was often in the hands of the local *ensi* (governor).

Cases were heard before a court consisting of three or four judges who were drawn from professional ranks: temple administrators, sea merchants, couriers, scribes, archivists, and city elders. An upper court was presided over by royal judges; this probably functioned as a court of appeal. Assisting the judges was the *mashkim*, whose function appears to have been that of court clerk.

For a case to come to court it was necessary for the victim to lodge complaint and to swear an oath that the complaint was a just one. He had to provide evidence that would justify his case and witnesses who could corroborate it. The judges appointed a date and time for the hearing, when the complainant was responsible for ensuring that his witnesses were able to attend. The witnesses gave their statements under oath, all of which were recorded on a clay tablet by the *mashkim*. When a verdict had been reached and the payment date of the penalty decided, these too were inscribed. The tablet was then countersigned by the judges, the clerk, the witnesses, and the litigants, and deposited in the court archive.

Above: This relief shows Ur-Nammu sacrificing before Shamash and receiving the commission to build his temple. It should be compared to the photograph on the following page of Hammurabi receiving the Law from Shamash, which is obviously a stylistic copy of this earlier relief.

THE ISIN-LARSA PERIOD, 2025–1763 BC

Isin and Larsa were important cities after the collapse of the Third Dynasty of Ur, as proved by many surviving documents from the latter. Control alernated between the two in this period, but neither could resist Hammurabi's Babylon.

Larsa, referred to in Genesis as Ellasar, lies near the modern town of Tall Sankarah about 19 miles southeast of Uruk (Warka) in southern Iraq. Isin's location is unknown, but its close association with Larsa suggests they may have been twin cities. Larsa flourished under the dynasty founded by King Naplanum (r.2025–05), who was a contemporary of King Ishbi-Erra (r.2017–1985) of Isin.

There was uneasy neutrality between the rival cities, with Isin initially the stronger of the two, according to documents recovered from Ur. Certainly there were closer links between Isin and Ur: Ishbi-Erra had been an official at the court of Ibbi-Sin, the last king of Ur's Third Dynasty, and could lay claim to control not only of Ur but also of Uruk and Nippur, as well as to trade routes linking Mesopotamia with Arabia and India.

The balance of power shifted under Gungunum (r.1932–06) and Abisare (r.1905–1895), the fifth and sixth kings of Larsa. Gungunum, son of the governor at Lagash, wrested control of Ur from Isin and thus placed the main seaport of Mesopotamia under Larsa's authority. By 1835, however, the Elamites had reasserted themselves. Silli-Adad, the 12th king of Larsa, ruled for one year before being deposed by Kutur-Mabuk, who placed his son Warad-Sin (r.1834–23) on the throne.

Thousands of business documents exist from

Above: Detail of Hammurabi receiving the Law from the sun god Shamash on the Stele of Hammurabi. Shamash was revered at Larsa, and after his conquest of the city-state, Hammurabi made restorations to his temple there.

Warad-Sin's reign, which indicate an extensive program of agriculture and stock-breeding, and long-distance trading in ivory, vegetable oil, hides, and wool from the Euphrates to the Indus Valley. Under Rim-Sin (r.1822–1763), Warad-Sin's son, the arts received particular encouragement and the old Sumerian scribal schools were revived. Rim-Sin, known as Eriaku to the Elamites and referred to in the Bible as Arioch, eventually conquered Isin during the 30th year of his reign by diverting its canals to Larsa, leaving Isin without water and placing Larsa in control of southern and central Mesopotamia.

The House of Justice

In 1763 Rim-Sin's rule was brought to an end when Hammurabi of Babylon defeated Larsa and substituted his own authority under his son Samsu-Iluna. Prior to this, Larsa and Babylon had exerted almost equal infuence—tablets from Mari say "10 or 15 kings follow Hammurabi of Babylon; the same number follow Rim-Sin of Larsa"—but thereafter Larsa was a subject city of Babylon.

Excavations carried out by Loftus in the mid-19th century AD describe the ruins of Larsa as dominated by a low circular platform, about 15 feet in circumference, rising gradually to a height of 72 feet. Loftus also found inscriptions that suggest the temple of the sun god Shamash was first restored by Hammurabi and later by Nebuchadnezzar II (r.605–562) and Nabonidus (r.555–39).

Further excavations at Larsa in 1933, under the direction of French archeologist André Parrot, revealed the ziggurat of El-Babbar, dedicated to Shamash, as well as ruins of the ancient mound of Senkereh and the Palace of Nur-Adad (r.1865–50), and a temple library. Parrot also found numerous tombs and extensive remains from the later Neo-Babylonian and Seleucid periods.

Among Parrot's most important finds, discovered in the so-called House of Justice, since it served as an early court of law, was the law code of Lipit-Ishtar. These, the earliest example of codified laws, were written during Lipit-Ishtar's reign as king of Isin (1868–57).

He rose to prominence from a humble origin as a farmer and shepherd at Nippur, and many of his laws refer to the management of farmland and livestock; but he also wrote what are the first child support laws in existence. According to these, if a man had children "by a harlot from the public square" then he was to provide "grain, oil, and clothing for that harlot [and] the children which the harlot has borne him shall be his heirs."

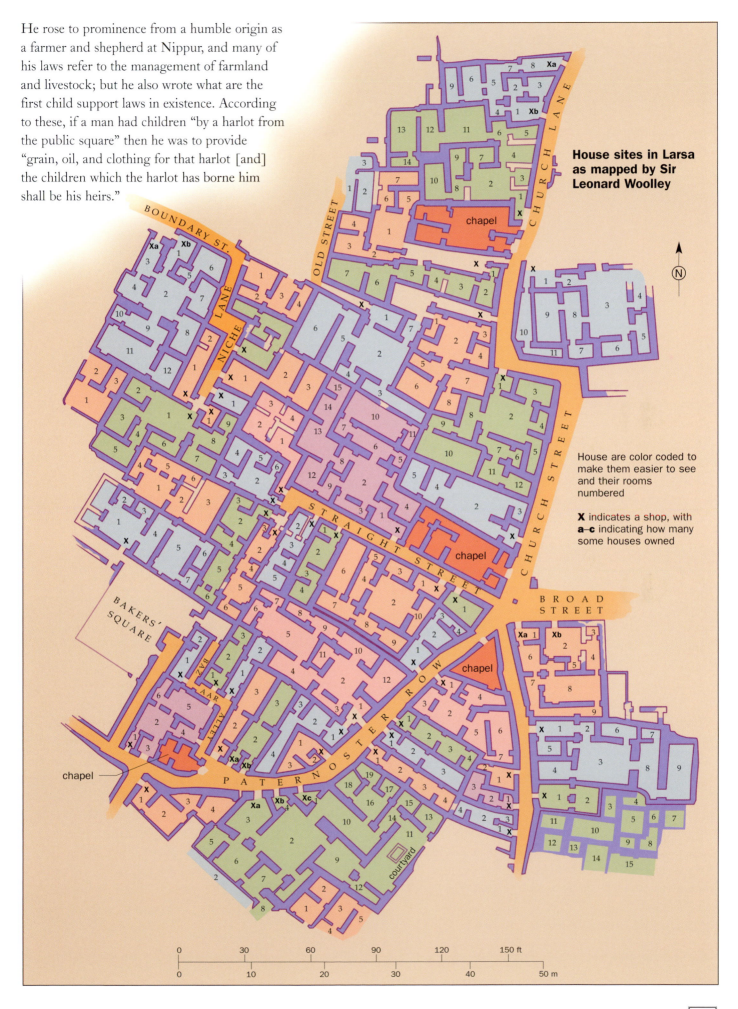

House sites in Larsa as mapped by Sir Leonard Woolley

House are color coded to make them easier to see and their rooms numbered

X indicates a shop, with **a–c** indicating how many some houses owned

CHAPTER 4

OLD BABYLONIA, 1900–1100 BC

The last of the old Sumerian dynasties collapsed in about 2000, leading to a century of economic and political decline during which various city-states vied for control of the area's resources. By 1900 Elamites from Persia had gained control of much of Mesopotamia, following conflicts between Sumerian Larsa in the south and Babylon in the north, although a long struggle was to continue until Babylonian control was fully established under Hammurabi in 1763.

Babylonian is, essentially, a union of the earlier Akkadian and Sumerian beliefs and political systems, with a new centralized government created in the capital city of Babil (Babylon). It is likely that this shift in the focus of government was linked with a change in course of the Euphrates that served to locate Babylon at the north end of its main stream, thereby giving the formerly insignificant village considerable economic influence. Babylon was previously of so little import that its name does not even appear in the Sumerian texts until the reign of Shar-kali-sharra in 2254–30.

This change in fortune was reflected in the ritual status of the city, which became known as the "gateway of the god," a reference to the principal Babylonian deity, Marduk, who was said to be the child of the Sumerian god Enlil. The period from the establishment of Babylon as the capital until the Hittite invasions in 1595 is referred to as Old Babylonian, to distinguish it from the later Chaldean or Neo-Babylonian period.

New systems of administration were put in place. Authority was taken away from individual states and vested in a monarchy that claimed divine origin. Laws were introduced to control crimes against the state (the Code of Hammurabi), and a new judiciary was funded through the introduction of direct taxation.

Civilization of trade

Other significant changes were the introduction of compulsory military service and the centralization of all state activity at Babylon. Money raised from taxes supported the new state infractructure and financed ambitious building programs that included a bridge across the Euphrates so the city developed on both banks of the river.

For the first 30 years of his reign, Hammurabi exerted his influence through diplomatic means. Hundreds of diplomatic letters from his reign and that of his son Samsu-Iluna (1750–12) have been recovered from the court archives at Babylon. Most of these refer to trade agreements and alliances and to the entertainment of visiting envoys from distant parts of the kingdom, although there are also references to trading activities well beyond the borders of Mesopotamia.

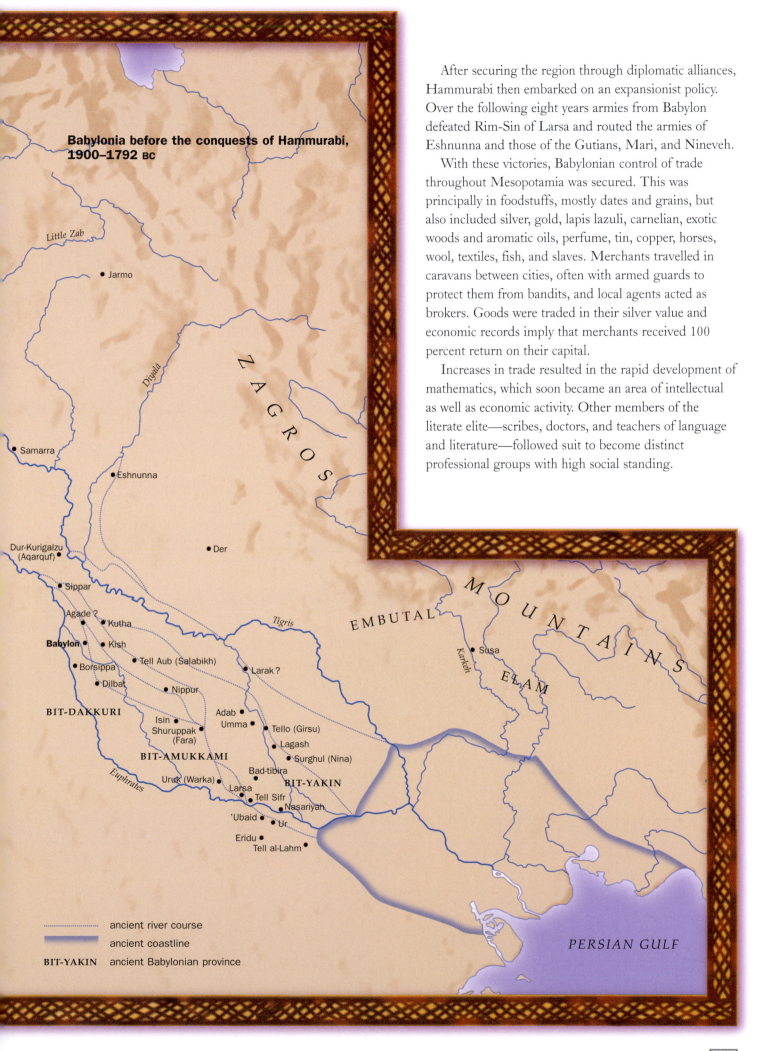

Babylonia before the conquests of Hammurabi, 1900–1792 BC

Little Zab

Jarmo

Samarra

Diyālā

Eshnunna

Dur-Kurigalzu (Aqarquf)

Der

Sippar

Agade ?

Kutha

Babylon

Kish

Borsippa

Tell Aub (Salabikh)

Dilbat

Larak ?

Nippur

BIT-DAKKURI

Isin

Adab

Shuruppak (Fara)

Umma

Tello (Girsu)

Lagash

BIT-AMUKKAMI

Surghul (Nina)

Bad-tibira

Euphrates

Uruk (Warka)

BIT-YAKIN

Larsa

Tell Sifr

Nasariyah

'Ubaid

Ur

Eridu

Tell al-Lahm

Tigris

Z A G R O S

E M B U T A L

M O U N T A I N S

Karkeh

Susa

E L A M

PERSIAN GULF

.... ancient river course

———— ancient coastline

BIT-YAKIN ancient Babylonian province

After securing the region through diplomatic alliances, Hammurabi then embarked on an expansionist policy. Over the following eight years armies from Babylon defeated Rim-Sin of Larsa and routed the armies of Eshnunna and those of the Gutians, Mari, and Nineveh.

With these victories, Babylonian control of trade throughout Mesopotamia was secured. This was principally in foodstuffs, mostly dates and grains, but also included silver, gold, lapis lazuli, carnelian, exotic woods and aromatic oils, perfume, tin, copper, horses, wool, textiles, fish, and slaves. Merchants travelled in caravans between cities, often with armed guards to protect them from bandits, and local agents acted as brokers. Goods were traded in their silver value and economic records imply that merchants received 100 percent return on their capital.

Increases in trade resulted in the rapid development of mathematics, which soon became an area of intellectual as well as economic activity. Other members of the literate elite—scribes, doctors, and teachers of language and literature—followed suit to become distinct professional groups with high social standing.

THE DEVELOPMENT OF MATHEMATICS

Babylonian mathematics developed from earlier, and much simpler, methods of counting and recording transactions that had been devised by the Sumerians and Akkadians. New, sophisticated disciplines included geometry, algebra, and calculation tables.

The first Sumerian mathematics system used representative clay tokens; one token was equivalent to one sheep, or to one measure of grain. As trading increased, the quantities of goods being exchanged meant dealing with larger numbers, leading to abstraction and the use of tokens that had multiple values. Thus the number 11 could be signified by one token that represented ten units and another representing a single unit, placed in a denominational position, similar to the place-values used in a decimal system. To facilitate counting the Akkadians invented the abacus, which also used this idea of positional notation.

In the more sophisticated Babylonian system, the base number was 60; sexagesimal has survived to the present day, where one hour is divided into 60 minutes and one minute into 60 seconds, and the 360 degrees of a circle are a simple multiple.

Several hundred mathematic and economic Babylonian tablets have been recovered from sites of the period, although relatively few of these are from Babylon itself. These tablets indicate that they had refined the Sumerian notions of measures of length, area, capacity, and weight and given them standard values.

While some tablets are official records, others are clearly the product of established schools of mathematics that list problems set by teachers and set out the solutions given by their students. They do not usually state a general procedure, but instead give worked examples.

Theory in practice

A typical problem would be to find market rate for goods, lengths of canals, weights of stones, areas of fields, or the number of bricks used in a construction. They include calculations of the number of workers and days necessary for building a canal, and the total wages for the workers. Some of the tablets go considerably beyond the skills needed for daily life,

1750–12 Reign of Samsu-iluna of Babylon, son of Hammurabi	**1741** Iranian Kassites make their first raid into Mesopotamia	**1680–50** Reign of Labarnas, who begins a Hittite dynasty	**1620–1590** The Hittites advance into Syria under the leadership of Mursilis I	**1595** Hittites invade Babylonia with Kassites led by King Kakrime of Mari	**c.1550** Indo-European Hurrians from Mitanni invade northern Mesopotamia	**1545–00** Kassite Burnaburiash II signs a treaty with Assyrian King Puzur-Ashur III	**c.1500** The Hittites are one of the first cultures to smelt iron

presumably intended for the use of an elite group of male mathematics students singled out for special attention or destined to enter the priesthood.

A notable feature of the advanced mathematical tablets is the use of tables, which gave the Babylonians advantages over any previous form of mathematics or calculation. They had multiplication tables, tables of square and cube roots (two tablets found at Senkereh in AD 1854 give squares of numbers up to 59 and of cubes up to 32), reciprocals (used in division), constants, and tables of coefficients or conversion factors. The latter were used to determine the relative values of goods traded from other areas and to convert the value of the goods into an equivalent weight of silver. They also had knowledge of pi and triangular geometry (1,200 years before Pythagoras), employed logarithms, and used tables to solve equations.

The greatest surviving evidence of mathematics being used in practice is in large-scale construction projects, such as pyramidal ziggurats and major canals. Generally the Babylonians seem to have thought in terms of algebra and trigonometry, rather than geometry; but despite the emphasis in theoretical mathematics on calculation,

Babylonians applied geometry to determine length, area, and volume.

Above: Babylonian clay tablet (2000–1600 BC) with cuneiform script and rectangular diagram with details of an algebraic-geometrical problem. and, **facing,** a similar tablet containing a complex algebraic equation.

Left: Although the Babylonians used a positional base-60 system, it had some vestiges of a decimal, or base-10 system. This is because the 59 numbers were built from a single symbol configured in nine different ways, and a "ten" symbol configured in five different ways.

1		11		21		31		41		51	
2		12		22		32		42		52	
3		13		23		33		43		53	
4		14		24		34		44		54	
5		15		25		25		45		55	
6		16		26		36		46		56	
7		17		27		37		47		57	
8		18		28		38		48		58	
9		19		29		39		49		59	
10		20		30		40		50			

c.1500	c.1500	1472	1460	1440–30	1430–1380	1400–1200	1380–59
The Egyptian empire extends to the River Euphrates	An alphabet is employed at Ugarit, Syria	Assyrian areas are still subject states, dominions annexed to the Hurrians of Mitanni	Egyptians under Thutmose III encounter Mitanni and ally against the Hittites	Karaindash extends Kassite empire south into Sealander territories	Kassite Kurigalzu I restores Ur and builds a palace at their new capital of Dur Kurigalzu	Imperial period of the Hittites	Kassites conquer Arrapha, giving them access to trade routes out of Mesopotamia

BABYLON

It was not until 1900 BC that Babylon gained any significance, when Sumu-Abum established a dynasty. Under its sixth king, Hammurabi, it became one of the greatest empires of ancient times.

Archaeological investigations at the site of the ancient city of Babylon (modern Hillah) suggest that it was originally a small, unnamed hamlet on the left bank of the Euphrates about 56 miles south of Baghdad. There is mention of a town with a similar name about 2300, when Sargon of Agade is said to have built sanctuaries there, but the tablet is

badly eroded and the inscriptions unclear.

The name "Babylon" is a Greek rendition of Babil or Bab-ili (Gate of God), which itself is the Semitic translation of the original Sumerian name, Ka-dimirra. In Kassite texts the name appears as Ba-ba-lam. The etymology is unclear, but most of these names seem to refer to the temple dedicated to Marduk (Bel-Merodach) who, under the Old Babylonian dynasty, was considered to be the principal deity.

During the revivalist period of the Third Dynasty of Ur, Babylon was just a provincial town under the authority of a local *ensi* (governor). Babylon only started to gain

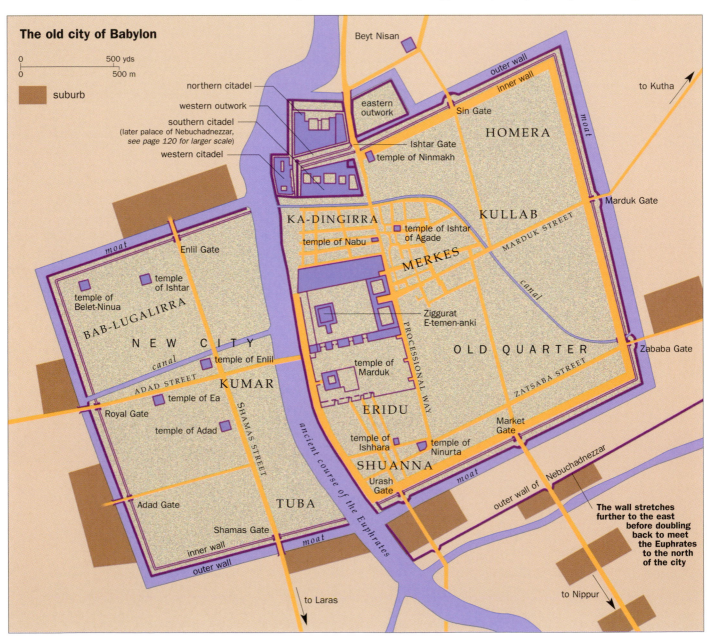

The old city of Babylon

0 — 500 yds
0 — 500 m

suburb

Beyt Nisan

northern citadel
western outwork
southern citadel
(later palace of Nebuchadnezzar,
see page 120 for larger scale)
western citadel

eastern outwork

outer wall
inner wall

to Kutha

Sin Gate

HOMERA

Ishtar Gate
temple of Ninmakh

moat

Marduk Gate

KULLAB

KA-DINGIRRA

temple of Nabu

temple of Ishtar
of Agade

MARDUK STREET

MERKES

canal

temple of Ishtar

temple of
Belet-Ninua

BAB-LUGALIRRA

Enlil Gate

Ziggurat
E-temen-anki

OLD QUARTER

Zababa Gate

NEW CITY

moat

canal

temple of Enlil

temple of
Marduk

PROCESSIONAL WAY

ZATSABA STREET

ADAD STREET

KUMAR

Royal Gate

temple of Ea

ERIDU

Market
Gate

temple of Adad

SHAMAS STREET

temple of
Ishhara

temple of
Ninurta

ancient course of the Euphrates

SHUANNA

Urash
Gate

moat

outer wall of Nebuchadnezzar

Adad Gate

TUBA

**The wall stretches
further to the east
before doubling
back to meet
the Euphrates
to the north
of the city**

Shamas Gate

inner wall
outer wall

moat

to Laras

to Nippur

importance as a city in 1900, when a western Semitic dynasty was established there under Sumu-Abum; although even he may have been in the service of some other Mesopotamian state. It was not until Hammurabi, the sixth king of its first dynasty, that Babylon was raised to the status of a holy city as the capital of a unified Babylonia. Hammurabi converted this municipal town into the spiritual center of an empire whose influence was to remain profound for at least the next 1,200 years. The Assyrian king Tiglath-Pileser came to Babylon in about 1100 to legitimize his right to rule over Mesopotamia, and Babylon was to became the seat of power for the Chaldean kings Nebuchadnezzar and Nabonidus until 539.

Although most of the ruins that can be seen today date from the Chaldean period, it became one of the largest and richest cities the world had ever known during the reign of Hammurabi. With a permanent population of some 50,000 people, it was most important city of the ancient Middle East.

Crippled by the Kassites

The grandeur of Babylon drew attention from other regions. While much of this was in the form of homage to Marduk, there was unrest from factions who sought to undermine Babylon's power and influence. During the reign of Samsu-Iluna, Hammurabi's son, there were revolts in southern Mesopotamia and numerous incursions by the Kassites from the north. The revolts were put down and the Kassite incursions repulsed, but they left Babylon weakened and vulnerable. Under Samsu-Iluna's successors the city suffered a serious decline in both power and territory.

It was plundered and burned by Mursilis, the fourth ruler of the Hittite empire, who carried Babylonian prisoners of war off to Anatolia and left the city open to Kassite occupation. Under the Kassites it was briefly restored as a major center before being ruthlessly destroyed by the Assyrian king Sennacherib in 689. Sennacherib tore down the walls, palaces, and temples, and threw their rubble into the Arakhtu canal that ran to the south of the city. Such a blatant act of desecration shocked the region and caused an Assyrian civil war, during which Sennacherib was assassinated.

Subsequently the Assyrians were overthrown and Babylon was declared independent under the leadership of the Chaldean (Neo-Babylonian) king Nabopolassar. He embarked on an ambitious rebuilding program, continued under Nebuchadnezzar and Nabonidus.

After the Chaldean period, Babylon again lost its status as a major city and became an administrative center of the new Persian empire. However, the monotheistic Persians rejected the old deities and disbanded the priesthood, leaving the temples to fall into disrepair.

Above: This photograph, taken in the early 1950s before any archaeological reconstruction began, shows a view of the ruins of Babylon. At the left is the Ishtar Gate and on the right the Ninmakh temple, thought to be the site of Alexander the Great's death.

BABYLONIAN ADMINISTRATION

The key to Babylonia's success was its efficient administrative system, which influenced all the empires that were to follow. With the aid of a series of advisers, the king had control over law, agriculture, diplomacy, war, trade, and more; regional governors had a smaller support system to manage their realms.

Right: Boundary disputes were a common feature of local life in ancient Mesopotamia, with so many cities nestling together and coveting every inch of irrigated land. This is one of the boundary markers of the 13th-century Babylonian King Nazimruttash.

In theory, the king was directly responsible for all affairs of state. These included major undertakings, such as declarations of war, down to the resolution of local problems, such as the distribution of land or grazing rights, or even assistance in a marital dispute. Matters were usually brought to the attention of the king through petition, when he would consult with various advisers and determine an appropriate course of action.

Among his advisers was a group of priests, or diviners, who were skilled in the interpretation of omens and predicted whether a particular action would result in a favorable outcome. Diviners were consulted on any matter that involved risk; thus they gave advice to the king before a journey and also accompanied the army during campaigns. Although kings sometimes disregarded a diviner's advice, this was discouraged by the priests. Cautionary tales were told of the disastrous consequences that had befallen the kings of old.

A preoccupation of the king was the management of affairs of state and the delegation of authority to regional officials, who reported directly to the royal court. These officials were responsible for local administration, collection of taxes, and maintaining order, for which they were rewarded with grants of lands and the revenues these generated. Such appointments were technically the king's prerogative, although he could be petitioned by the citizens of a region with their own nominees, which they usually accompanied with valuable gifts to ensure favorable reception.

The king's representatives were responsible for hearing appeals from farmers concerning the pasturage of their flocks of goats and sheep, especially when poor weather meant that alternative sustenance needed to be sought from

a neighboring region. Merchants, too, were under the protection of the king, who maintained small garrisons in rural areas to ensure their safe passage, put down local disputes, and act as a police force.

Versatile scribes

Regional governors usually had a number of officials to assist them. Among these was a regional military commander, tax inspectors, local priests, and scribes and couriers for sending dispatches and reports back to the capital.

Essentially, administration in the capital was a more elaborate form of that exercised in the provinces, but with the addition of a number of ambassadors and envoys from foreign nations at the royal court, some of whom had permanent attachments. Their role was primarily to maintain or establish friendly relations between different rulers, centered on trade and military relationships.

In the military sphere, co-operation sometimes came in the form of a direct alliance but more frequently involved the loan of troops for a specific campaign, over a limited period. Trade was promoted through the exchange of gifts between kingdoms, the assurance of safe international passage for trading caravans, and the guarantee of markets for goods that were unavailable locally. The royal court had interpreters on hand to ensure that communications between the king and foreign rulers were kept open and free of dispute or misunderstanding.

The most important officials at royal and provincial courts were undoubtedly the scribes, since without them Babylonian administration would have floundered. They played a vital role in communicating royal decisions to the provinces and in return sending reports back to the capital. They recorded treaties and agreements with foreign powers, kept records of merchants' transactions, provided data for the priests, and functioned as mathematicians, calculating the labor forces and wages required in public building works. They also acted as quartermasters during military campaigns. It is certain, given the variety of roles they needed to fulfil, that scribes were trained for specific duties in scribal schools that employed specialist tutors in subjects as diverse as mathematics, astronomy, and medicine.

Above: Inscription on a brick in a Babylonian wall.

HAMMURABI'S CONQUESTS

When Hammurabi ascended the throne, Babylon's influence extended over an area with a radius of less than 50 miles. At the end of his reign he controlled a region extending from the Persian Gulf to Nineveh, and from the Euphrates to the Zagros mountains.

Hammurabi was an empire-builder, yet tantalisingly little is known of what he was like as a person. He was descended from an ancient line of nomadic desert sheikhs and claimed that he could trace his ancestry back over 24 generations. Cuneiform tablets depict Hammurabi in consultation with envoys and ambassadors from other nations, but treat his military accomplishments in a cursory fashion, in date form without further elaboration. There is no suggestion that he maintained a vast court of noblemen and advisors, nor is there architectural evidence in the form of grand palaces to imply that he had an ostentatious lifestyle. Almost all of his architectural achievements were in the field of public works, such as the building of canals.

His other great achievement was the establishment of a set of laws, the Code of Hammurabi, intended to protect the rights of the weak and disadvantaged. While it would be a mistake to claim that Hammurabi was a truly benevolent king, it is apparent that one of his concerns was the well-being of his subjects. He appointed royal judges to administer the law, and they reported directly back to him rather than being answerable to local committees, as had been the case with the Sumerians.

Hammurabi's main field seems to have been diplomacy. Numerous clay tablets recording his diplomatic activities indicate that he took personal control

Right: Statuette of Hammurabi kneeling in adoration.

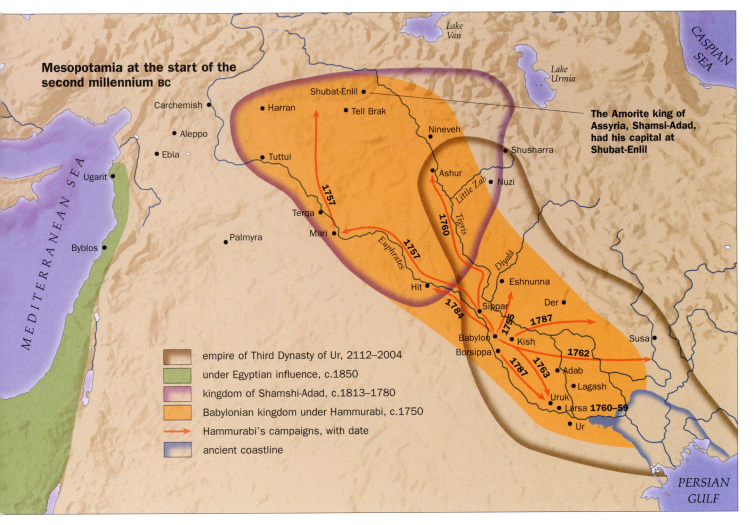

The Amorite king of
Assyria, Shamsi-Adad,
had his capital at
Shubat-Enlil

empire of Third Dynasty of Ur, 2112–2004
under Egyptian influence, c.1850
kingdom of Shamshi-Adad, c.1813–1780
Babylonian kingdom under Hammurabi, c.1750
Hammurabi's campaigns, with date
ancient coastline

over state affairs; meeting diplomats, sending
dispatches, arranging military deployments, and
overseeing his public works programs. It is
apparent that he held an open court, accessible
to his own subjects as well as foreign
ambassadors, and that grievances could be
presented before him for his adjudication.

A flood of invaders

Hammurabi was a determined individual who,
perhaps, had difficulty in delegating authority to
others. Nevertheless, during his early years on
the throne his rule was overshadowed by that of
Shamsi-Adad of Assyria, who controlled a
number of loosely allied states. There
are suggestions that Babylon was
under Shamsi-Adad's control as
a vassal state, with Hammurabi
only functioning as a titular head.
On Shamsi-Adad's death, control of
his coalition passed to Hammurabi,
consolidated by his defeat of Rim-Sin of
Larsa in 1763. Two years later he conquered
Mari and gained control of the trade routes
into Syria.
His reluctance to grant any form of
autonomy to his army commanders suggests

that Hammurabi was a brilliant military
strategist, although there is little direct evidence
to support this assertion. Our only clue comes
from a fragment of a clay tablet recording a
campaign against an unknown city, which states
that the city was defeated by "a great mass of
water." This is unlike contemporary accounts of
other Mesopotamian campaigns, which were
dependent on siege warfare, and implies that
Hammurabi had contrived to breach his
enemies' defenses by damming their water
supply and causing an artificial flood.

We are left with the impression of a proud
and domineering ruler who was prepared to
listen to others but reluctant to act on their
advice. His skills as a diplomat and strategist
ensured that he was able to avoid any direct
challenge to his authority; but this was to be the
weak point of his empire. After Hammurabi's
death his son and successor, Samsu-Iluna, was
unable to live up to his father's expectations. He
lacked Hammurabi's charismatic hold over his
subjects and lost their trust, leading to a period
of unrest, incursions from beyond Babylonia's
borders, and civil disobedience from its own
citizens.

THE CODE OF HAMMURABI

The Code of Hammurabi was not the first set of laws in Mesopotamia; however, it was the most extensive and the first to address the problems of the ordinary citizen. Based on "an eye for an eye," punishments were clearly defined and commensurate with the guilty party's wealth.

Left: Stele of Hammurabi detailing his law code, with a relief at the top depicting the king receiving the law from the god Shamash.

The Code of Hammurabi is carved into the surface of a black diorite stone monument eight feet high. It begins and ends with addresses to the gods, invoking their wrath on the head of any law-breaker, and contains 282 judgments on a variety of topics. It is evident these were actual judgments that had been handed out and which were intended to act as examples of legal precedent in future judgments.

The principle of the laws is that of *lex talionsis* (an eye for an eye, a tooth for a tooth), in which retribution is made according to the nature of the original crime. Thus if a man shall "put out the eye" of another, his punishment would be to lose an eye of his own. In practice, there were several qualifications to this basic rule.

The most important distinction in the code is the division of the population into three groups: the *amelu*, *muskinu*, and *ardu*. The *amelu* were an aristocratic, land-owning group with full citizenship who enjoyed certain rights and privileges, but were subject to higher fines and heavier punishments for their crimes. Beneath them were the *muskinu*, a term that has come to mean "beggar" in modern usage but more properly refers to someone who is not a land-owner. Their punishments were less severe, and they had reduced liability in the payment of taxes and in making offerings to gods.

The *ardu*, or slaves, were captives or free citizens who had been sold into slavery for indebtedness. Although they enjoyed a number of privileges, including the right to acquire property, any compensation paid to them went to their master.

Justice for widow and orphan

The code also dealt with the sale, lease, loan, and barter of property, which had to be substantiated by documentation and the sworn oath of witnesses. Similarly, a house could be rented for a year or more, with the rent paid half-annually in advance. Contracts were issued for hired labor, with statutory fixed wages decided by the state. Loan contracts were also made, with repayments at 20–30 percent.

Marriage contracts, governed by the code, gave considerable rights to women over dowries, ownership of property, and custody of children. If a wife was unable to bear children, the husband could take a second wife with his first wife's agreement; an invalid wife remained the responsibility of her husband whose duty it was to care for her and ensure that her needs were met. Children had responsibility for the care of elderly parents, although they could opt out by purchasing a slave to undertake care on their behalf.

Adultery and incest were punishable by death. The death penalty might also be imposed for theft and burglary, for illegal entry to the temple or palace treasuries, for handling stolen goods, for kidnapping, harboring fugitive slaves, for the disorderly conduct of a tavern, and for causing death by the careless building of a house. It was also the sentence for undertaking any action that caused another person to be put in danger. Exile, disinheritance, public whipping, and permanent removal from office were frequently imposed punishments.

In most cases it was incumbent on the court to prove that any criminal act had been carried out with deliberate intention. Suspicion of a crime was not sufficient to result in conviction, although carelessness and neglect might be punishable. The judges, witnesses, and other interested parties signed the decision, and an oath was taken to pledge that the verdict would be adhered to. In an epilogue to his laws, Hammurabi set out his reasons for formulating them, so "that the strong may not oppress the weak [and] to see that justice is done for the orphan and widow."

Making fair laws for all

The number of the quoted law is shown in square brackets.

In a society for which agriculture was the mainstay of the economy (as indeed it was in all societies until the dawn of the Industrial Revolution in the 18th century AD) it is not surprising that Hammurabi's Code made extensive provisions for pay structures within the agrarian field. He laid down strict guidelines for hire fees and laborer payment. So we hear that for his hire an ox-driver was to be paid six *gur* of corn per year [258], while a field-hand could be hired for no less than the period from April to August at a daily rate of six *gerahs* in money [273], and from August until the end of the year at the rate of five *gerahs* per day (to take into account the shorter days). The hire fees for an ox for threshing grain was 20 *ka* of corn per day [268], for an ass also 20 *ka* [269], and for a "young animal" ten *ka* of corn [270]. An ox, cart, and driver could be hired for 180 *ka* of corn per day [271] and the cart alone for 40 *ka* [272].

Over the duty of care by the hired hand, Hammurabi showed how reasonable was his thinking. Laws 265–7 state: "If a herdsman, to whose care cattle or sheep have been entrusted, be guilty of fraud and make false returns of the natural increase, or sell them for money, then shall he be convicted and pay the owner ten times the loss. "If the animal be killed in the stable by God (an accident), or if a lion kill it, the herdsman shall declare his innocence before God, and the owner bears the accident in the stable. "If the herdsman overlook something, and an accident happen in the stable, then the herdsman is at fault for the accident which he has caused in the stable, and he must compensate the owner for the cattle or sheep."

Some laws show concern for the good goverance of the justice system, even at the highest level: "If a judge try a case, reach a decision, and present his judgment in writing; if later error shall appear in his decision, and it be through his own fault, then he shall pay twelve times the fine set by him in the case, and he shall be publicly removed from the judge's bench, and never again shall he sit there to render judgment [5]."

There was to be short and swift justice for thieves: "If any one is committing a robbery and is caught, then he shall be put to death [22]." But compassion for the victims of robbery: "If the robber is not caught, then shall he who was robbed claim under oath the amount of his loss; then shall the community, and… on whose ground and territory and in whose domain it was compensate him for the goods stolen [23]." A similar compassion extended to inheritance laws: "If a man be… [killed in battle], if his son is able to enter into possession, then the field and garden shall be given to him, he shall take over the fee of his father [28]. "If his son is still young, and cannot take possession, a third of the field and garden shall be given to his mother, and she shall bring him up [29]."

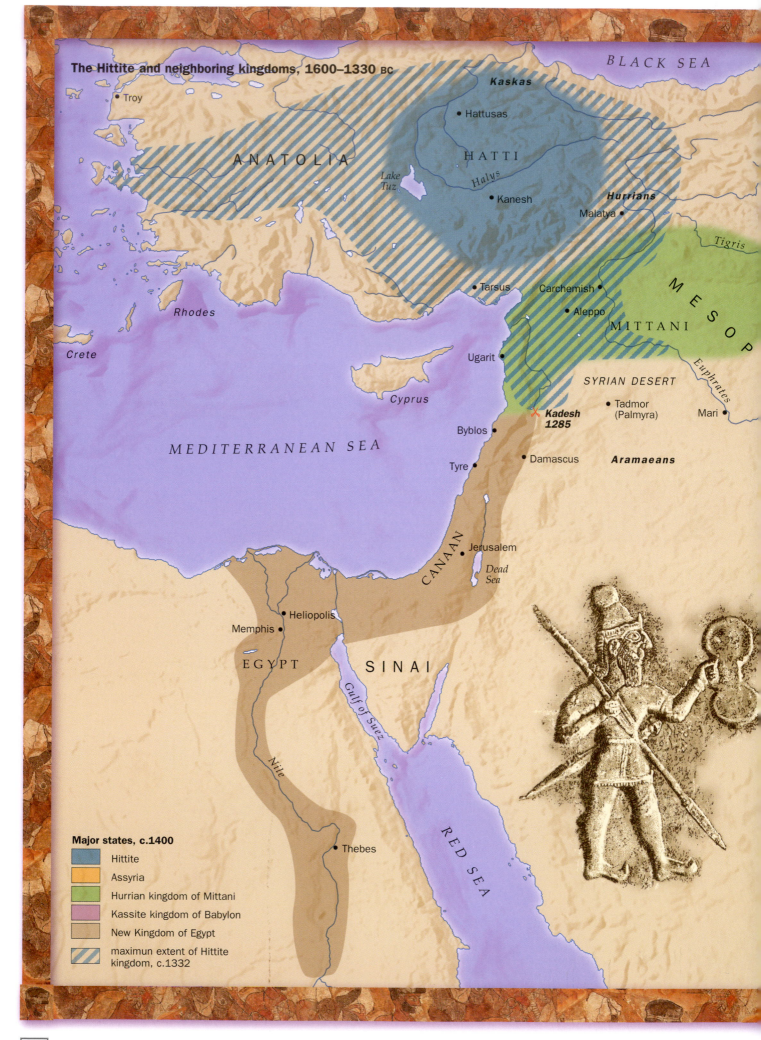

The Hittite and neighboring kingdoms, 1600–1330 BC

BLACK SEA

Kaskas

Troy

ANATOLIA

Hattusas

HATTI

Lake Tuz

Halys

Kanesh

Hurrians

Malatya

Tigris

Tarsus

Carchemish

Aleppo

M E S O P

MITTANI

Rhodes

Crete

Ugarit

SYRIAN DESERT

Kadesh 1285

Tadmor (Palmyra)

Euphrates

Mari

Byblos

MEDITERRANEAN SEA

Cyprus

Tyre

Damascus

Aramaeans

Jerusalem

CANAAN

Dead Sea

Heliopolis

Memphis

EGYPT

SINAI

Gulf of Suez

Nile

Thebes

RED SEA

Major states, c.1400

- Hittite
- Assyria
- Hurrian kingdom of Mittani
- Kassite kingdom of Babylon
- New Kingdom of Egypt
- maximun extent of Hittite kingdom, c.1332

CHAPTER 5

THE HITTITE INVASIONS, 1600–1300 BC

Lake Van

Lake Urmia

Nineveh

Arbil

ASSYRIA

Ashur

Diyala

Der

Sippar

Babylon

BABYLONIA

Nippur

Uruk

Ur

Chaldeans

Left: Carved relief of a Hittite warrior from Sendschirli Schamial.

By the end of the third millennium BC a group of people known as the Hittites had moved into the high central plateau of Anatolia, where they expelled the original Hattian population but adopted Hatti names for their kings. Their early history is obscure. Where they came from is unknown and until recently their language remained undecipherable, although it is now accepted that they spoke an Indo-European language and had migrated into the area.

By 1750 they had established their capital town of Hattusas, at Boghazköy in modern Turkey, some 130 miles east of Ankara. The first king of this new Hittite dynasty was Labarnas, whose rule began in 1680, and he was succeeded by Hattusilis (man from Hattusas) who reigned 1650–20.

From Hattusas the Hittites advanced into Syria under the leadership of Hattusilis's successor, Mursilis I (r.1620–1590), who was Labarnas's grandson by adoption. With the conquest of Syria completed, Mursilis advanced down the Euphrates to sack Babylon in 1595, effectively bringing the ruling dynasty of Hammurabi to a close and ending Babylonian rule in Mesopotamia.

Babylonia continued to be important, since the Hittites wholeheartedly adopted religion, many of the laws, and literature of the Babylonians. There is, in fact, considerable doubt over whether the Hittites attempted to impose any of their own values and beliefs on the peoples they conquered, and less evidence still that they tried to force absolute rule. It is probable that they left existing governors in place and did not interfere with the priesthood and the practice of Babylonian cults.

The Hittites claimed ownership of all land in the name of their king. Under Babylonian law, individual families held land and paid taxes to the king, who owned only the royal estates. The Hittite system, however, turned former landowners into tenant farmers who paid annual rent to the king but had no property rights.

A fiscal empire

The Hittites modified the law system that they inherited. Babylonian justice meted out the death penalty for innumerable offenses, although it is apparent that many of these sentences were reduced on appeal to the payment of fines. The Hittites imposed capital punishment only for serious crimes against the person, such as murder and rape. Many modern scholars have claimed that Hammurabi's laws are harsh and those of the Hittites are more merciful. However, we should bear in mind that the Hittite laws are merely a refinement of those established by Hammurabi.

The willingness of Hittites to adapt is also evident in the texts they left behind them. The majority of the 10,000 clay tablets recording legal and economic transactions that were discovered in Hattusas are written in Assyrian-Babylonian, with a minority in the Hittite's own Indo-European language.

At its height between 1600 and 1200, the Hittite empire extended from Mesopotamia to Syria and Palestine. They fought a long and bitter war with Egypt over the strategically important city of Kadesh, eventually defeating the Egyptian army but lacking the resources to consolidate their gains.

Despite the vast extent of the empire, it appears that Hittite interests were primarily economic. Unfortunately their motives may never be completely clear. The Hittites left very few accounts of their own history, and they are hardly mentioned in the Hebrew scriptures. Even the Egyptian records refer to them only as "barbarians," although this is an obviously biased observation.

AMBITIONS OF MURSILIS AND TELEPINUS

The Hittite empire was built on aggressive expansion. Dispossessing the Hatti, ending Old Babylonian rule, and gaining eastern Mesopotamia and more, the Hittites over-stretched themselves and had to use diplomacy to survive.

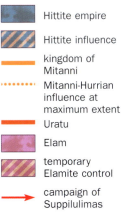

Under their first king, Anittas, the Hittites moved into Anatolia, where they sacked several cities and displaced the original Hatti population. Under Anittas's successor, Labarnas, the old Hatti city of Hattusas became the Hittite capital in about 1750. Gradual expansion from Hattusas was aided by the use of two new inventions: iron weapons, superior to the bronze previously used, and the horse-drawn chariot.

The invasions of the Hittite king Mursilis I in 1595 spelled the end of the Old Babylonian kingdoms. But Mursilis was unable to retain a firm hold over his new conquests, primarily because the Hittites were too few to take direct control of such a vast area. Under Mursilis the Hittite empire encompassed all of Syria and extended to the Aegean in the west and to all the territories of Mesopotamia in the east, as well as making incursions into Assyria. Instead of a consolidated rule, they left local leaders in place and demanded annual tribute from them. While this did not lead to open rebellion, feelings of discontent were openly expressed, which tended to undermine the authority of the Hittite kings. This culminated in the assassination of Mursilis by his brother-in-law, which triggered a series of "palace revolts."

The revolts left the Hittite kingdom in disarray and permitted the Hurrians, who originated in the area around the Caspian Sea in Iran, to establish themselves in Cilicia, where they created the kingdom of Mitanni (*see also pages 88–91*). In an attempt to stabilize their position, the Hittites agreed a treaty with the Mittani that placed much of the land east of the Hittite center under Hurrian control.

A pharaoh's hand

This deliberate policy of reduction was carried further by Telepinus, who was Hittite ruler from 1525 to 1500. Under Telepinus the Hittites relinquished control of much of the western part of their kingdom and all territories east of the Taurus mountains. In their place, the Kaska occupied the Black Sea area, while

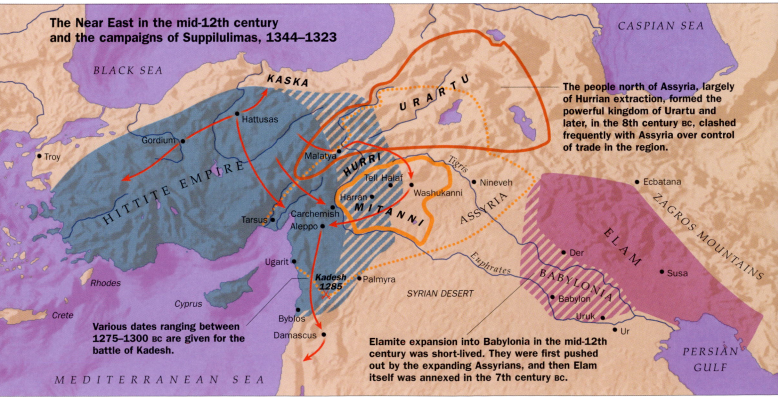

Legend:
- Hittite empire
- Hittite influence
- kingdom of Mitanni
- Mitanni-Hurrian influence at maximum extent
- Uratu
- Elam
- temporary Elamite control
- campaign of Suppilulimas

The Near East in the mid-12th century and the campaigns of Suppilulimas, 1344–1323

CASPIAN SEA

BLACK SEA

KASKA

URARTU

Hattusas

Gordium

Troy

Malatya

HITTITE EMPIRE

HURRI

Tell Halaf

Nineveh

Ecbatana

The people north of Assyria, largely of Hurrian extraction, formed the powerful kingdom of Urartu and later, in the 8th century BC, clashed frequently with Assyria over control of trade in the region.

Harran

Washukanni

Tarsus

Carchemish

MITANNI

Tigris

ASSYRIA

ZAGROS MOUNTAINS

Aleppo

Ugarit

Kadesh 1285

Palmyra

Euphrates

SYRIAN DESERT

Der

ELAM

Susa

Rhodes

Cyprus

BABYLONIA

Crete

Byblos

Babylon

Uruk

Various dates ranging between 1275–1300 BC are given for the battle of Kadesh.

Damascus

Elamite expansion into Babylonia in the mid-12th century was short-lived. They were first pushed out by the expanding Assyrians, and then Elam itself was annexed in the 7th century BC.

MEDITERRANEAN SEA

Ur

PERSIAN GULF

Hurrians and Assyrians carved out powerful niches for their kings.

Under King Suppilulimas I in 1344, the Hittites struck back. The Kaska were defeated and areas in Syria under Hurrian control were retrieved without Hurrian resistance. New tribute laws were enacted that effectively bound the conquered cities to the Hittite empire as vassals.

Not all the Hittite neighbors gave in readily. Egypt, under the pharaohs Ramesses I and his successor Seti, fought long, hard, and indecisive battles with the Hittites, culminating in c.1285 with the battle of Kadesh, which both sides claimed as a victory. An uneasy diplomatic peace was negotiated with the marriage of the daughter of King Hattusilis II to Ramesses II.

The war of attrition between the Hittites and Egypt had drained the resources of both, and Hattusilis II was the last strong Hittite ruler. Under his successors the kingdom waned, while the Assyrians came to the forefront. Ashurnasirpal and his successor Shalmaneser II conquered Syria, Anatolia, and then Palestine, exacting heavy tributes from the Hittites. Only Carchemish, the last stronghold of the Hittites, resisted; but this city fell to the Assyrian king Tiglath-Pileser in 717 and Hittite rule over the region came to an end.

Biblical references to the Hittites can be found in the Old Testament, although these refer to a period when Hittite power was in decline. The most significant reference is to Abraham, who is said to have bought a field and cave from Ephron the Hittite: this site grew in importance to become the town of Hebron.

Above: Aerial view of the ruins of Hattusas, the Hittite capital.

Below: Detail of a Hittite wall-painting depicting the organizers of a sacrifice and a bull.

TRADE IN THE MEDITERRANEAN

The Hittites are generally depicted as aggressive expansionists, who created an empire from which they could exact tribute from conquered states. However, much of their wealth came from trade, creating a mercantile empire that spanned the Mediterranean.

Two Hittite relief sculptures of, **below**, a merchant holding weighing scales and, **facing**, two merchants bargaining, dating from the 10th–8th centuries.

There is little in historical record to suggest that the Hittites claimed either political or religious dominion over subject states. On the contrary, the Hittites seemed to accept foreign gods as being as valid as their own, and generally kept local dignitaries in positions of power and authority. A more recent suggestion is that Hittite power can be more closely linked to the establishment of merchant colonies.

This assertion is borne out by the fact that at the time of Hittite control of Syria the area was the crossroads of world commerce. Artifacts recovered from Hittite sites show that they took over many of the earlier forms of trade agreement records, such as cuneiform writing and the use of cylinder seals.

Key Hittite cities, such as Carchemish, had bazaars that traded goods from across the entire region, and the Hittites had a trade monopoly on a number of new materials and resources, such as iron. It is significant that Hittite traders are recorded in a number of carvings and inscriptions of the period.

Hittite trade contacts were expanding at the expense of a diminishing Egyptian sphere of influence. The non-aggression pact signed between the Hittites and Egypt in 1272, after the battle of Kadesh (c.1285), is not only the oldest known historical document of its kind, but also allowed the Hittites to move into new markets. This was to have long-lasting effects on the development of cities such as Tyre and Byblos.

Central to these new developments was a small Syrian village near present-day Ras-el-Shamra, its name recorded as Ugarit at the time. According to the records, Ugarit was a vassal state of the Hittites and paid an annual tribute in gold, silver, and purple wool; as such it was little different from other cities under Hittite control.

Peace and prosperity

The Hittite-Egypt peace accord allowed Ugarit to increase its international trade, thus also spreading Hittite influences throughout the region. Records found at Ugarit document trade in numerous foodstuffs, among them barley and wheat, olives, dates, honey, cumin, and wine. They also traded metals such as copper, tin, lead, bronze, and iron, and had a flourishing livestock market in sheep, cattle, donkeys, horses, and geese. Timber was an important export, as was the sale of finished wooden goods such as chests, beds, and other

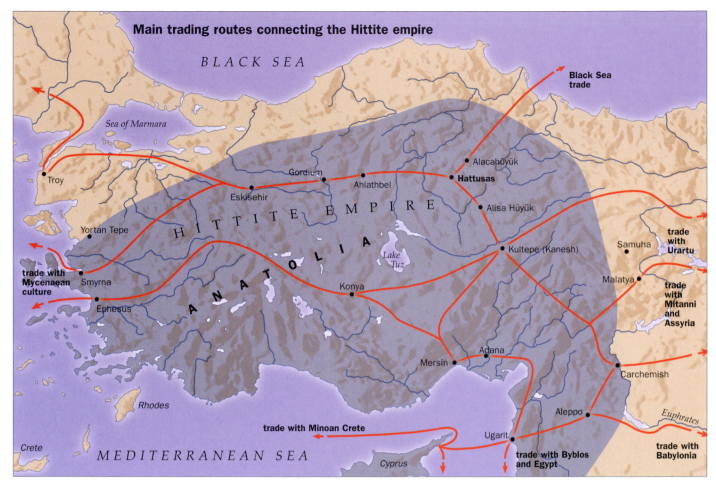

Main trading routes connecting the Hittite empire

BLACK SEA

Black Sea
trade

Sea of Marmara

Troy

Gordium

Alacahüyük

Hattusas

Eskişehir

Ahlathbel

Alisa Hüyük

HITTITE EMPIRE

Yortan Tepe

trade
with
Urartu

Samuha

Kultepe (Kanesh)

A N A T O L I A

Lake
Tuz

Malatya

trade
with
Mitanni
and
Assyria

trade with
Mycenaean
culture

Smyrna

Konya

Ephesus

Adana

Mersin

Carchemish

Rhodes

Aleppo

Euphrates

trade with Minoan Crete

Crete

MEDITERRANEAN SEA

Ugarit

Cyprus

trade with Byblos
and Egypt

trade with
Babylonia

furniture; there was even a flourishing ship-building industry. Exotic goods such as elephant tusks and hippo teeth came from further afield, some from as far away as Afghanistan and central Africa.

The cosmopolitan nature of Hittite cities is apparent at Ugarit, which seems to have become the main import-export center for the entire eastern Mediterranean. There were numerous foreign nationals and diplomatic personnel from the Hurrians and Assyrians, as well as people from distant regions such as Crete and Cyprus. Although acting as an independent city, the activities of Ugarit's traders were nevertheless controlled by the Hittite kings.

We are left with the impression that the Hittites traded with all the civilizations of the Mediterranean, and that it was largely though them that Mesopotamian ideology, politics, law, and economics spread throughout the region. When the Hebrews migrated to Canaan under Moses they encountered a people, the Canaanites, who had been under Hittite domination but were nevertheless essentially Mesopotamian in their culture and outlook. The Hittites, like the Assyrians who followed them, adopted and adapted many of the beliefs and ideas of the people they conquered and thus allowed them to be perpetuated.

CONQUERING AND ABANDONING BABYLONIA

Although experienced traders and determined conquerors, the Hittites struggled to form the administration required to sustain an empire. They worked with the Kassites to take Babylon, but had to abandon new conquests to secure their northern territories.

Below: A procession of Hittite gods. The numerous local cult deities were combined during the the imperial period (1400–1200) into a huge state pantheon, headed by the storm god—over 800 names have been discovered, including many Akkadian and Hatti deities.

Hittite expansion was of major importance in the Middle East, but they never consolidated their position or made their empire secure. This was due to a number of factors: the size of the kingdom prevented absolute control; administration was left in the hands of local authorities, whose self-interest was in securing their positions rather than strengthening Hittite ideology; and levying taxes or tribute on vassal states left open the possibility of disaffection. There were also outside pressures—particularly from the Hurrians, Assyrians, and Egyptians—dissipating Hittite resources. After Mursilis I,

Telepinus, and Suppilulimas I, weak kings led to the eventual disintegration of the kingdom.

While we should not underestimate the significance of Hittite achievements, we should be aware that they were vulnerable on a number of fronts. They were militarily capable: Mursilis's overthrow of Hammurabi, the most powerful of the Babylonian kings, and Hittite resistance to Ramses I under Hattusilis II attest to the fact. They expanded trade networks to an unprecedented degree. They rewrote Mesopotamian law to address the needs of the individual in a more humane way than even Hammurabi had done. But they never installed an effective administration, and their history is littered with references to depositions and assassinations.

A withdrawal from duty

Even Hittite mythology speaks of dissent and internal disagreement. Teshub constantly tries to

1375	1365	1359–33	1352–36	c.1350	1345–23	1344–22	c.1335
End of the early Kassite period, beginning of the later period	Assyria gains its independence under King Ashuruballit I	Burnaburiash II becomes "Brother of the Pharaoh" Akhenaton, who occupies Syria	Although married into the Hurrian dynasty, Akhenaton offers no support against Hittites	King Shuppiluliuma founds a new Hittite kingdom	Although made Babylonian king by Assyria, Kurigalzu I rebels against their overlordship	Hittite Suppilulimas I retakes Syrian areas	Mattiwaza of the Mitanni is made a puppet-king of the Hittites

dethrone his father, Kumarbis, Father of the Gods. Telepinus—elevated to the status of deity—goes off hunting when state problems need to be addressed, and a bee is sent out to force his return. Mursilis II published a prayer in which he asked the gods to forgive the indiscretions of his father and himself, and begged them to withdraw the plague that was afflicting innocent people. Although powerful, the kings struggled to control events outside their experience.

When the Hittites moved south from their capital at Hattusas to lay siege to Babylon, they were accompanied by warriors from the Kassite kingdom. We do not know who these people were—the Egyptians only refer to them as barbarians and savages. They spoke an Indo-European language, related to that of the Hittites, and there may have been some affinity between them. Other authorities suggest that the Kassites were responsible for the introduction of more efficient iron weapons and horse-drawn chariots, although these innovations are more generally believed to be of Hittite invention. Elsewhere there are implications that the Kassites were simply mercenary warriors employed by the Hittites.

The truth of these matters may never be resolved. The important fact here is that the Hittites and their Kassite allies attacked and destroyed Babylon, leaving the city desolate, its agricultural base destroyed, and the great canals that fed it in ruins. Hammurabi's personal fate is unknown, but many members of his court were carried away in chains. Curiously, the Hittites then withdrew

from the domains of their new conquests, failing even to put a governor in place, and returned to their mountain fastnesses in an attempt to secure their hold in the northern regions, on the upper reaches of the Euphrates and Tigris. Babylonia was left unprotected and open to Kassite domination.

Above: An 8th-century relief sculpture of Taru (storm god) and King Warpalawas.

1333	1332–08	c.1300	1290	1285	1275–40	1274–45	1272
Karahardash, grandson of Assyrian Ashur-Uballit, is assassinated	Puppet ruler Kurigalzu II leads Kassite rebellion against the Assyrians	The Assyrians conquer eastern Mitanni	The area east of the Euphrates is an Assyrian province	Egyptian and Hittite rulers both claim victory at the battle of Kadesh	Choga Zanbil, the largest man-made structure in Iran, is built for Elamite Untash Napirisha	By Shalmaneser I's reign, Assyria includes Babylonia, n. Syria, and w. Mesopotamia	Egypt makes peace with the Hittites

CHAPTER 6

KASSITES, ELAMITES, MITANNI—THE STRUGGLE FOR DOMINATION, 1570–1157 BC

When the conquering Hittites swept into Babylonia and ended the rule of Old Babylonian king Hammurabi, they were accompanied by nomadic warriors led by the Iranian Kassite king Agum II Kakrime (r.1595–45), ruler of Mari. The Hittites were unable to secure their hold over Babylon, partly because they were numerically small and had over-extended their power base, far from their capital at Hattusas. The political vacuum left at Babylon was quickly filled by a new Kassite governorship.

The term "Kassite" refers to several distinct entities: to an Iranian ethnic group with origins in the Zagros mountains; to their language, which was different from that spoken in Mesopotamia; to a dynasty of kings; and to the period of their Babylonian occupation. They had apparently settled in the Hamadan-Kermanshah district of Iran by 1800, with their first raid into Mesopotamia occurring in 1741. By the 17th century BC kings with Kassite names were recorded on clay tablets recovered from the middle Euphrates region.

The Kassite period is generally divided into two phases: an early period from 1595 to 1375, for which there are few historical records, and a later period from 1375 to 1157. There is a clear succession record for the later period, as well as extant copies of contracts and peace accords with neighboring states and extensive architectural evidence.

In the 16th century Babylonia was divided between the Kassites in the north around Babylon, and Sealand occupation of Ur and Uruk in the south. Feudal warlords who exercised little political or religious control dominated much of the Sealand region. In the Kassite area, however, Agum II had revived the cult of Marduk. The original statue of the Babylonian god was removed by the Hittites, but Agum restored him as equivalent to the Kassite god Shuqamuna. His successor, Burnaburiash II (r.1545–00), extended Kassite political influence into Assyria through the signing of a peace treaty with the Assyrian king Puzur-Ashur III.

Peaceful solutions

Under Ulamburiash (r.1470–65) and Agum III (r.1465–45) the Kassites reincorporated Sealand into Babylonia and embarked on an ambitious rebuilding program. At Uruk, Karaindash (r.1440–30) erected a temple to Inanna, decorated with bas-relief tile ornaments. Kurigalzu I (r. c.1400–1375)

restored Ur and built a new royal residence at Dur-Kurigalzu near Babylon.

Competing rivals for Mesopotamia, 1400–1157

From the late 15th century through to the late 13th century BC the Kassites enjoyed a period of increased prosperity. In addition to restoration and rebuilding projects and the founding of new cities, a literate administration was reinstalled and the political and economic stability of the region assured. The Kassites became renowned traders, famed for their jewelry and textiles, as well as their knowledge and supply of medicine. Despite the assertion of many scholars that Kassite rule stemmed from chaotic and disorganized migration, this was the longest period of peace and growth in Mesopotamian history.

Kassite prosperity was largely a result of their conservatism.

They remained as a small minority in the region, but readily embraced Babylonian culture and did not engage in expansionist wars. Much of their success appears to have been the result of diplomacy, as evidenced by the numerous peace treaties and accords they made with neighboring groups. They actively sought support from local leaders and granted land-holding rights to favored individuals. These are recorded in carved boundary markers known as kudurru stones, which also functioned as ownership contracts, although these did not grant any additional political rights. The Kassite period established the groundwork for the future development of later Chaldean (Neo-Babylonian) culture.

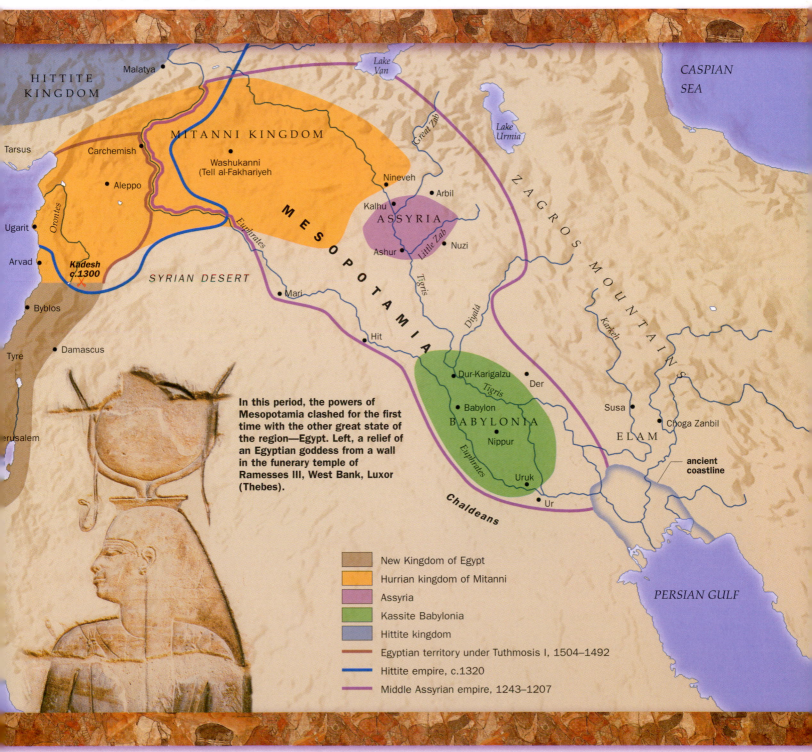

In this period, the powers of Mesopotamia clashed for the first time with the other great state of the region—Egypt. Left, a relief of an Egyptian goddess from a wall in the funerary temple of Ramesses III, West Bank, Luxor (Thebes).

New Kingdom of Egypt
Hurrian kingdom of Mitanni
Assyria
Kassite Babylonia
Hittite kingdom
Egyptian territory under Tuthmosis I, 1504–1492
Hittite empire, c.1320
Middle Assyrian empire, 1243–1207

A SUMERIAN RENAISSANCE

When the Kassites took control of Babylonia, they embarked on an extensive rebuilding program that helped to establish their political and economic control of its domains. Among their first acts was the renaming of Babylonia as Karanduniash (or Kar-Duniash).

Below: Now in the modern northwestern suburbs of Baghdad, the ziggurat of Dur-Kurigalzu photographed in the 1950s before the extensive reconstruction of its base.

The Kassites' motive for rebuilding Babylonia was to restore some of the old Sumerian deities to their earlier positions, although during this process the deities were often renamed or associated with the newcomers' own gods. It also helped assert Kassite dominion over existing Mesopotamian trade routes.

Some dispute exists over whether the new name of Karanduniash referred to the entire region or just the city of Babylon itself. Generally the prefix "kar" is understood by Mesopotamian scholars to mean "city." However, it has wider associations with "lands that are under cultivation" and may therefore have referred to agricultural regions that were previously subject to Babylonian control.

It is certain that the name had royal associations and referred to the imposition of regal prerogatives over the old Babylonian empire, since the name of Karaindash, Kassite

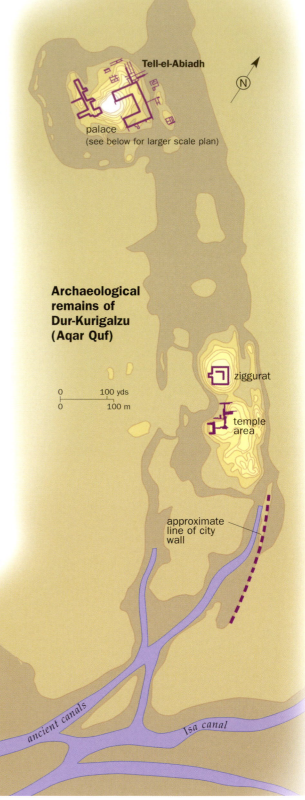

Tell-el-Abiadh

palace
(see below for larger scale plan)

Archaeological remains of Dur-Kurigalzu (Aqar Quf)

0   100 yds
0   100 m

ziggurat

temple area

approximate line of city wall

ancient canals

Isa canal

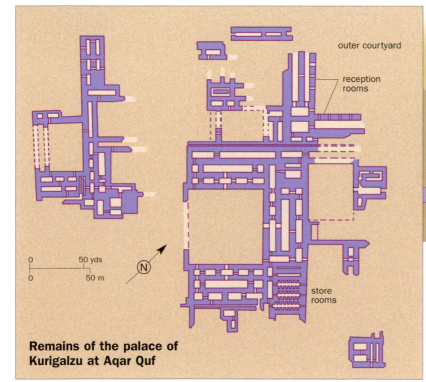

outer courtyard

reception rooms

store rooms

0   50 yds
0   50 m

Remains of the palace of Kurigalzu at Aqar Quf

king 1440–30, derives from the same word root. Under Karaindash, the Kassite empire was extended to the south into territories formerly held by the Sealanders, and Kassite hegemony was reinforced through the rebuilding and rededication of the temple of Inanna at the former Sumerian capital city of Uruk. The revitalization of Sumerian deities is apparent in the molded brick frieze on this temple, depicting a series of gods and goddesses carrying vases that overflow with water. This theme is often encountered in earlier Sumerian architecture, a reference to fertility and to the waters of the Euphrates and Tigris.

Dividing religion and state

As part of their use of architecture to depict Kassite dominance, they erected a new capital west of Babylon which they called Dur-Kurigalzu (Fortress of Kurigalzu), named after King Kurigalzu I (r.1400–1375). This also served to separate the functions of religion and culture, which remained Sumerian in character, from the imposed administrative functions of the new Kassite regime. Thus Babylon remained the most significant religious and cultural center, while the administration of the southern regions of the kingdom was moved to Kurigalzu, where it remained until the beginning of Kassite collapse in 1170.

Kurigalzu (modern Aqar Quf) is about nine miles west of Baghdad and contains two large mounds. One of these is a ziggurat made from sun-dried brick interwoven with reed matting, fronted by a low platform and a series of courtyards that formed a religious precinct. In a second, equally imposing mound are the remains of a huge palace and royal storehouse and treasury.

Many exquisite examples of Kassite art have been recovered from here, including a decorated gold mace head, gold bracelets with paste inlay, inlaid glass vessels, and terracotta figurines. The royal residence at Kurigalzu has a number of secondary temples dedicated to the cults of Enlil, Ninli, and Ninurta; the presence of Sumerian gods in a Kassite city of this importance reflects the degree of integration between Kassite and Sumerian ideologies.

King Kurigalzu also played an important role in the rebuilding and restoration at Ur, where he is named in documents of the period as a patron of the architectural arts and of other public works. He was involved, too, in extensive building projects at Uruk and Eridu, where he was responsible for the restoration of ancient sanctuaries and the building of new ones.

Below: Detail of musicians from a Kassite boundary marker stone.

CRIPPLED BY THE ASSYRIANS

From 1380 BC onward the Kassites attempted to enlarge and consolidate their empire. Alliances with Assyria were ill-judged, leading to power struggles and war that left them open and vulnerable to the otherwise transient Elamites.

Right: Column statue of the pharoah Akhenaten, found at Karnak temple, Luxor (Thebes). In keeping with the short-lived revolution he made in Egyptian religion—breaking the power of the Karnak priests of Amun-Ra—Akhenaten brought in a mannered style of representation, leaving scholars wondering whether his portraits are really indicative of his appearance or merely an exaggerated convention.

Facing: A boundary stone of Melishipak (r.1187–72), the 25th Kassite king of Babylon.

The Kassite empire was strengthened through the appointment of local state-approved dignitaries and governors, a series of conquests over unruly, threatening, or strategic states, and by means of diplomatic alliances and royal marriages. The ancient city of Arrapha (modern Kirkuk) was conquered by King Kadashman-Enlil (r.1380–59), giving access to some of the major trade routes out of Mesopotamia. His successor Burnaburiash II (r.1359–33) formed strong links with Egypt's pharaoh Akhenaton, who was in occupation of Syria. These links were so close that several references to Burnaburiash's reign give him the title "Brother of the Pharaoh."

While helping to strengthen Kassite trade and influence beyond the region, links to Assyria and Egypt were not always welcomed by the wealthy landowners in Mesopotamia, who felt that their own power to affect decisions made by the Kassite ruling families was being undermined. Many thought that interference in affairs of state, particularly by the Assyrians, was growing to an unprecedented extent through royal marriage alliances. In 1333 Karahardash, son of Burnaburiash and an Assyrian princess, and therefore the grandson of the Assyrian king Ashur-Uballit, was assassinated; and in the same year the Assyrians overthrew his successor, Nazibugash, in retaliation for Karahardash's death.

Assyrian attempts to control the Kassite region led to their installation of Kurigalzu II (r.1332–08). He was the second son of Burnaburiash, and through his relationship with the Assyrian throne was expected to act as a puppet king. However, Kurigalzu ignored Ashur-Uballit's dictates and listened instead to the protests of his own commanders. He led a rebellion against the Assyrians, which initiated a series of minor wars and skirmishes between the Kassites and Assyria. At the same time, Kurigalzu opened hostilities against the Elamites in Iran, who had started to infiltrate Kassite regions and were themselves engaged in a power struggle with Assyria.

1250	**1225**	**c.1200**	**1158**	**1157**	**1154**	**c.1100**	**c.1000**
Shalmaneser I founds the town of Kalhu (Nimrud)	Tukulti Ninurta attacks Babylon, in retaliation for Kassite campaign against Assyria	Weakened by the Sea Peoples, the Hittites fall to the Kassites and Assyrians	Elamite King Shutruck-Nahhunte of Susa defeats the Kassites and invades Babylon	The Elamites are driven from Babylon but Kassite unity is shattered	Assyrian empire extends into s. Mesopotamia, conquering the Kassites	In Babylon Assyrian Tiglath-Pileser confirms his rule over Mesopotamia	The Assyrian empire begins to use conquest to expand northward and westward

Desecrating Babylon

Although Kassite power within the area remained firm, largely present to protect its borders rather than to acquire new territory, long years of attrition began to impact on the ability of the Kassite kings to defend the region. This led to increasing protest within Mesopotamia itself. While this fell short of an actual revolt, it was sufficient to persuade King Kashtiliash IV (r.1233–25) to launch a major campaign against Assyria in an attempt to reassert the authority of Kassite kings. His armies were repulsed by Tukulti Ninurta of Assyria (r.1244–08), who then invaded Mesopotamia and launched an attack on Babylon in 1225. The city walls were torn down. Babylon was looted and burned, and part of its population was deported. Tukulti Ninurta appointed a new puppet governor.

Assyrian occupation of Babylon was short-lived and there was a brief respite under Adad-shum-usur (r.1216–1187) and Melishipak (r.1186–72), but the Kassite dynasty never fully recovered and was left nursing an economically weak state; a situation exacerbated by local landowners. Having been made wealthy through the land grants of the Kassite kings, they threatened to fragment the state unless their demands for further grants were met.

The Elamite king Shutruck-Nahhunte, who crossed the River Ulai in 1158 from his capital at Susa and overran Babylon, delivered the final blow. The golden statue of Marduk was carried off triumphantly to Susa, as was the victory stele of Narim-Sin and the monument containing the Code of Hammurabi.

Although the Elamites were expelled in the following year, Kassite power was over by 1157 and thereafter political authority became decentralized. The smaller provinces reverted to tribalism, leaving the former Kassite lands open to Assyrian domination under Ashur Dan I (r.1178–33) and his successors. Tiglath-Pileser (r.1115–1077) was able to lead the Assyrian occupation armies across the Euphrates without meeting resistance.

THE ELAMITES

According to Mesopotamian texts a people known as the Elamites occupied the eastern part of their land, in the province of Khuzestan in southwestern Iran. At the height of their power the Elamites were renowned as traders, but their history was stained by war.

Although indigenous to eastern Mesopotamia, the Elamites spoke a language unrelated to Sumerian, Semitic, or Indo-European, and which even today is not fully understood. They also practiced a form of matrilinear descent, with their rulers referred to as "son of a sister," rather than following the general Mesopotamian custom, whereby a son succeeded his father.

Their country was rich in natural resources, including timber, alabaster, marble, metal ores, and precious stones such as lapis lazuli, which were difficult to obtain outside the region. They were widely respected for their skills in metalworking, glazing bricks, weaving, tapestry, and embroidery. Trade links connected them with centers as far away as Baluchistan, Afghanistan, and India.

Yet Elamite history is marked by conflict with neighboring groups. Even at the period of the first kings, about 2700, there were fights between Elam and Ur. Sumerian clay tablets record numerous battles between different Sumerian cities and the Elamites. Later they fought with Babylonia, when Hammurabi crushed their forces in 1764; but immediately after Hammurabi's death the Elamites restarted hostilities to regain their independence. They came into conflict with the rising power of Assyria, and in 1158 under King Shutruk-Nahhunte, they defeated the Kassites and sacked Babylon.

After punitive retaliatory raids by the armies of Nebuchadnezzar I of Babylon (r.1124–03), Elamite power waned. There was a resurgence in 750, but the kingdom continued to be threatened

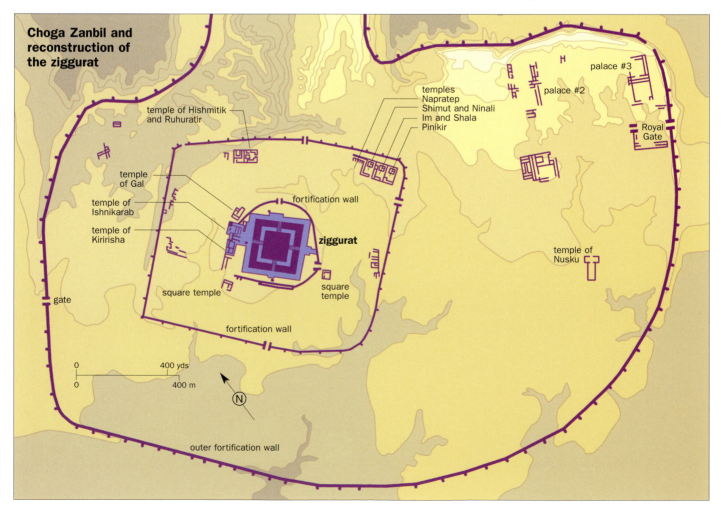

Choga Zanbil and reconstruction of the ziggurat

temple of Hishmitik and Ruhuratir

temple of Gal

temple of Ishnikarab

temple of Kiririsha

gate

square temple

fortification wall

ziggurat

square temple

fortification wall

temples
Napratep
Shimut and Ninali
Im and Shala
Pinikir

palace #3

palace #2

Royal Gate

temple of Nusku

0   400 yds

0   400 m

N

outer fortification wall

by Assyria and never regained its former greatness. Then in 645, Ashurbanipal of Assyria invaded Elam and sacked its major cities.

Susa and Choga Zanbil

The capital city was Susa, one of the oldest cities in the world. Urban structures have been uncovered here that date back to at least 4000 BC, and it is probable that a settlement was established as long ago as 6000. The ruins at Susa cover an area of about 500 acres, with the earliest building, a large temple platform, dating to the fourth millennium.

It was ravaged and destroyed by Ashurbanipal of Assyria in 640, but was restored during the Achaemenid period by Darius of Persia, who claimed it as his favorite residence. Later it was part of the Seleucid empire, when it was renamed Seleucia and a Greek-style palace was erected. Susa remained important until the 13th century AD, when it was sacked by the Mongols.

The other major Elamite site is Choga Zanbil, which was excavated between 1951 and 1962 by the French archaeologist Roman Ghirshman. Located about 25 miles south of the old capital at Susa, it is the largest man-made structure in Iran. It was built under Untash Napirisha (1275–40), who named it Dur-Untash (Fortress of Untash). A walled sanctuary with a large ziggurat, the royal quarters in its eastern section contain palaces, brick-vaulted royal tombs, and a gateway complex of five concentric towers. Choga Zanbil was devoted to Inshushinak, Lord of Susa, who is believed to appear each night on the flat roof

of the temple.

As at Susa, Choga Zanbil was destroyed by Ashurbanipal during the Assyrian invasions of 640. Unlike Susa, it was abandoned and apparently remained unfinished. Much of the area it encloses had not been built on. Ashurbanipal claimed to have sown its lands with salt to avenge the humiliation the Mesopotamians had suffered at the hands of the Elamites over the years.

Two other important Elamite cities are mentioned in the texts, Awan and Simash, but the sites of these have yet to be located.

Above: The ruined lower courses of the middle-Elamite ziggurat at Choga Zanbil.

Below: Remains of Elamite buildings at Susa (modern-day Shush, Iran).

INCURSION OF THE MITANNI, 1500–1275 BC

The weakening of Semitic states in northern Mesopotamia after about 1550 enabled incursions of the Indo-European Hurrians. Although little remains of the Mitanni kingdom, we know their history entwines with that of the Hittites and Egyptians.

Right: Statuette of Idrimi, a king of Alalakh in the 16th century BC. Alalakh was a small state subject to Aleppo, itself subject to the Mitanni kingdom.

Below: One of many friendly letters written by King Tushratta to the pharaoh Akhenaten found at Akhenaten's capital of Tell el-Amarna, Egypt.

Little is known of the Hurrians' early history, leading to a great deal of speculation. Generally they appear to have been isolated dynasties with Indo-Aryan names, and the appearance of a number of deities such as Mitra, Varuna, Nasatya, and Indra, together with other Sanskrit references, has fueled suggestions that they were once part of the Aryan peoples who eventually settled in India.

The principal Hurrian kingdom was that of the Mitanni, located near the source of the Habor (the modern Khabur river), a tributary of the Euphrates in northeast Syria and an

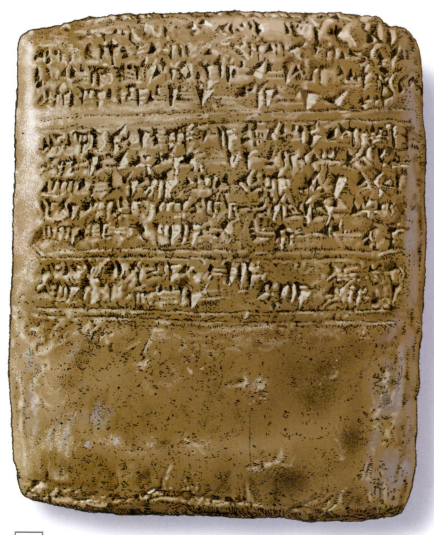

important communications route between Mesopotamia and Anatolia. Known to the Egyptians as the Naharin, the Mitanni ruled over a vast region that extended from Kirkuk and the Zagros mountains, through Assyria, to the Mediterranean.

Few architectural remains have been found that can be clearly identified as Mitanni, and in those that have been discovered there is little of merit. Temples are modest structures, lacking the vast religious infrastructures evident elsewhere in Mesopotamia. Their capital city of Wassukkani, or Vasukhani (Mine of Wealth), has yet to be located, although it is supposed that it must lie somewhere within the Khabur valley.

The virtual absence of city sites and temple buildings may be explained by the Mitanni's feudal nature, led by a warrior nobility with a judiciary patterned after the Babylonian system. A chariot-warrior caste, the *maryannu*, occupied the highest echelons of society and had vast country estates where they bred horses. Although land ownership was theoretically held only by the royal lineage, some of the *maryannu* amassed great wealth and could afford luxurious private residences decorated with frescos. These mansions could easily qualify as palaces in the Mesopotamian context.

The estates were also used for sheep raising to supply a thriving wool industry. Many of the *maryannu* "adopted" the lands of poorer neighbors for a fixed fee to avoid the penalties of illegal purchase, and the wool from adopted lands was delivered to the mansions to be made into textiles that were exported on a large scale.

Egyptian enemies and allies

The idea of the warrior-leader was also incorporated into Mitanni mythology and religion, where the terrible countenance of the gods predominates over any benevolent aspect of their character. The principal deity, a weather god known as Teshub, had deposed his own father Kumarbi in his attempts to grasp power, and owned a chariot drawn by the twin bull gods Seris (day) and Hurris (night). There is also evidence for cults of sacrifice, and for rituals of magic and the use of oracles.

There are few extant Mitanni records that can tell us anything about their early history; but the Egyptian chronicles suggest that for much of this period they were in constant struggle with Egypt over control of the Syrian territories. These persisted at least until the 18th pharaonic dynasty, when in 1460 Egyptian armies under Thutmose III advanced as far as the Euphrates, where they encountered the Mitanni army of Sausatatar. Instead of a pitched battle, the two rivals formed an alliance against the re-emerging threat posed by the Hittites.

After 1460 the Mitanni and Egypt forged even closer links. Thutmose IV (r.1400–1390) and Amenhotep III (r.1390–53) were married to daughters of the Mitanni kings Artatama I and Shuttarna II. Tushratta, son of Shuttarna, married his daughter, Tadukhipa, to the pharaoh Akhenaten (or Amenhotep IV,

r.1352–36). Akhenaten, however, failed to give Tushratta military support when the Mitanni kingdom was invaded in three separate campaigns under the Hittite king Shuppiluliuma.

Above: Egyptian pharaoh Thutmose III made an alliance with the Mitanni in order to jointly face the rising threat of the Hittites.

CAUGHT BETWEEN THE HITTITES AND ASSYRIA

Under the leadership of Thutmose III, the Egyptians attempted to extend their territories into Syria, which kept the expansionist policies of the Mitanni kingdom in check. But Egypt and the Mitanni together faced the growing military might of the Hittites.

Below: Monumental head of Ramesses II at Luxor (Thebes) temple, Egypt. The pharaoh claimed to have smitten his enemies, but it was a draw.

Pharaoh Akhenaten (Amenhotep IV) and King Tushratta decided on a policy of alliance and power sharing in the region, in the hope that this would prevent Hittite incursions. Yet despite the pact of friendship between Egypt and Mitanni, the Mitanni kingdom was unable

to resist the formidable armies of the Hittite king Shuppiluliuma. This was primarily because Akhenaten reneged on his promise to give Tushratta military assistance against the Hittites. Why this should have been is unclear, since it left Egypt's defenses weakened and undermined their own influence in the area, although it is known that Akhenaten's interests were in religious reform rather than military expansion. Shuppiluliuma correctly surmised that Akhenaten would be more concerned with this than meeting his obligations to Tushratta.

Shuppiluliuma took advantage, seizing northern Syria and laying siege to the Mitanni capital at Wassukkani. Wassukkani was overthrown and in the subsequent chaos Tushratta was assassinated, although debate continues as to whether this was done on the orders of Shuppiluliuma or by the hands of enemies within Tushratta's own court.

His successor, Artatama, though related through marriage to the Egyptian pharaohs, made a treaty with the Assyrians, another dynastic power that was rapidly gaining strength in the region. Artatama was quickly deposed by Shuppiluliuma and replaced by Mattiwaza ("He whose wealth is prayer"). Rather than being in the mold of the traditional chariot-warrior ideals of the Mitanni, Mattiwaza was a deeply religious man. Like Akhenaten, he relied on the intercession of the gods to resolve the Hittite-Mitanni dispute. Mattiwaza's character was very different from that of his father, Tushratta, and he was never more than a titular head of a new vassal state of the Hittites. Even the name of the capital city was changed to a Hittite word, Hanigalbat.

Kassites enter the fray

From this period on, Mitanni was little more than a pawn in a power game between the Hittites and Assyria. Under Ashur-Uballit I, who had ascended the throne in 1365, Assyria had regained its independence and was attempting to secure its political and economic position in the region. An Assyrian army under Ashur-Uballit's leadership conquered parts of Mitanni, and re-established a diplomatic

relationship with the Egyptian pharaohs.

Shortly after, the Assyrian annexation of Mitanni was completed under the leadership of Adad-Nirari I and Shalmaneser I. By about 1290 the entire area east of the Euphrates had become an Assyrian province. An Assyrian administration was installed, and parts of the local population were deported and their lands taken by Assyrians.

Meanwhile Egypt, under pharaohs Seti I and Ramesses II, continued to skirmish with the Hittites along the Syrian border; eventually reaching a peace accord after the battle of Kadesh in 1285. For reasons that are not clear, Egypt withdrew, leaving the regional dispute to be played out between the Hittites and Assyrians. Hittite power was undermined when their former allies, the Kassites, turned against them and occupied Babylon, which was then seized from the Kassites by the Assyrian armies of Ashur-Dan. By 1200 Hittite power was completely broken, and the Assyrians had embarked on building a new Mesopotamian empire.

CHAPTER 7

THE ASSYRIAN EMPIRE, 1420–609 BC

The earliest references to the Assyrians are of a Semitic speaking people entering the area in about 3000 BC. Their status is a matter of debate. Theirs may have been an independent nation that allied itself to the more powerful groups of the region, or a vassal state under the control of the Babylonians. The name given to the Assyrian rulers, *Ishhaku*, implies the latter, since it refers to a priest-prince or governor rather than a ruling monarch.

By about 1800 the earliest Assyrian rulers, Ishmi-Dagan and his son Shamshi-Adad I, although not yet forming a dynasty, had united the cities of Ashur, Nineveh, and Arbil. Together with Nimrud, these cities would later form the core of Assyrian civilization. Shamshi-Adad had already begun to form an administrative system, with the kingdom divided into districts. Hammurabi of Babylon mentions both Ashur and Nineveh in letters, but these also give details of his defeat of Ishmi-Dagan, Shamshi-Adad's son, and note that Assyria was merely a province of Babylonia.

Although some scholars have placed the beginning of the Assyrian empire as early as the 17th century BC, it is apparent that as late as the 15th century Assyria was still essentially a subject state. In 1472 the Assyrian dominions are listed as being annexed to Mitanni, and officials at the Assyrian court are given Hurrian (Mitanni) names. Even after Egyptian influence began to extend into Syria and the Mesopotamian valley, Assyria was ruled by outside powers. Correspondence by the pharaoh Thuthmose III (r.1480–1427) lists Assyria as a tributary nation.

It is not until after 1420 that royal inscriptions refer to Assyria as an independent entity. During this period diplomatic exchanges between Assyria, Babylonia, Syria, Mitanni, and Egypt were frequent, and it is evident from these that the kings of Assyria were now ranked equally with those of Babylonia. In 1365 the newly enthroned Assyrian king, Ashur-Uballit, exchanged gifts and wrote to the Egyptian pharaonic family as their equal.

Thebes, capital of Upper and Lower Egypt and the southernmost point of Assyrian conquest, was sacked by Ahsurbanipal in 663.

Ashur and established the Assyrian royal residence at Nineveh. Under Tukulti-Ninurta I (r.1244–07) Assyrian power was further extended to the north and northwest; but he was assassinated by his nobles, who were dissatisfied at his long campaign absences, and Ashurnadinapli (r.1207–03) was made king.

The Babylonians counterattacked and defeated the Assyrians, but this was reversed under Ashur-Dan in 1180. His grandson, Ashur-Resh-Ishi (r.1133–15) mounted a campaign during which Nebuchadnezzar I was defeated and Babylon destroyed. Tiglath-Pileser I (r.1115–1077), a brilliant

Urartu became a rival to Assyria in the 8th century until it was subdued by Sargon II in 714.

The first capital of Assyria was Ashur (c.1363–c.878), then it moved to Kalhu (–707), then to Dur-Sharrukin for two years, and then to Nineveh (705–612), when it was sacked by the Babylonians and Medes.

Babylonia remained the religious and cultural center of the empire, despite the military dominance of Assyria.

The expansion of Assyria
- c.1400
- 934–912, Ashur-Dan II
- 883–859, Ashurnasipal II
- 680–627, maximum extent

Ongoing conquests

During the early part of the reign of Ashur-Uballit (1365–29), relations between Assyria and Babylonia were friendly, but conflict arose after the son of Ashur-Uballit's daughter (who was married to the Babylonian king) was murdered by Nazibugash, a Kassite usurper to the Babylonian throne. Ashur-Uballit clearly felt that Assyrian power was sufficient to enable him to intervene in the accession. He deposed Nazibugash and put Kurigalzu II on the throne.

Kurigalzu's allegiance to the Assyrians was short-lived, and by the end of his reign (1345–23) he was openly hostile. As a result, Enlil-Nirari of Assyria (r.1329–19) annexed the northern part of Babylonia. Adad-Nirari (r.1307–1274) and Shalmaneser I (r.1274–45) defeated the remaining Babylonians and added considerable territories by extending Assyrian power westward to encompass northern Syria and western Mesopotamia. Shalmaneser restored the temple at

strategist and one of the greatest Assyrian monarchs, succeeded Ashur-Resh-Ishi and took Assyria to great military successes.

For many scholars the New Babylonian era begins in 1100, with the conquests of Tiglath-Pileser. Others have placed this date almost 200 years earlier, and see the new empire beginning to take shape with Adad-Nirari's defeat of the Babylonians. Adad-Nirari described himself as the "defeater of the ferocious ones—the hordes of the Kassites, the Qutians, the Lullumeans and the Subarians." Kassites here refers to the Babylonians; the other defeated forces are the Gutians and mountain tribes of the Zagros and Taurus ranges.

ASSYRIAN DAILY LIFE

History portrays the Assyrians as a war-loving race. The archaeological record refutes this simplified image, offering a more accurate picture of a largely agrarian society, with a rigid but respected social structure.

The Assyrians were not a single race, but a nation containing a bewildering mix of ethnic identities and speaking a number of Semitic dialects. The most potent unifying force appears to have been religion, centered on belief in a chief deity named Ashur—the country they

or which they were employed to cultivate. It was a nation of farming villages and country towns, with a few cities.

Land was originally owned by extended families, who grouped together as village communities and implemented state projects, such as road building and digging irrigation canals. In times of war, they provided manpower for military service. Theoretically, the people who worked the land were inseparable from it; thus a sale of land included its workers.

The villages had ties to a local town, under the administration of a court-appointed

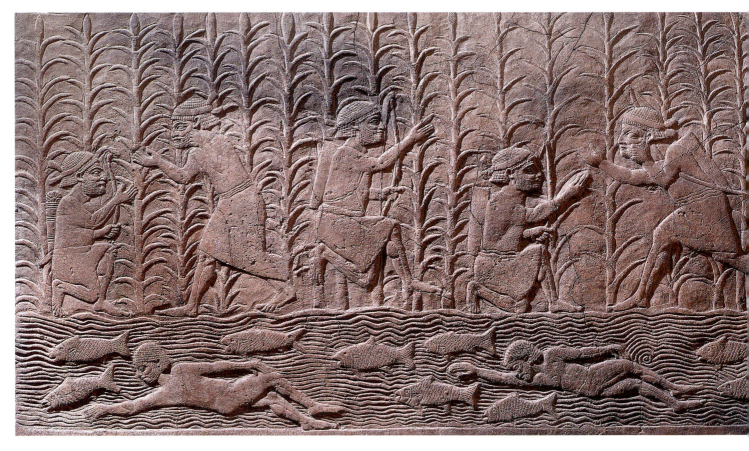

Above: For the majority of Assyrians life was spent in agricultural pursuits. This bas-relief is one scene of several showing ordinary folk going about their daily tasks, in this case harvesting grain and fishing.

dominated was known as the "lands of Ashur," hence Assyria.

Many of the carvings of the period depict warfare, but these were records of Assyrian achievements and victories rather than everyday life. The mainstay of the Assyrian economy was farming and the activities of ordinary men and women centered around their fields, crops, and livestock. A large part of the population, probably the majority, consisted of peasant farmers who were tied to the lands they owned

governor whose duties included acting as a judge in local disputes, collecting taxes, and arranging festivals. The town in turn was responsible to one of the cities that answered directly to the king.

Bonded into marriage

Assyrian society was decidedly patriarchal. Women were under the jurisdiction and authority of a male head of family, and later came under that of the father-in-law into whose house they moved, following a marriage arranged by the male members of the two families. They had few property rights. Even jewelry given to the bride as a marriage gift was the property of her husband. Girls could legally be married at ten years of age, although marriage contracts from the period suggest the average was 16; which, incidentally, was also the age at which a boy became eligible for military service.

Marriage was usually monogamous, but this refers to legal status—it was not uncommon for men to have concubines or use prostitutes. The Assyrians were very open about sexual matters between legally married couples; although adultery might be severely punished. Prostitution was not considered to be disreputable, and there were religious prostitutes associated with the temples. Respectable women were veiled in public and wore clothing that covered their bodies, distinguishing them from the revealing clothing and lack of a veil that marked a prostitute. Men generally wore a short tunic. In private both men and women were frequently naked or only scantily clad.

Within this structure there were two indistinct social groups, free and non-free, with innumerable subtle gradations of status that reflected the wealth and influence of any particular individual. Non-free status, although generally translated to mean "slave," often indicated no more than a position of subservience to someone of higher authority.

Ultimately, every aspect of state life was linked to the king, whose power was in theory absolute; but unlike the earlier Sumerian kings, they were not considered to be divine. The king's palace was both the official royal residence and the seat of government, with a large retinue of administrative staff and courtiers. This was a politically stable society. There were royal intrigues concerning succession to the throne, but there is no record of public dissatisfaction or revolt.

Below: A relief from the Palace of Sargon II depicting men loading boats with cut timber. Companion scenes show the transport of logs by river and unloading them ready for building work.

ASHUR

Ashur is both the name of a city and of the Assyrians' principal deity, and is also the word from which the term Assyria derives. Capital of the kingdom for half a millennium, modern knowledge comes from an excavation in the early 20th century, after the site was presented to Germany.

Inset below: Detail of offering bearers from a sculpted relief series in the throne room of Shalmaneser III.

Ashur (modern Qala'at Sharqat) is situated within a spur on the west bank of the Tigris, some 60 miles south of Mosul in Iraq. The city was founded in about 2500 BC by settlers from Syria, but the presence of

Sumerian statues and a temple of Ishtar from this period suggests that it was originally a Sumerian outpost. At this time it was probably ruled by local leaders, but its location on the border between the rain-fed and irrigation agricultural zones that divide Mesopotamia meant that the city could take advantage of caravan routes running both north–south and east–west. Although it probably began as a military post, Ashur became a trading settlement of international importance.

Its most significant period was from the 14th to ninth centuries BC, when it was the capital of the Assyrian kingdom. The city's importance is reflected in the fact that it remained as the religious center of ancient Assyria even after the political rise of more powerful cities, such as Nimrud and Nineveh, and was renowned as the place where Assyrian kings were both crowned and buried. After the ninth century the capital was removed to Nimrud (modern Kalakh, and referred to as Calah in biblical texts) under the leadership of King Ashurnasirpal II (r.883–59).

Ashur was presented to German Emperor Wilhelm II as a diplomatic gift by Ottoman sultan Abdul Hamid II in the early 1900s, leading to excavations for the Deutsche Orient Gesselschaft led by archaeologist Walter Andrae between AD 1903 and 1911. Andrae's team found that many of the structures at Ashur were too large for them to excavate properly; however, they dug a number of trenches and uncovered and recorded most of the principal monumental buildings. The dates and descriptions that they gave for Ashur are still generally accepted today.

A series of threats

On the northern side of the city is a high escarpment that offers natural defense, while massive fortified buttressed walls with a total length in excess of 2½ miles encircle the inner city. A large part of the eastern wall is occupied by extensive quays built during the reign of Adad-Nirari (r.1307–1274). Sennacherib (r.704–681) added to the fortifications by building a semi-circular watchtower, known as the *mushlalu*, the first known structure of its kind.

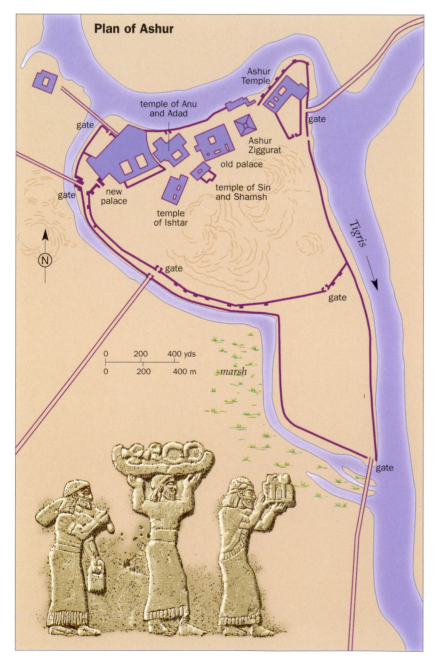

Plan of Ashur

Within the protective wall are 34 temples dedicated to a number of deities, among them Ashur-Enlil, Anu-Adad, Sin-Shamash, Ishtar, and Nabu. There are three palace complexes, the oldest built by Shamshi-Adad (r.1813–1781) and later used as a royal burial ground. Shamshi-Adad was also responsible for building the largest of the three ziggurats at Ashur.

A new palace was added by Tukulti-Ninurta I (r.1244–07), and there were later rebuildings carried out during the reign of Shalmaneser III (858–24), who also added a new outer wall and strengthened Ashur's southern and western fortifications. In the northwest corner there is an extensive residential area, presumably home to high status citizens, since many of the sites have their own family burial vaults.

In 614 Ashur was one of the first Assyrian cities to be captured and looted by the Babylonian-Mede army, after which it was abandoned and left in ruins. There is some evidence for a partial reoccupation during the Parthian period in the mid-second century.

Ashur has been placed on the World Heritage list of sites in danger, following an outcry over a proposed dam that would have flooded major parts of the city. Although these plans have been temporarily suspended, Ashur is still largely unprotected and considered to be under threat.

Below: The remains of Ashur, the first capital city of ancient Assyria.

THE NEW KINGDOM

About 1000 BC, the rulers of Ashur began to lead military campaigns west and north in their attempts to secure tribute, seize bounty, and control resources such as metal and horses. This new Assyrian kingdom had the might and administration to control a larger empire.

Below: A relief from Shalmaneser III's throne commemorates his pact with the Babylonian king, Marduk-zakir-shumi (r.855–19), whose brother rebelled in 850. The king called on Assyria for assistance. Shalmaneser defeated the rebels, entered Babylon, and temporarily established the city as a vassal.

Under Tukulti-Ninurta (r.1244–07) and Tiglath-Pileser I (r.1115–1076), Assyria began its first major conquests, defeating the Mitanni, the Kassites, and conquering Babylon. Assyrian dominance was extended into Syria and Armenia, although it was not yet secure enough to form a stable empire. Building on the foundations set by these earlier kings, the new Assyrian kingdom began c.1000 and struck out in different directions.

Ashurnasirpal II (r.884–59) moved the capital from Ashur to Kalhu (Nimrud), which he dedicated to the war god Ninurta and populated with deportees from cities he had captured. From Kalhu he launched 11 military campaigns using the first armies to apply cavalry tactics, but which have become infamous for their ferocity and merciless treatment of conquered peoples. Ashurnasirpal had whole communities impaled. Rebel leaders were flayed alive, others were burned, or had their severed heads displayed in large piles.

Under Shalmaneser III (r.858–24), son of Ashurnasirpal, "the land of Omri" (Israel) was defeated; Omri's King Jehu is recorded as paying tribute to the Assyrians in 842. Though not as merciless as Ashurnasirpal, the rulers that followed expanded Assyrian territory to the Euphrates and beyond. All of Syria and Palestine was conquered, as were Armenia, Babylon, and southern Mesopotamia, their conquered peoples deported to different parts of the Assyrian empire.

In 745, Tiglath-Pileser III (r.745–27) made fundamental changes to Assyrian administration. The most important organized

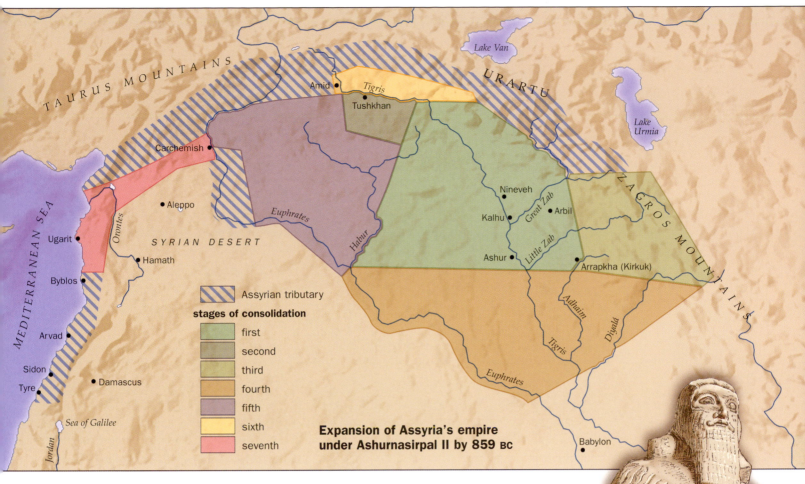

Assyrian tributary

stages of consolidation

first
second
third
fourth
fifth
sixth
seventh

**Expansion of Assyria's empire
under Ashurnasirpal II by 859 BC**

Above: Statue of
Ashurnasirpal II.

the entire empire into provinces, each of which paid a fixed tribute to the state treasury that financed public building wars and underwrote the state's military expansion program. His radical departure from previous Assyrian ideology may be partly explained by the fact that he was probably a usurper of the throne. The records claim that he was abandoned and brought up by a gardener (an official, supervisory position) before rising through the ranks of the aristocracy to seize ultimate power.

Feats of Esarhaddon

Sargon II (722–05), Sennacherib (704–681), and Esarhaddon (681–69) built new capital cities at Khorsabad and Nineveh and expanded the empire from Iran to the Mediterranean. Sargon built Khorsabad (Dur-Sharrukin) between 717 and 707 as a new capital to replace Nimrud; there is no evidence for any previous occupation of the site. Its role as a capital city was short-lived—after Sargon's death, his son Sennacherib relocated the administration to Nineveh.

Throughout his career, Sargon personally military campaigned against unrest in his kingdom. After his conquest of Israel, northern kingdom of the Hebrews, Sargon was responsible for their relocation. Among his

other achievements, he called a siege on Babylon and forced Medes to pay tribute to Assyria. Sennacherib followed his father's lead in subduing Babylonians and successfully resisted an invasion by a large Egyptian army. However, he was a brutal and much resented leader who was killed by a court assassin. There was a dynastic revolt, in which his younger son Esarhaddon emerging as the new Assyrian leader.

Although somewhat vain, Esarhaddon was a popular king. He rebuilt Babylon (naming himself as its king) and gained the trust and loyalty of the Babylonian army, although this began to dissipate under the rule of his son and successor Ashurbanipal (669–27). There were revolts in Babylon and border problems with Egypt and Elam, all of which Esarhaddon overcame.

After Esarhaddon, the kingdom started to crumble under pressure from the Babylonians. In 616 the Babylonian king Nabopolassar (630–05) made an alliance with the Medes and launched a series of attacks against Assyria. In 614 the Babylonian-Mede armies sacked Ashur, and in 612 they defeated and destroyed Nineveh. The Assyrian court fled to Harran, which was to be their last stronghold, meeting their end in 609.

TIGLATH-PILESER AND SARGON

Two of the most important military commanders of the Neo-Assyrian empire were Tiglath-Pileser III (r.745–27) and Sargon II (r.722–05), both of whom came to the throne from uncertain backgrounds and in violent circumstances.

Prior to Tiglath-Pileser's accession, Assyria had been in a state of gradual decline. Tiglath-Pileser, referred to as Pul in the Bible, came to the throne following a revolt in 745 prompted by the threat of invasion from the north. It is unclear whether he was a member of the royal family, with some records claiming direct descent and others mentioning him as the abandoned child of a court official. In either case, he was already a mature and experienced administrator on the date of his accession. He changed his name from Pul to the throne name

of Tukulti-Apil-Esharra ("I am supported by the son of the god Esharra"), which has been simplified to Tiglath-Pileser by modern scholars.

Under Tiglath-Pileser, Assyrian dominions were extended and consolidated. Effective control was first secured over much of Syria, followed in 736 by an invasion of the state of Urartu, whose king had begun to form a coalition of local leaders that threatened Assyria's hold over northern trade routes. In 729 Tiglath-Pileser invaded Babylonia, on the pretext of quieting rebellious factions there and maintaining peace. Having secured the rebels, he had himself declared king of both Assyria and Babylonia.

Tiglath-Pileser then took the unprecedented step of removing any sense of autonomy from his subject states. Assyrian kings before him had entered into treaties with local leaders, who swore their allegiance but continued to exercise authority within their own regions. In an attempt to prevent local leaders forming more powerful coalitions such as that of Urartu, Tiglath-Pileser installed regional governors who were appointed by and directly answerable to the royal court at Kalhu (Nimrud). As part of this plan he built paved roads that connected the provincial centers with the capital, and introduced way-stations so that couriers could quickly convey messages back to the court. While he was a great military strategist, Tiglath-Pileser is remembered primarily for his introduction of an effective administration.

Leading from the frontline

Sargon II's reign was markedly different. On Tiglath-Pileser's death his son, Shalmaneser V (r.727–22), had taken over the throne, but he was a weak king whose main concern appears to have been the court's revenues. He introduced restrictive taxation and labor laws in Ashur and was consequently threatened by an insurrection that gave Sargon the opportunity to seize power in a violent coup. There is little evidence that Sargon had any legitimate claim to the throne. He adopted the name Sharru-Kenu—the legitimate or true king—perhaps as a way of

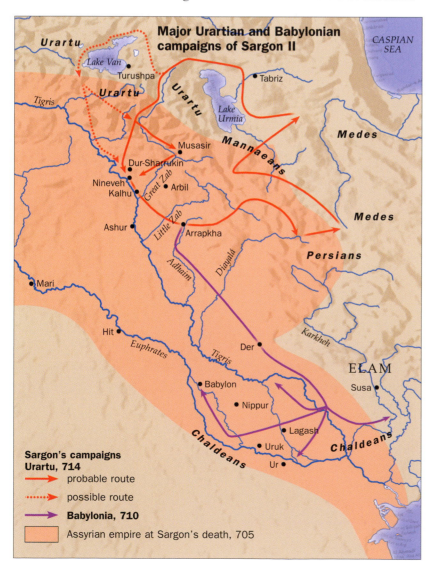

Major Urartian and Babylonian campaigns of Sargon II

Sargon's campaigns
Urartu, 714
→ probable route
┈┈▶ possible route
Babylonia, 710
▮ Assyrian empire at Sargon's death, 705

bolstering his doubtful lineage.

Sargon's immediate concern was to deal with the unrest within Assyria that he had inherited from Shalmaneser V, as well as troubles fomenting in Babylonia and Palestine. A coalition of rebels in Syria led by Yau-bi'idi was ruthlessly suppressed; a bas-relief depicting Yau-bi'idi's flayed skin was made at the new palace of Dur-Sharrukin (Khorsabad) to act as a warning to ambassadors from other regions. Sargon faced intermittent interference from Egypt in the affairs of Palestine and Syria. While much of this was dealt with diplomatically, Sargon's forces fought and defeated an Egyptian army in Gaza in 720, and it became necessary to maintain frontier garrisons and establish a buffer zone between Assyria and Egypt to prevent further conflict.

Meanwhile, Urartu was again growing in influence. Frequent border clashes led Sargon to take an army on a forced march into Urartu territory, where they came upon their enemy in a deep mountain pass. The Assyrians were at a disadvantage, but undeterred, Sargon led a chariot charge that broke their ranks. As a punishment, his forces ravaged the region. Towns were burnt, dams and canals broken, orchards and forests devastated.

Sargon's army was defeated in 720 by the Babylonians, but ten years later, after the news of his other conquests had reached Babylon, he was able to retake Babylonia without resistance. Sargon II was killed in battle at a mountain district of Persia in 705.

ASSYRIAN HUNTING

Although hunting was an economic activity in ancient Assyria, it had far greater significance as a ritual act performed by the Assyrian kings, through which they demonstrated their power and success over the wild beasts of the land.

Above: Detail from a series of reliefs depicting Ashurbanipal enjoying the sport of kings—lion hunting. **Facing above**, Ashurpanipal confronts his "divine" opponent in the arena, but armed attendants ensure the king comes to no harm.

Ritual hunting can be traced back through texts and bas-reliefs to the beginnings of the Old Assyrian kingdom and was to continue until the collapse of the Assyrian empire in about 609. Some of the most exhaustive texts refer to the reign of Tiglath-Pileser I (1115–1077) and give an inventory of the animals that the royal hunting parties pursued. Among the various game animals that were hunted are bears, hyenas, lions, tigers, leopards, deer, and wild goats; bison, water buffalo, wild pig, and gazelle; wild sheep, lynx, cheetah, wild ass (onager), wild ox, elephant, and even ostrich.

In one of the texts, Tiglath-Pileser is described as visiting the Mediterranean city of Arvad, where he commandeered a boat and harpooned a *nahiru* (sea-horse) while at sea. The *nahiru* is generally assumed to have been a dolphin or some species of whale. Tiglath-Pileser's fascination with wild animals, and particularly foreign species, led him to accept gifts of these from visiting ambassadors and to his establishment of several large zoos which contained apes, crocodiles, and animals captured in the Syrian desert.

The killing of large numbers of wild animals is often recorded. Tiglath-Pileser apparently killed up to 800 lions at a time, and Ashurnasirpal II (884–59) claimed that "Ninurta [god of war and the hunt] and Nergal, who love my priesthood, gave me the wild animals of the plains, commanding me to hunt. Thirty elephants I trapped and killed; 257 great wild oxen I brought down with my weapons, attacking from my chariot; 370 great lions I killed with my hunting spears."

A crippled target

To the king, the "great beasts" were considered to be divine and for him to kill as a display of power. Lions were trapped and brought in cages to a hunting arena, where they were released and set upon by his soldiers and trained mastiffs. The king's own role was largely ritualized, since he stepped in at the last moment to deliver the coup de grâce with a spear or dagger. Even then, trained bowmen were nearby to ensure that the king came to no harm.

The texts and bas-reliefs paint a slightly different picture from this ritualized hunt. They tell us that the kings engaged in the pursuit of

gazelle and wild boar, and in the slaying of wild oxen and lions. Only a few references are made to ritual enclosures and most of these hunts are depicted as taking place in the field; some references are even made to certain uninhabited territories and forests being reserved exclusively for the royal hunting privilege.

There are further references to the need to dispatch threatening wildlife when humans expanded into animal habitats. Inscriptions on the bas-reliefs of hunting from Ashurbanipal's throne room at Nineveh, which are now in the British Museum, note that an unusually rainy period had triggered an increase in the lion population. There were resultant attacks on people and livestock, and it was the king's duty to challenge and defeat this danger to his subjects.

There can be little doubt that the hunting activities of Assyrian kings depleted the wild livestock population. Sometimes numbers fell so low that lions were caught in Africa and brought to Assyria; at other times lions were bred at zoos specifically to be released into the enclosures for ritual hunts. The Assyrian lion sub-species is now extinct.

Below: Hunt attendants carrying cages, with trained mastiff dogs.

ASSYRIAN MILITARY ORGANIZATION

An outstanding feature of the Assyrian period was its military organization—the first culture to employ a standing army. A carefully managed and versatile force, unnecessary bloodshed was avoided.

The Assyrian army was noted for its organization and discipline. It was a complex force with specialist units that could be called on for specific duties. Each division had its own commander, intelligence officers, and interpreters, as well as a diviner who foretold events. A pioneer corps was responsible for road building in difficult terrain and for constructing rafts and bridges when they were needed. An elite royal bodyguard providing personal security for the king.

The bulk of the army consisted of bowmen, slingsmen, swordsmen, pike-bearers, and light and heavy infantry, as well as permanent units of charioteers and cavalry. Ethnic regiments retained their traditional weapons and the dress of their own region, thus there might be a contingent of bowmen from one specific area.

There was also a section that dealt exclusively with the logistics of transporting military equipment and basic provisions (primarily corn and oil). These were carried on pack-donkeys or on carts drawn by teams of oxen. Among the equipment that needed to be transported were armored battering rams, large wheeled machines that provided sufficient cover for several men to operate the ram, which was suspended from heavy chains so that it could be swung back and forth.

With the regular army augmented by conscripts, the Assyrians were able to field armies of 200,000 or 300,000 men. The greater part of these was composed of levies raised under provincial governors, who also had responsibility of providing provisions while the army was in territories they controlled.

Professional soldiers lived on a military base or *ekal masharti* (palace for marshalling forces) in the capital cities. The *ekal masharti* consisted of a large courtyard for military maneuvers, surrounded by a number of buildings used as barracks and store rooms for provisions and equipment. Smaller garrisons were maintained at border crossings and other key points.

Battles of body and mind

There was a distinct war season, sanctioned by the god Ninurta, that followed harvesting in July; a time when peasant labor was available for military service. Several texts indicate that the king had a ritual responsibility to undertake at least one military campaign each year, although some of these were training exercises.

Military campaigns might be conducted as local concerns, involving only the soldiers from a garrison town, but on other occasions they were grand affairs led by the king. Usually the Assyrians surrounded the enemy town and shouted at them to surrender. This was a form of psychological warfare, in which the Assyrians proclaimed that their gods had predicted victory and that resistance was useless.

If the town refused to surrender, a siege was made. A fortified camp was set up outside the town and its essential services were cut. When the town was sufficiently weakened, the battering rams were brought into play or the

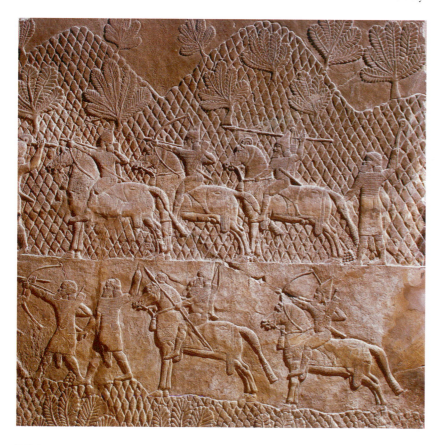

Below: Created in c.668–630 BC, this relief shows the Assyrian army, with infantry and mounted soldiers using spears and bows against the enemy.

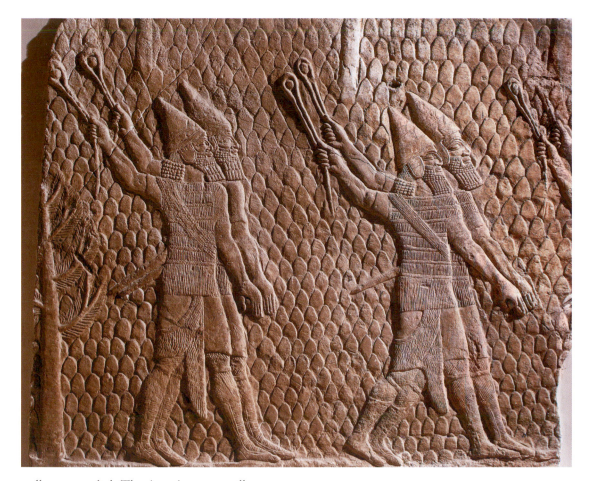

walls were scaled. The Assyrians generally avoided open conflict, when casualties were likely to be high, but nevertheless had a highly efficient cavalry and skilled charioteers that were used when the occasion demanded.

Psychological warfare was also employed after a victory, when the flayed skins of rebel leaders were publicly displayed to discourage others. It is significant too that at royal palaces bas-reliefs of Assyrian victories predominated in the halls that served as audience chambers.

These reliefs have given rise to claims that the Assyrians were barbaric. While atrocities were committed—including the severing of hands, burning alive, putting out of eyes, and the cutting off of noses and ears—sadistic revenge was rare and such extremes were only used against those who had encouraged their followers to rebel. The usual punishment of prisoners was deportation to a distant part of the kingdom where they would be less likely to foment further trouble.

FORCED MIGRATIONS

One of the most important, but also among the most controversial and least understood, policies of the Assyrians was the mass deportation of subject peoples. While it's easy to criticize such a radical policy, their motives were understandable and their actions measured.

Below: The siege of Hamath by the Assyrians. The defenders may be on the ramparts, some falling to their death, while Assyrian soldiers shelter under shields, and others make a sneak attack by swimming the Orontes.

This issue is an emotive one, not least because it is linked with the deportation of the "Ten Tribes of Israel" from Samaria 722–20 during the reigns of Shalmaneser V (727–22) and Sargon II (722–05). It was carried out on a vast scale during the reign of Sennacherib (704–681), who is said to have deported 20,000 inhabitants of the city of Judah, and continued under Esarhaddon (681–69).

It had begun much earlier, with the deportation and enlistment of defeated Ururarti men (tribal groups that later confederated as the Urartu kingdom, c.900) into the army of Shalmaneser I (1274–45). Under these various kings the Chaldeans were moved to Armenia; the Jews and Israelites to Assyria and Media; and the Arabs, Babylonians, and Persians to Palestine. Various scholars have described this policy as reprehensible, inhumane, and indiscriminate.

Yet it is important to view this from the Assyrian point of view. Numerous surrounding small tribes and alliances frequently challenged the rule of the Assyrian kings. Although the Assyrians were militarily capable of suppressing these uprisings, stability could only be ensured

by relocating populations in less troubled regions and by breaking up the petty dictatorships of feudal lords.

There were also sound economic reasons for the relocations, since the acquisition of larger territories required more intensive exploitation of agricultural lands and made it necessary to populate unproductive areas. Other deportees were settled in cities where their craft skills could be employed, and some were given high-status positions within the Assyrian court as scribes and interpreters. There is nothing in the records to suggest that these relocations were indiscriminate or intended to be punitive. If anything, the implication is that they were carefully planned movements intended to place new populations in areas where their skills could be most usefully employed.

Supply and demand

We should also be wary of accusations that the practice was inhumane. In the political and cultural climate of the era, migrations of entire populations were commonplace and relocation did not carry the negative connotations that might be applied today. The deportees went to environments that were similar to those they originated from, and concern was shown for their welfare. These were not forced marches in shackles and chains, but well supervised movements during which the comfort and health of the deportees was of paramount importance: provision lists indicate that they were better clothed and better fed than many rural Assyrian families.

In the countryside, the resettled populations worked alongside and as part of the existing rural communities, with the same rights and obligations as anyone else. Difficulties in resettling were recognized. New immigrants and deportees were provided for by the state until they had established themselves in their new homes, and state officials were appointed to oversee any integration problems.

The Assyrians did not break up ethnic communities or separate family members, and all deportees remained technically free persons

who were settled and treated as independent groups, able to practice their own beliefs and speak their own language. The only controlling factor appears to have been an expectation of loyalty to Ashur, although Ashur's identity could be broadly interpreted to encompass other local and foreign gods.

Many of the later deportations were linked to an Assyrian ideal of cultural mixing. For the Assyrians, ethnic purity was an irrelevance and ethnic differences were not seen as significant. A proud boast at Ashurbanipal's court was the number of languages that were spoken there and that all people, of whatever ethnic group, background, or culture, were equal.

Many of the leading craftsmen in cities such as Nineveh were foreign, as were some of their most important architects. People from outside Assyria constantly added to the mix of nations that were represented in these cosmopolitan cities. Even the Assyrian language changed dramatically as new words were assimilated.

Above: This relief shows the population of a conquered city beginning their deportation to a foreign land for resettlement.

NINEVEH

Nineveh is located on the River Khawsar, on the east bank of the Tigris. Dominated by the Kuyunjik mound and Sennacherib's palace atop it, the ancient city's grand facilities were encompassed by a high wall.

About 250 miles north of Baghdad, Nineveh is at the main crossing of the Tigris in the northern plain and at the center of a rich agricultural region. According to Genesis, Nineveh was founded by Nimrod, and it is later mentioned by Jonah as the flourishing capital of the Assyrian empire—"an exceeding great city of three days' journey [in circumference]." The prophet Nahum is recorded as foretelling Nineveh's ruin and utter desolation.

Despite these Biblical references, the site of Nineveh was unknown until AD 1842. It had been briefly surveyed in 1820 by the British archaeologist Claudius J. Rich but its

significance was not realized. Subsequent excavations by the French consul Paul Emile Botta in 1842 and British archaeologist Austen Henry Layard from 1845 to 1854 have confirmed the site's identity, and extensive work was done until 1931. Recently the Iraq Department of Antiquities has stabilized many of the walls and installed a protective roof over the major buildings.

At its center is an ancient tell, Kuyunjik, which had been occupied from the seventh millennium BC. By the third millennium it was an important city with a prestigious temple dedicated to the goddess Ishtar. It was maintained by a number of successive kings under the Agade dynasty (2300), by Shamshi-Adad of Ashur (1800), and in the mid-second millennium by the rulers of Mitanni.

Feeding flora, raiding culture

With the revival of Assyrian power in 1000, Nineveh became a royal city. It was Sennacherib's capital in 700, and he was responsible for laying out the inner city and its perimeter walls. These were about 50 feet high and enclosed an area 7½ miles in circumference. A total of 15 gates, each named after an Assyrian deity, punctuated the walls. Only five of these have been excavated, but it is likely that all were marked with colossal carvings, such as the winged bulls flanking the reconstructed Nergal gate. At the center of the city, atop Tell Kuyunjik, is the Southwest Palace (Sennacherib's palace), which covers nearly 10 acres and contains at least 80 rooms that were decorated with stone reliefs and painted frescos.

Sennacherib's heir, Esarhaddon (r.681–69), built an arsenal on the river wall south of the main citadel mound. The site has never been excavated. since later legend claimed it to be tomb of the prophet Jonah. It is still revered as Tell Nebi Yunus, or the Mound of Jonah.

Ashurbanipal built a second palace on Kuyunjik, and it was here that the famous bas-reliefs of an Assyrian lion hunt were discovered (*see pages 102–3*). Many of the reliefs of Ashurbanipal and his grandfather Sennacherib were removed to the British Museum and the

Below: The reconstructed walls of Nineveh.

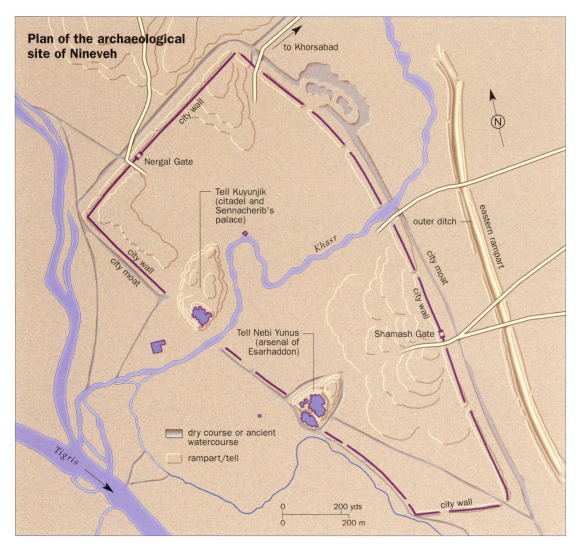

Plan of the archaeological site of Nineveh

to Khorsabad

N

city wall

Nergal Gate

Tell Kuyunjik (citadel and Sennacherib's palace)

Khasr

outer ditch

eastern rampart

city moat

city wall

city wall

city moat

Shamash Gate

Tell Nebi Yunus (arsenal of Esarhaddon)

dry course or ancient watercourse

rampart/tell

Tigris

0   200 yds
0   200 m

city wall

Louvre in the 19th century. Ashurbanipal was also responsible for building a state library and for other public construction works.

The excavations that have been carried out to date indicate that Nineveh contained public squares and parks, wide boulevards, a botanical garden, and a zoo. The oldest known aqueduct brought water from hills 30 miles away to irrigate exotic plants and trees in the parks and gardens. At the height of its power, the city and its suburbs extended almost 30 miles along the river bank.

In 612 Nineveh fell to the combined forces of the Babylonians and Medes, who burned the city and slaughtered or enslaved its inhabitants. Although Assyrian dominance was over, occupation of the site continued intermittently for a further millennium, until Nineveh was eclipsed by Mosul on the opposite bank of the river. During a brief reoccupation in the Parthian period, the remnant of the city adopted a Greek constitution and a temple to Hermes was built. Nineveh is still subject to misfortune—Sennacherib's Palace was ransacked in the 1990s. The Assyrian reliefs were broken from the walls, and fragments continue to appear for sale on the black market.

Below: Reconstruction of the palaces of Nineveh by architectural scholar James Fergusson, painted in 1853.

THE LIBRARY OF ASHURBANIPAL

He was looking for bas-relief panels, but what 19th-century archaeologist Austen Henry Layard found instead was extraordinary. Ignored for 40 years, the thousands of tablets had been assembled by King Ashurbanipal, organized in much the same way as we would recognize a library today.

Right: This stela of Ashurbanipal depicts the king with a basket raised above his head, piously engaged in the task of rebuilding Babylon after its destruction by his grandfather Sennacherib in 689 BC. Kings of the 3rd millennium had also depicted themselves in this way.

In AD 1849–51, British archaeologist Austen Henry Layard came across a vast number of clay tablets while searching along the walls of King Ashurbanipal's palace at Nineveh. He shipped them back to the British Museum, where they lay unremarked on until the German scholar Carl Bezold published translations of them in five volumes between 1889 and 1899.

Many of the tablets exist only in fragmentary form, but it is estimated that there were originally between 20,000 and 30,000. Of these some 5,000 remained in good enough condition to translate, containing about 1,500 complete texts in total. Layard's discovery is now known as the Library of Ashurbanipal, one of the most remarkable finds from the Assyrian period.

Ashurbanipal (r.669–27) was a scholar rather than a statesman, with a passionate fascination for literature. He was known to the Greeks as Sardanapalus and is referred to in the Bible as Asnappeer or Osnapper. Ashurbanipal had trained as a scribe and high priest of the god Ashur, and was fluent in Sumerian and Akkadian.

Ashurbanipal's Library may have been founded on an earlier library begun by Sennacherib, who was following in a tradition of regal record keeping and archives. Ashurbanipal is however the first king to have organized these records as a library and the first to have made a concerted effort to gather literature from other sources. He had texts sent from distant regions or had copies of them made, several of the latter believed to be by his own hand.

Archaeological techniques of the 19th century AD were, unfortunately, less systematic than those of today. Many tablets were removed without accurately recording their original position or their relationship to other finds. Because of this the significance of the Library at Nineveh remained hidden for several decades. More recent studies suggest that the library contained several rooms arranged according to subject matter: history/government, religion/magic, geography, science, and poetry.

A royal concern

Modern translations suggest that some tablets were a form of catalog that classified the general contents of each room. There was a separate state archive, kept in a secure area, containing copies of treaties and charters, as well as records from Assyrian spies and emissaries.

The largest category is what has been termed omen texts, largely concerned with divination.

722	720	717	717	700	689	681–69	671
Sargon II completes siege of Samaria, Palestine; its "Ten Tribes of Israel" are deported	Sargon II's army is defeated by the Babylonians but he takes Babylonia a decade later	Carchemish, last stronghold of the Hittites, falls to Tiglath-Pileser's Assyrians	Sargon II begins work on Dur-Sharrukin as his new Assyrian capital	Nineveh receives new buildings and city walls when Sennacherib makes it his capital	Assyrian king Sennacherib destroys Babylon	Esarhaddon puts down revolts in Babylon and the Egyptian and Elam borders	Esarhaddon of Assyria conquers Egypt

Left: Ashurbanipal, protected from the sun, rides in his chariot accompanied by attendants.

There are some 300 of these tablets, comprising approximately a quarter of the library's holdings. The next largest category consists of Akkadian/Sumerian texts that give details of cuneiform signs and sign combinations and provide lists of Sumerian words with their Akkadian translations.

Other categories include incantation texts, mainly chants and formulas that had a religious or medical function; instruction manuals or handbooks for priests in training; legal documents; "wisdom literature," consisting of poetry and proverbs; and a number of autobiographical annals. There is also a large collection of myths and epics, which are essentially Babylonian in origin and include the Myth of Creation (the basis for Assyrian New Year festivities) and the Epic of Gilgamesh.

That Ashurbanipal was personally responsible for selecting and cataloging works is clear from annotated instructions to scribes to outline the tablet's general contents and importance. He also notes that the library was intended as a repository of knowledge that could be readily accessed. He does, however, leave a stern warning for anyone who might be tempted to abuse its resources: "May all the gods curse anyone who breaks, defaces, or removes this tablet with a curse that cannot be relieved, terrible and merciless as long as he lives, may they let his name, his seed be carried off from the land, and may they put his flesh in a dog's mouth."

c.650	**645**	**640**	**c.628**	**626**	**616**	**616**	**615**
The Library at Nineveh is built by King Ashurbanipal of Assyria	Ashurbanipal invades Elam and sacks its cities, reaching Susa five years later	Persia is a vassal state of the Medes	Zarathustra, founder of the Zoroastrian religion, is born	Nabopolassar makes himself king of the new Chaldean empire	Babylonian king Nabopolassar forges an alliance with the Medes	Nabopolassar defeats Assyrian army near Carrhae and a second army near Kirkuk	Assyrians force the Babylonians to abandon a siege of Ashur

NIMRUD

The prehistoric village that first occupied the site is deeply buried and has never been explored, but much has been found at Nimrud, also known as Kalhu. The site is dominated by palaces and temples from its time as a capital and administration center of Assyria.

Above: Assyrian winged deity.

Right and facing: Three ivory reliefs from the temple of Nabu.

In 1250 Shalmaneser I (r.1274–45) founded a provincial town on the east bank of the Tigris about 19 miles south of Mosul, in a location that had been the site of a third-millennium village. During the Middle Assyrian period it became an administrative center, Kalhu (Calah in the Old Testament), but it is better known today as Nimrud.

Kalhu was chosen as the new capital by Ashurnasirpal II (884–59) and served in this capacity for 150 years. During this time several new palaces and administrative buildings were erected over the citadel mound that remained from Shalmaneser's time. Kalhu had an elaborate sewage system, and extensive orchards and public parks

The site of the inner city of Nimrud encloses an area of about 500 acres, with all the major buildings on the citadel mound at its southwest corner. There is a temple dedicated to Ninurta, the patron god of Kalhu, which adjoins a well-preserved ziggurat on its southern side.

Ashurnasirpal's palace (the Northwest Palace) was built from mud brick and is decorated with numerous plaster reliefs and wall paintings that depict tribute bearers. The doorways of the palace are flanked by colossal winged lions and bulls, which lead into Ashurnasirpal's throne room. South of the throne room are a number of reception rooms lined with sculptures, which have been restored by the Iraq Department of Antiquities.

The date of the palace's completion can be fixed exactly at 879, since there is a stela on which this is commemorated. The stela also records a banquet given by Ashurnasirpal for the builders and architects who had worked on the palace. A feast was provided for 63,000 people, including 47,000 workers who had been brought to Kalhu from conquered lands.

Temple of writing

Most of the mound is occupied by palaces and temples of various dates. The largest single building is the temple of Nabu, the god of writing. This has two chambers dedicated to Nabu and his consort, and is surrounded by smaller buildings that served as the priests' quarters and housed the domestic staff of the temple. Surviving ivory fragments—now in the

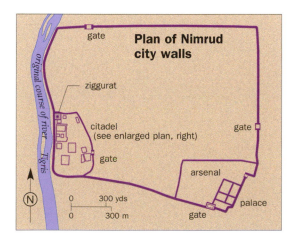

Iraq Museum—are probably the remains of booty or tribute payments. Although stripped of the original gold and lapis lazuli decoration, these small carvings are exquisite. They include a concave ivory mask representing a woman's face in profile, and a carving in the round of the head of a roaring lion. Southeast of the citadel is a royal arsenal built by Shalmaneser III (r.858–24), known today as Fort Shalmaneser. This has barracks, workshops, and stores, as well as its own royal palace.

Nimrud was abandoned as the Assyrian capital at the end of the eighth century, when the capital was transferred to Khorsabad and then to Nineveh, but it continued to be a major center and provincial capital until it was destroyed by the Babylonians and Medes between 614 and 612. A later Hellenistic village

was erected on the ruined citadel, but that was abandoned by 150.

Austen Henry Layard carried out the major excavations at Nimrud between 1845 and 1851. He was, however, digging without permission of the French consul who held authority in the area and was forced to bribe local chieftains into providing him with a labor force and keeping the extent of his activities secret. Most of the relics he removed from Nimrud are now in the British Museum.

During the 1950s a series of brick containers or boxes were discovered beneath the floor of a chamber in the Northwest Palace, in which were a number of clay tablets containing state letters and records. Recent Iraqi excavations have also revealed the tombs of some of the queens of Assyria.

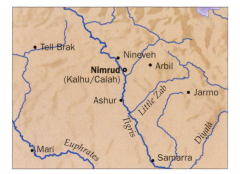

The palace of Ashurnasirpal II was organized around three courtyards. State apartments and the major throne room were situated around the first courtyard. The second was surrounded by rooms devoted to the internal business of the palace, while the innermost courtyard belonged to the harem.

DUR-SHARRUKIN

Although there had been no trace of any earlier occupation at Dur-Sharrukin, Sargon II intended it to replace Nimrud as his new capital of Assyria. The otherwise insignificant city lasted only as long as his reign, abandoned even before existing building works were completed.

Facing: Relief from Khorsabad depicts Sargon at a victory banquet.

In 717 Sargon II (722–05) founded a new city called Dur-Sharrukin ("Sargon's fortress") north of the ancient city of Nineveh and about 12 miles northeast of Mosul. It may be that Sargon wanted to begin his reign free

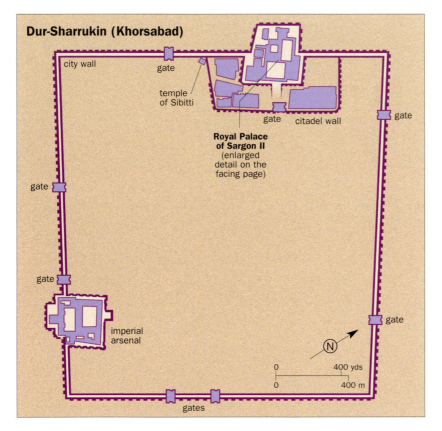

Dur-Sharrukin (Khorsabad)

city wall

gate

temple of Sibitti

gate   citadel wall   gate

Royal Palace of Sargon II (enlarged detail on the facing page)

gate

gate

gate

gate

imperial arsenal

N

| 0 | 400 yds |
| 0 | 400 m |

gates

from the yoke of his predecessor, Shalmaneser V (727–22), and therefore chose a location that had no previous associations. However, Dur-Sharrukin was destined never to become an important center, and appears simply to reflect the whim of a solitary monarch.

Dur-Sharrukin (modern Khorsabad) is almost square in plan, with each side about a mile long and laid out so that the corners of the square point

Tell Brak

Nineveh   Dur-Sharrukin

Nimrud   Arbil

Ashur   Little Zab   Jarmo

Tigris   Diyala

Mari   Euphrates

Samarra

approximately in the cardinal directions. Originally protected by a high fortified wall, seven gates gave access to the inner city, which contained a second fortified interior wall surrounding a terrace near the northwest side. This fortified terrace, about 46 feet high and straddling the exterior wall, formed a citadel within the city and contained a temple and a ziggurat, as well as the most important building: the Palace of Sargon.

Although little of the palace plan can now be traced, it has been ascertained that it was built with three main sections. In the center was the residence of the king and his immediate retinue, forming the administrative hub of the city. The harem in the southern corner gave separate provision for four wives. The eastern corner was occupied by domestic quarters that included a kitchen, bakery, and wine cellar, as well as stabling. South of the terrace and linked to it by a stone bridge was the temple of Nabu, while just outside the citadel on its southwest side was the temple of Sibitti (the Pleiades). Within the city a small arsenal contained a secondary palace.

Sunken treasures

It is apparent from texts that the gods worshipped at Dur-Sharrukin were only brought in when Sargon took up residence in 707. The city was not completed at the time of his death (705), since several of the buildings remained in an unfinished state. Even in the completed ones, there is often no discernible sign that they were ever occupied. Following Sargon's death Dur-Shurrukin was abandoned, and his son and successor Sennacherib (704–681) moved the capital to Nineveh.

Despite its very short period of use, Dur-Shurrukin is an archaeologically significant site. It was excavated by the French in 1843 and again in 1851–55 under the consul Paul Emile Botta and the archaeologist Victor Place. They found numerous friezes showing processions of courtiers, which are now in the Iraq Museum. There was also a wealth of carved stone reliefs lining the palace walls, and massive statues of Sargon and winged bulls. Among the carvings are scenes of everyday life, rituals, ceremonies, and

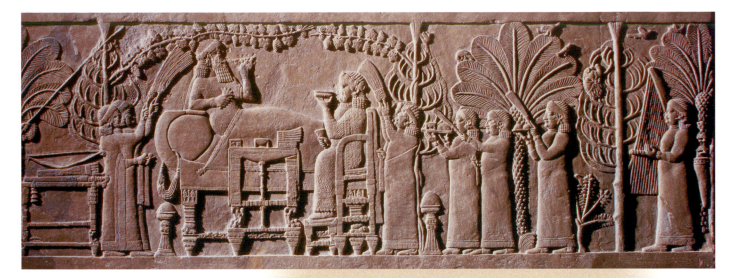

the more frequently depicted military campaigns.

Botta and Place removed most of these items for shipment to the Louvre in Paris. Place's collection was aboard a boat that sank in the Tigris during bad weather, and remains on the river bed. Botta's finds safely reached their

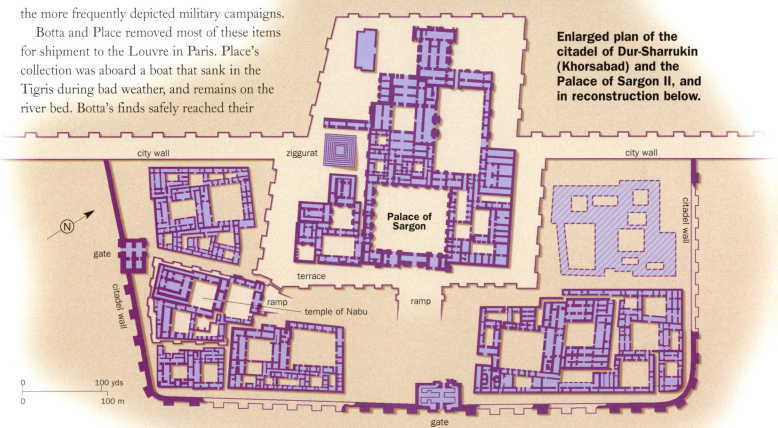

Enlarged plan of the citadel of Dur-Sharrukin (Khorsabad) and the Palace of Sargon II, and in reconstruction below.

city wall   ziggurat   city wall

citadel wall

N

gate

Palace of Sargon

citadel wall

terrace

ramp   temple of Nabu   ramp

0   100 yds
0   100 m

gate

destination and formed the basis for the first Assyrian museum open to the public.

Between 1928 and 1935 further excavations were carried out by the Oriental Institute, University of Chicago, in co-operation with the Iraq Department of Antiquities. Excavation director Professor Edward Chiera and his colleague James Henry Breasted found a number of good but hardly startling Assyrian carvings, until, in 1932, they discovered a hoard of hundreds of cuneiform tablets written in the Elamite language, together with a listing of kings from 2200 to 730 BC.

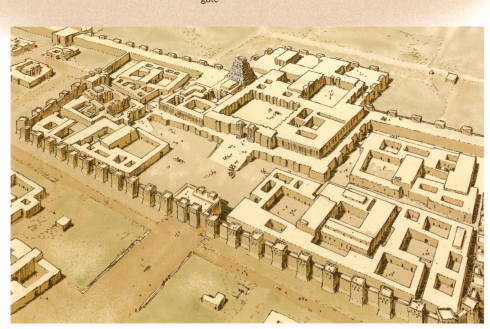

THE RISE OF NEW BABYLONIA

Assyrian central authority was weakened by the death of King Ashurbanipal, revolts, and an attempted coup by a governor that resulted in Babylon declaring its independence. Allied with other groups, both sides sought an advantage in a developing power struggle.

The death of the Assyrian king Ashurbanipal in 627 left the line of succession in doubt and led to the establishment of an interim government under Sin-Shum-Lishar and Sin-Shar-Ishkun. This gave disaffected groups opportunity to protest, and in some instances to stage an outright revolt, against Assyrian leadership. Taking advantage of this, Sin-Shum-Lishar obtained the support of some Assyrian garrisons in Babylonia and staged a coup, but Nabopolassar, a general at

Right: A decorated brick fragment depicts two Assyrian men of the late period, one carrying a sack or a jar on his shoulder.

Babylon who had been appointed by Sin-Shar-Ishkun, thwarted his attempt.

In the following year Nabopolassar (630–05) declared Babylon independent of Assyria, defeating an army that was sent to quell the uprising and naming himself as king of Babylonia and of the emerging Chaldean (Neo-Babylonian) empire. Realizing that Babylon alone could not withstand the might of the Assyrians, Nabopolassar embarked on a series of diplomatic missions in which he sought the alliance of other regional groups. From Babylon he began planning campaigns against the Assyrian religious center at Ashur and their administrative center at Nineveh.

Egypt, concerned with its own interests in the area and eager to maintain the balance of power, came out in support of Assyria. In 616 Nabopolassar defeated an Assyrian army south of Carrhae (Harran) in northern Mesopotamia, but was forced to withdraw when an Egyptian army arrived to reinforce the Assyrian position. During his withdrawal he met a second Assyrian army near Arrapkha (Kirkuk), which he engaged and defeated.

In the following year Nabopolassar's army laid siege to Ashur, but was forced to retreat in the face of fierce Assyrian opposition. At this point it is probable that the Assyrians and their Egyptian allies might have suppressed the Babylonians, since their armies were numerically superior and could rely on established field support. But a new group entered the conflict. These were the Medes, Indo-European tribes from Iran, under the leadership of Umakishtar (Cyaxares).

Avoiding the consequences

The chronicles state that in 614 a Median army laid siege to and defeated Ashur, but Nabopolassar arrived too late for his troops to be involved. It is more likely that the siege was made by a combined Babylonian-Mede force,

614	613	612	609	609	605	605–562	587
Ashur is abandoned after it is looted by an allied Babylonian-Mede army	Nabopolassar puts down pro-Assyrian rebellions along the Euphrates	Nineveh is taken by the Medes and Babylonians	At Carrhae the Assyrian dynasty is ended by Nabopolassar	Egypt allies with Assyria against Babylonia and Judah at the battle of Megiddo	Babylon defeats Egypt and Assyria at the battle of Carchemish	Reign of Nebuchadnezzar of Babylon	Nebuchadnezzar sacks Jerusalem and expels the Jews

and that the story of Nabopolassar's tardy arrival was a convenient way of exonerating him from any blame for looting the holy city.

Following this battle, a treaty between Nabopolassar and Umakishtar cemented the Babylonian-Mede friendship. As a token of the linking of the states, the Babylonian crown prince Nebuchadnezzar (Nabopolassar's son) was married to Amytis, the daughter of Umakishtar's son Astyages. This may have been a symbolic rather an actual marriage, since Amytis was a child well below marriageable age.

In 613 Nabopolassar came under attack from tribes living along the Euphrates who had allied with the Assyrians. It was only with great difficulty that he contained the rebellion—there is no mention of Mede support at this time. It is possible that the Medes were engaged elsewhere, against Scythian incursions along their borders in northern Iran.

In May 612 the Medes and Babylonians laid siege to Nineveh. Three months later the city fell, after the attacking army had dammed the rivers that supplied it and caused a flood that broke through one of the perimeter walls. Sin-Shar-Ishkun (621–12), who had remained in control of Nineveh, is believed to have committed suicide, although some reports say that he died in the fighting. Looting continued for nearly a month, until the city was burned and its inhabitants slaughtered or deported.

Despite the loss of both Ashur and Nineveh, a new king, Ashur-Uballit II (612–09) was able to set up a refugee Assyrian kingdom in Harran, which was supported by the Egyptian pharaoh Necho I. Ashur-Uballit's control lasted for three years, until Harran was abandoned and the Assyrian empire was brought to an end.

Above: Carved relief of a line of Mede dignitaries on the side of a stepped walkway.

562–60	560	559–29	556	c.550	555–39	547–46	539
Amel-Marduk succeeds Nebuchadnezzar	Amel-Marduk is assassinated and succeeded by brother-in-law Nergal-Ashur-Usur	Reign of Cyrus II of Persia	Labashi-Marduk favors the priesthood and is killed in a military coup	Zoroastrianism is the religion of the Persian empire	Reign of Nabonidus, who elevates the status of Sin, the moon god	Cyrus takes the Lydian capital of Sardis, deposing Croesus, and founds Pasargadae	Cyrus II of Persia defeats the Babylonian army near Baghdad

CHAPTER 8

CHALDEA: NEO BABYLONIA, 612–539 BC

Following its destruction by the Babylonian-Mede armies of Ashur in 614 BC and Nineveh in 612, the remnants of the once-powerful Assyrian empire fled to Carrhae (Harran) under the leadership of Ashur-Uballit II (r.612–09). Carrhae was an obvious choice for their retreat: It had been a powerful and well garrisoned provincial capital, controlling the trade routes from the Mediterranean Sea into the heart of Assyria, and was a sanctuary of the moon god Sin and his consort Nikkal.

Ashur-Uballit was not isolated but had widespread support in the remaining provinces of Assyria, as well as among some of the Babylonian towns. In fact, Nabopolassar's hold over much of his new-found kingdom was rather tenuous. Even his Mede allies could not be entirely relied upon, as is evident from their failure to support him in suppressing rebellious tribes along the Euphrates.

Despite the rhetoric employed by Nabopolassar, claiming he "marched to Assyria victoriously," the expulsion of Ashur-Uballit's forces from Carrhae took nearly three years. Even then it was accomplished by an army largely comprised of Scythian warriors who, despite Mede fears and the Scythians' former Assyrian allegiance, had chosen to side with the Babylonians. The three allies divided the former Assyrian territories—the Scythians were to control Asia Minor, the Medes held power in Anatolia, while Nabopolassar occupied central Assyria and the middle Euphrates.

Problems with the Assyrians were not yet over. Ashur-Uballit convinced Pharaoh Necho II to support his cause, and in June 609 a large combined Assyrian-Egyptian army attempted to retake Carrhae. They were nearly successful, but in August their supply lines broke down and they had to lift the siege. The Assyrian army regrouped at Carchemish, an important river crossing on the Euphrates for caravans engaged in the Syria-Mesopotamia-Anatolia trade, where there was a heavily fortified town. They

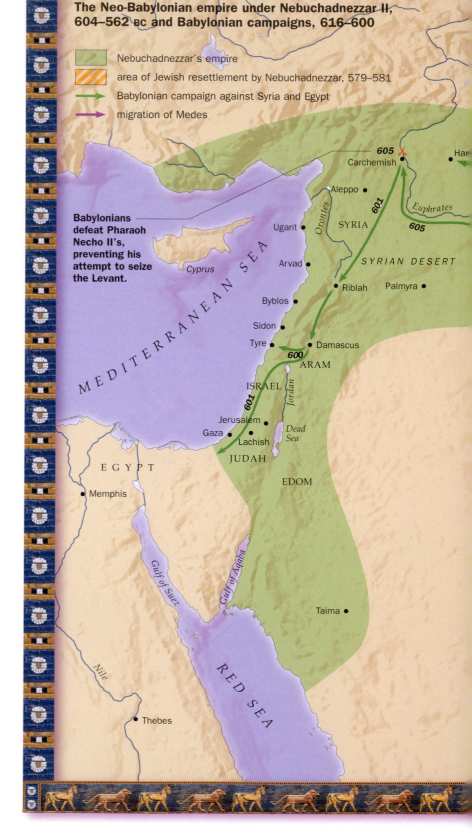

The Neo-Babylonian empire under Nebuchadnezzar II, 604–562 BC and Babylonian campaigns, 616–600

- Nebuchadnezzar's empire
- area of Jewish resettlement by Nebuchadnezzar, 579–581
- → Babylonian campaign against Syria and Egypt
- → migration of Medes

Babylonians defeat Pharaoh Necho II's, preventing his attempt to seize the Levant.

Left: Stele of Nabodinus, last of the Neo-Babylonian kings, who raised the Assyrian deity Sin (moon) above Marduk the dragon.

Nisibis

608
608

Tigris

MANNEA

Dur-Sharrukin
Nineveh
Arbil
Kalhu

Medes, 614–612

Ashur
Arrapha

615-612

Mari

Tigris

Diyala

Karkeh

Euphrates

605

Der

Babylon

Susa

BABYLONIA

ELAM

Uruk

Ur

Judah and Israel, 597 BC

Sidon
Damascus
Tyre
Dan
Akko
PHOENICIA
ARAM-DAMASCUS
Sea of Galilee
MEDITERRANEAN SEA
Megiddo
Beth-shean
ISRAEL
Jordan
AMMON
Ashkelon
Jerusalem
MOAB
independent of Israel, 843 BC
Gaza
Lachish
Dead Sea
PHILISTIA
JUDAH
Babylonian empire
EDOM
independent of Judah, 843 BC

The kingdom of Judah held sway over Israel after the Assyrian decline in the 630s until its king was defeated by the Egyptians at Megiddo. In turn, the Babylonians defeated the Egyptians at Carchemish in 605, after which Judah became a vassal state of Babylon. Nebuchadnezzar crushed a revolt in 597 and deported many Jews to Babylonia. A second revolt ten years later resulted in the sack of Jerusalem and the removal of the entire population to Babylonia, where they stayed until the Achemenid Persians let them return in 539.

intended to wait for Egyptian reinforcements that had been promised by Necho.

Taking up the sword

Nabopolassar was by now an elderly man, too weak to command an army in the field. Learning of the Assyrian and Egyptian plans from spies in their camps, he appointed his son Nebuchadnezzar as commander-in-chief and sent emissaries to King Josiah, whose Jewish forces were loyal to Babylon.

Josiah was killed at the battle of Megiddo; his troops also engaged the Egyptian army at Riblah, delaying them long enough to prevent them from reaching Carchemish ahead of Nebuchadnezzar. With the Assyrian defenders defeated, Nebuchadnezzar turned against the Egyptians and routed them, pursuing them to Hamath, where most of the Egyptians were killed. Nebuchadnezzar's actions finally eliminated any threat from Assyria, removed the Egyptians from their Syrian territories, and enabled him to annex both Syria and Palestine.

While he was engaged on this campaign, news reached Nebuchadnezzar of Nabopolassar's death, forcing him to make a hasty return to Babylon. At the burial ceremony arranged for his father, Nebuchadnezzar acceded to the throne as the new king of the Neo-Babylonian empire, which he was to rule from 605 until 562.

Although this new empire was short-lived and over by 539, when it became part of the Persian (Achaemenid) empire under Cyrus II, it was a period of majestic splendor. Babylon was rebuilt by the finest architects, who constructed the famous Hanging Gardens (*see following spread*), and became the largest settlement in Mesopotamia. There were new palaces and temples, and a massive ziggurat gave rise to the myth of the Tower of Babel (*see pages 124–125*). Even after Babylonian power ended, the city remained important. It was a royal city of the later Seleucid empire in 281 BC and was occupied until the 11th century AD.

NEBUCHADNEZZAR'S HANGING GARDENS

Nebuchadnezzar II is known to us from cuneiform inscriptions and from the Bible and Jewish sources. Renowned as a military strategist and frequently shown as a general leading his armies into battle, contrastingly he was also depicted as a devout and pious man of peace.

Upon his hasty return to Babylon following the death of his father Nabopolassar, Nebuchadnezzar II (r.605–562) immediately succeeded to the throne of Babylonia. There was little opposition to his accession, but to secure his legitimacy Nebuchadnezzar re-invented his past and, despite his father's disclaimer of royal descent, asserted that his ancestor was the Akkadian king Naram-Sin.

During his long reign, Nebuchadnezzar's Babylonian armies and Greek mercenaries defeated the Egyptians, secured control of Syria and Palestine, captured Jerusalem, and invaded northwestern Arabia. In addition to his royal duties, he was also a high priest of Marduk and the god's son, Nabu—Nebuchadnezzar translates as "Nabu will protect my sovereignty." It is significant that most of his campaigns were to ensure the security of Babylonia and prevent incursions across its borders. The only immediate threat within the empire came from the Medes, and Nebuchadnezzar resolved this diplomatically by forming an alliance with their rulers.

With his borders secured, Nebuchadnezzar embarked on the reconstruction of the Babylonian empire. Years of internal strife coupled with numerous wars had left much of the country's agricultural land neglected and allowed many of its temples to fall into disrepair. Nebuchadnezzar was responsible for restoring more than 40 temples in major cities such as Borsippa, Sippar, Ur, Uruk, Larsa, Dilbat, and Baz, as well as for

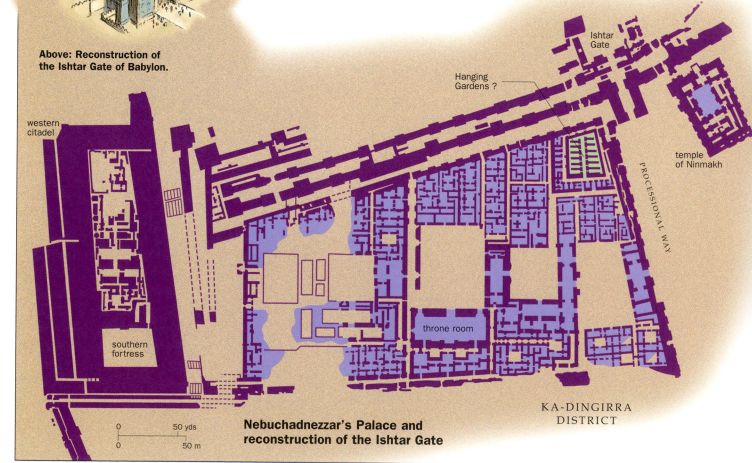

Above: Reconstruction of the Ishtar Gate of Babylon.

western citadel

Ishtar Gate

Hanging Gardens ?

temple of Ninmakh

southern fortress

throne room

PROCESSIONAL WAY

KA-DINGIRRA DISTRICT

0   50 yds
0   50 m

Nebuchadnezzar's Palace and reconstruction of the Ishtar Gate

a complete overhaul of the canal system, including the building of a major new canal that connected the Euphrates and Tigris.

A reconstructed land

Under his rule, Babylonia was restored as the most important economic and military power of Mesopotamia, but Nebuchadnezzar is best known for the rebuilding of Babylon itself. This included the dedication of new temples, strengthening the city's fortifications, and the construction of an entire new quarter. Nebuchadnezzar's palace was magnificent. It had more than 600 rooms, whose brick walls were inscribed with Nebuchadnezzar's name as the protector of Babylonia, and which contained gold and lapis lazuli-encrusted sculptures and carvings made by the best craftsmen of the day.

His architects were also responsible for one of the world's greatest architectural masterpieces: the Hanging Gardens of Babylon. Legend records that Nebuchadnezzar had these

Above: Foundations of the Hanging Gardens and, **below**, a doorway in the palace.

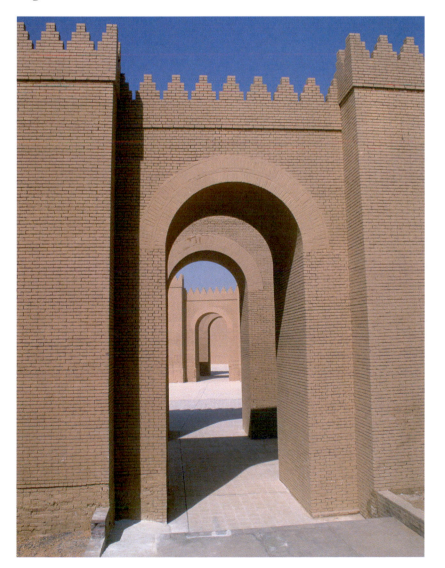

built at the request of his wife Amytis, daughter of the Median king Umakishtar, who pined for the trees and hills of her northern homeland. According to later Greek historians, the gardens consisted of a series of irrigated terraces several hundred feet high, planted with trees "of all description."

The gardens would have been an amazing engineering feat. Water needed to be raised from the nearby Euphrates, collected in a pool on the top terrace, and then released through a series of small dams to water the terraces below. Each terrace had to be many feet in depth to accommodate the roots of the fully grown trees, and the mud brick construction of the period was protected by lead liners to prevent it dissolving.

Unfortunately for science, Herodotus, who described Babylon's palaces, canals, and fortifications in 450, made no mention of the Hanging Gardens. Modern archaeologists have been unable to locate them with certainty, but a recent discovery has been made of vaulted brick-built chambers that have bore holes in their walls. These might be channels that contained the chains and pulleys needed to raise water to the top terrace, but further study is necessary to provide positive identification.

Nebuchadnezzar's palace, too, is the object of current debate, since the old palace was largely obliterated by a new one built by Saddam Hussein. Many of the baked bricks now bear inscriptions that dedicate the palace to Saddam's rule as the new Babylonian king.

NEW BABLYON

Babylon has veered from being the center of mighty empires to the symbol of the most repressive regimes, and in the Bible is synonymous with everything that is sinful against God and His kingdom. Modern studies of the city from Nebuchadnezzar's reign revealed much of its construction and layout.

Babylon must be one of the most maligned cities on earth. Coveted and occupied by numerous kings and rulers since its inception in about 3000 until the time of Alexander the

Above: The Ishtar Gate as it was in 1950 before the recent restoration work began.

Great, and more recently as the center of Saddam Hussein's Iraq, it has seen successive periods of glory, destruction, and rebuilding.

Little remains today of the original city built by Hammurabi and rebuilt by Nabopolassar and Nebuchadnezzar. Yet at the height of its power during Nebuchadnezzar's reign it was

the largest city in the world. Herodotus tells us that "Babylon surpassed in splendor any city in the known world," and states that the outer walls were 56 miles long, 80 feet thick, and almost 330 feet high. He says that the road on the top of the wall was wide enough for a four-horse chariot to turn, and that the whole was surrounded by a moat 164 feet across.

Modern archaeological studies suggest that Herodotus was prone to exaggeration. Even so, the statistics are still impressive. A 39-foot wide moat encircles the entire site, and there are three fortified walls around the city. The outer wall, beyond the moat, is 23 feet thick and the space between the two inner walls is wide enough to have functioned as a military road. The inner wall is further reinforced with towers at 59-foot intervals, with eight gates and drawbridges leading into the city itself.

The Euphrates runs through the city center. Major temples were concentrated close to the river, although there are an estimated 1,179 temples and shrines scattered throughout the city's precincts. The most important is Marduk's temple of Esagila and its associated ziggurat of Etemenanki (the "house that is the foundation of heaven and earth"), which lie about ⅔ mile south of the principal royal palace. There are a number of shrines at Esagila, but the main one originally had walls covered with gold and contained a gold figure of Marduk seated on a golden throne. The amount of gold used in this shrine alone is estimated to have weighed about 22 tons. Outside the temple is a golden altar with a second brick altar on which frankincense was burned.

A magnificent palace

Babylon contained several palaces. Of the three main royal palaces, the Summer Palace (South Palace) of Nebuchadnezzar was considered by

Herodotus to be "the most magnificent building ever erected on earth." It has five courtyards leading to the royal quarters and harem, administrative offices, and military and residential buildings. The throne room had cedar beams in the roof, glazed tiles on its walls, and was adorned with gold, silver, and precious stones. A second large royal palace, sometimes referred to as the Museum Palace, was filled with antiquities from all parts of the realm.

The city was laid out on a grid plan, roads running parallel or at right angles to the Euphrates. The most important of these was the Processional Way, a 69-foot wide elevated roadway that leads from the Ishtar Gate to the ziggurat and temple of Marduk. It is made from 39-inch square stone slabs lined with red and white bricks that lead into drainage channels on either side, and runs between walls decorated with glazed tiles and a lion frieze. During the annual Babylonian New Year festivities, an image of Marduk was carried through the city along this route in a procession led by Nebuchadnezzar.

Above: Detail of one of the horse reliefs on the Ishtar Gate, showing the intricate molding of the bricks that were used.

Left: A doorway in Nebuchadnezzar's Palace fully restored to the original color scheme painted onto the molded brick reliefs of the bull Adad and Marduk the dragon.

TOWER OF BABEL

Although based upon a religious building in Babylon, the biblical story of the Tower of Babel originated outside the empire. The real tower was a ziggurat dedicated to the god Marduk, and its construction celebrated diverse peoples.

According to Genesis, after the Flood the people resettled in Shinar where they founded a city and attempted to build a tower whose top would reach into heaven. The tower was toppled by the winds, the people were scattered, and their languages confused so that they could no longer understand one another. Reference to the word "balal" reinforces this story through Hebrew etymology, since this means "to confuse or confound." The confusion of languages is seen in a negative light, as retribution for people's sins and vanity.

The origin of this story has not however been found in Babylonia, where Babel, the original name of Babylon, is a contraction of the Assyrian word Bab-ili ("Gate of the God"); it is a later, probably Christian addition. Accounts of the confounding of languages and the diversity of speech are found in the myths of many nations, but there is nevertheless reason to believe that the Genesis story was predicated on the great ziggurat of Etemenanki at Babylon.

The ziggurat (or stepped pyramid) of Etemenanki was begun by Nabopolassar and completed during the reign of Nebuchadnezzar II as a shrine to the god Marduk. According to Nebuchadnezzar's inscriptions, it was made so that "its top might rival heaven," but this should probably be interpreted to mean that Marduk's power would reach the sky.

As with other Mesopotamian ziggurats, Etemenanki was not built from stone, which is rare in the region. Instead it was constructed from trodden clay with a 50-foot-thick outer covering of sun-dried mud and straw bricks, held in position with bitumen as mortar. In the arid conditions of the Mesopotamian plain such a structure is relatively stable; however it is susceptible to water damage, which softens the bricks and causes them to crumble. Elaborate drainage systems are therefore required, as well as regular maintenance and periodic rebuilding.

Banded levels

The Etemenanki ziggurat was built in seven stages, connected by stairways that alternate along each side at the different levels, so climbing to the top required one to make a complete circuit of the building. Each stage was a different color. Based on assumptions from other Mesopotamian periods (since there is no direct evidence at Babylon), from base to top these may

Below: Reconstruction of the sacred precinct of Marduk in Babylon, with the great ziggurat of Etemenanki at its heart.

have been white, white, red, bronze, silver, gold, and blue.

At its summit, probably on the seventh stage, was a small temple or shrine, although some scholars have argued that this was an eighth level. Nebuchadnezzar tells us that the outside of the shrine was covered with blue glazed tiles, and the interior had a cedar roof and walls plated with gold and embellished with alabaster and lapis lazuli. Inside was an altar with a solid gold statue of Marduk seated on a golden throne, together with a gold couch and footstool.

There is also reference by Nebuchadnezzar to diversity of language. He tells us that he called upon "various peoples… from the mountains and the coasts" to help with its construction. Many of them were people from conquered nations, such

as Israel, who were relocated in Babylon to serve as a labor force during Nebuchadnezzar's rebuilding programs; although there is no evidence that the Babylonians saw this mixing of languages and cultures in the same negative light as the biblical tradition. Some clay tablets recovered from Babylon give details of the provisions supplied to Babylonian, Jewish, and other workers to ensure that they were housed comfortably and remained fit.

Surrounding the ziggurat platform was a protective wall built using a similar construction to the fortified walls of Babylon. It was wide enough to contain several brick-built chambers that functioned as store rooms, shrines for pilgrims, and quarters for the ziggurat's priests and officials.

Below: The legend of the Tower of Babel has exercised the imaginings of artists throughout the centuries. This version by Pieter Brueghel the Elder (c.1520–69) is perhaps the best known.

BABYLONIAN DAILY LIFE

The Babylonians did not separate secular and spiritual life; their gods had human attributes and were closely involved in the everyday life of Babylon's 200,000 or so occupants. However, spiritual bias was evident in the prestige and wealth of temple officials.

Babylon during Nebuchadnezzar's time was a devoutly religious city. Apart from its numerous temple complexes, there were small altars on the approaches to temples, at each of the city gates, and at crossroads, where prayers could be offered. In addition, it has been estimated that there were as many as a thousand small roadside shrines, although only a few have been excavated.

The city covered approximately $1\frac{1}{3}$ square miles, wholly contained within protective walls and divided into a number of districts. The two main districts were the old city on the west bank of the Euphrates and the new city on the east, which were connected by bridges. An ancient canal, the Libil-hegalla, flowed through the city, as did a number of smaller canals that brought water from the Euphrates for the gardens and orchards on the west bank, and provided fresh water for its suburbs. There was farmland beyond the walls, but unlike earlier Mesopotamian cities there were few residential areas in the countryside.

The people who lived here were diverse, culturally and socially; many of the foreigners came from lands that the Babylonians had previously conquered. This had been a feature of Babylon since Hammurabi's reign. There were Hurrians, Kassites, Hittites, Elamites, and some Egyptians and Assyrians, many of whom were married into Chaldean families. During Nebuchadnezzar's reign there was also a sizable Jewish population. Babylon had a large number of temporary immigrant workers who had been pressed into service as labor gangs during its extensive rebuilding. Other laborers kept the

canals in good order.

The landed elite

Socially there was a division between free men and slaves, and between temple personnel and the laity. In practice, these distinctions were often blurred. Agricultural workers, for example, might be paid laborers or indebted slaves, but they could also be captured soldiers who had no rights as citizens yet remained technically free men.

Status as a slave did not necessarily entail undue hardship, and the living standard of a slave in a wealthy household was considerably higher

Right: The remains of a mud-brick column stand in Babylon.

531	525	522	c.520	518	499	495	490
Cyrus II gives the rule of Babylon to son Cambyses II	Cambyses II conquers Memphis and invades Egypt	Cambyses dies traveling to stop a rebellion; Parthian governor Darius I seizes power	First reference to Parthia/Parthava, part of the Persian empire	Works begins on Darius the Great's new capital of Persepolis	Greek cities rebel against Persian rule	Darius quells the Greek rebellion and invades mainland Greece	Athens and Sparta defeat Persians under Darius at Marathon

than that enjoyed by a poor but free citizen. Usually male slaves undertook much of the manual labor, the exact nature of which depended on their owner's profession. Choice of profession was limited by hereditary principle and a man generally followed that of his father. Female slaves were maids to the lady of the house, and sometimes the concubines of the owner or one of

shipping fleet.

Temple and court officials resided within the precincts of the temples and palaces, where special quarters were reserved for them according to status and the duties they had to perform. These precincts also housed most of the military and provided accommodation for visiting diplomats and dignitaries.

Ground-plan of private houses of the Neo-Babylonian period

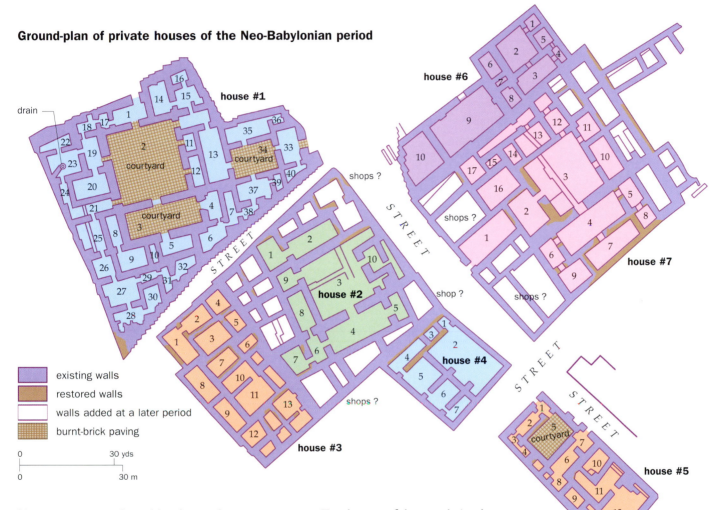

existing walls
restored walls
walls added at a later period
burnt-brick paving

0 ———— 30 yds
0 ———— 30 m

his teenage sons; when older they took over duties such as grinding corn and collecting water.

The temples formed a virtual state within a state. The only formal education took place at them and was reserved for those who would enter temple service or be attached to the royal court. Temple officials were the biggest owners of land and real estate, with some 50 percent of Babylon under their direct control. Their senior representatives had authority that rivaled that of the king. They also had vast business interests and owned a sizable proportion of Babylon's

For the rest of the population homes were distinguished mostly by size. Most were single-story and all had blank outer walls up to 6½ feet thick to protect against the heat of the sun. A single entrance doorway opened onto an inner courtyard; living quarters and bedrooms ranged from the courtyard, as did a large room on its northern side that served as a kitchen, with a bathroom at the south fitted with drainage and a soakaway. Bathing was usually a matter of being doused with water, followed by a brisk rub down and the application of olive oil and perfume.

486	486	480	479	466	449	413	401
Darius the Great dies and is succeeded by his son Xerxes	Persian empire reaches its greatest extent	Xerxes defeats a Spartan army at Thermopylae and sacks Athens	The Greek Delian League defeats Persia at the Battle of Plataea	The Delian League shatters the Persian army and navy at the River Eurymedon	Artaxerxes and Pericles agree the Peace of Kallia treaty between Persia and Greece	Persians under Darius II ally with Sparta against Athens	Artaxerxes II assures his reign by killing his brother and rival Cyrus at Cunaxa

THE DECLINE OF CHALDEA

The firm rule of Nebuchadnezzar was not matched by his successors, who passed in a matter of years. The aged Nabonidus was an unpopular and unstable leader who upset the delicate balance between state and priesthood, ultimately leaving Babylon open to invasion.

Nebuchadnezzar kept a firm grip on affairs of both state and religion and retained control of the Chaldean empire throughout his reign, but discontent had been festering beneath the surface. On his death, his son and successor Amel-Marduk (Evil-Merodach, r.562–60), was unable to prevent the suppressed rivalry between the priests and the state from breaking into open disagreement.

Partly to blame was Amel-Marduk's leniency. Against the priests' wishes, he had Judah's king, Jehoiachin, released from prison and gave him a seat of honor in the Babylonian court. The priests branded Amel-Marduk as "lawless and impious"; with the incitement of the religious establishment, Amel-Marduk's brother-in-law Nergal-Ashur-Usur (Neriglissar, r.560–56) hatched a plot to have him assassinated and seized the throne.

Nergal-Ashur-Usur reigned for only four years, apparently dying from natural causes. He was succeeded by his son Labashi-Marduk (Labosoarchod, r.556), who incurred the displeasure of the military commanders, who accused him of "not knowing how to rule." Although details are uncertain, it seems that Labashi-Marduk supported the priests against the military. Factions developed between the secular and religious elites, and he was overthrown and killed by a military coup after only nine months in power.

The military faction placed the elderly Nabonidus (Nabu-Naid, r.555–39) on the throne; however, he proved to be an eccentric and intractable ruler whose opposition to the priests of Marduk was to create even greater divisions. His love of history led him to excavate earlier sites and collect antiquities, with which

Below: Wall decoration from the Processional Way of Babylon—rebuilt in the Pergamon Museum, Berlin, Germany—and, **facing**, the rebuilt, but unadorned, walls of the Processional Way in Babylon itself.

Plan of the palace of Nabodinus, near the North Harbor at Ur

See page 29 for Ur city plan and palace position

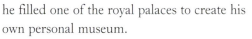

courtyard

courtyard

gate

```
0                    30 yds
0                    30 m
```

he was aging and senile and "imagined he was a goat and ate grass." In Daniel this assertion of insanity is made of Nebuchadnezzar II; however, there is no corroborating evidence that Nebuchadnezzar went into exile, whereas that for Nabonidus is certain. Some serious matter must have pre-occupied him, since he did not even return to Babylon for his mother's funeral.

Whatever the truth, Nabonidus left Babylon in the charge of his son, the prince-regent Belshazzar (Bel-Shar-Utsur). A cuneiform tablet (the Nabonidus Chronicle) tells us that while the king stayed in Temā, his crown prince, his officials, and his army remained in Babylon. The annual New Year's ceremonies during which images of Marduk and Nabu were carried in procession through the city did not take place in this period.

In 539 Cyrus II of Persis (Persia) defeated the Babylonian army in a battle on the Tigris near present-day Baghdad. Belshazzar was killed, and Nabonidus hurried back to Babylon to find Cyrus's army marching unopposed into the city. Cyrus promised to have exiled deities returned and to repatriate the Jews to their homeland, and was welcomed by the city. The center of political power shifted from Babylon to Cyrus's capital at Pasargadae.

he filled one of the royal palaces to create his own personal museum.

More significantly, he raised the status of the Assyrian moon god, Sin, above that of Marduk. It is probable that he was encouraged by his mother, who was the high priestess at the temple dedicated to Sin and supposedly lived to over a hundred years of age. Her significance is indicated by the fact that Nabonidus arranged for her to be given a queen's funeral on her death in 547. Nabonidus installed his daughter as the high priestess of Sin at the temple in Ur, and rebuilt the temple of Sin at Harran.

A welcome conquest

Naturally, Nabonidus was opposed by the priests of Marduk, and it may have been through their actions that he was forced to spend ten years in exile at the oasis of Temā in northern Arabia. Some claim he was in Temā to put down an Arab rebellion, while others state he was recovering from a physical illness, or that

CHAPTER 9
THE FIRST PERSIAN EMPIRE, 539–312 BC

Cyrus II's defeat of Babylon in 539 marked the beginning of the rise of a new dynasty, that of the Achaemenids. Under this dynasty the Persians expanded to create the greatest empire ever known. By 486 they controlled parts of Greece, Egypt, all of Mesopotamia and the old Assyrian empire, southern Russia, Afghanistan, and northern India.

Their rise to power was startling. They barely feature in the historical record prior to the sixth century BC, and then only as disparate Indo-European groups speaking a language similar to Sanskrit. They had no political or cultural cohesiveness. Some were nomads, others had small settlements of wooden brush-covered huts. Living just north of the Persian Gulf (modern Iran), they had not been involved in earlier power struggles in Mesopotamia, Palestine, or Egypt, and were simply seen as vassal states to the Medes.

Their sudden rise to power over what was then the whole known world was centered on a religion first expounded in about 600 by the prophet Zarathustra (Zoroaster in Greek). This claimed that the universe was under the control of two gods: Ahura-Mazda, the creative god, full of light and good, and Ahriman, the god of everything dark and evil. Cyrus II (r.559–29) was a devout follower of Zarathustrianism and the first king to believe he had a religious duty to defeat evil by conquering Ahriman's dark forces of the world. He became chief of an obscure tribe in southern Persia in 559, and just five years later had conquered the rest of Persia and defeated the Medes. He won a war against Lydia in Asia Minor, before capturing Babylon in 539.

He was succeeded by his son, Cambyses II (r.529–22), who carried his father's religious zeal to Egypt and added this to the Achaemenid realms. His son, Darius I (r.522–486), put down a revolt by Chaldeans and Medes, and introduced the idea of self-governing provinces (satrapies), whose deities were seen as supportive of the good forces of Ahura-Mazda.

Enter Alexander

The Persian-Greek wars began in 500, when Darius attempted to conquer Greece. He met fierce resistance from Athens and Sparta, culminating in a humiliating Persian defeat at Marathon in 490. Four years later he faced a revolt in Egypt, during which Darius was killed.

His successor, Xerxes I (r.486–65), defeated a Spartan army in 480 but was forced out of Europe by the Greeks the following year. Xerxes was murdered in 465, and in 449 Artaxerxes (r.465–25) agreed a peace treaty between Greece and Persia. The Persians attempted to use Greek rivalry

Head of an
Achaemenid prince,
6th century BC.

Map Legend

- Persia, 559
- gains by Cyrus II, 559–550
- gains by Cyrus II, 550–530
- gains by Cambyses II, 530–522
- gains by Darius the Great, 521–486
- vassal state
- extent of Persian empire, 496
- the Royal Road

between Athens and Sparta to their own advantage. In 413 Persian King Darius II (r.423–04) sided with Sparta in their war with Athens; but in 394, under Artaxerxes II (r.404–359), this policy was reversed and the Persian navy delivered a crushing defeat against Sparta's fleet.

Such intrigues were also felt within the Achaemenid court. Artaxerxes II only consolidated his power after warding off a challenge from his brother Cyrus, killing him at the battle of Cunaxa in 401. Egypt was once more in revolt at punitive taxes being imposed by the Persians. Rebellions and intrigues plagued the dynasty, until in 340 a

Macedonian general, Alexander, set out to conquer Persia.

Alexander's rise was as spectacular as that of Cyrus II. With only a tiny army, he invaded Egypt and crossed the Euphrates in 331 to enter Mesopotamia. Darius III (r.336–30), with an army of more than a million men against Alexander's 7,000 cavalry and 40,000 foot soldiers, was defeated in the battle of Gaugamela, leaving Alexander in possession of the empire.

CYRUS II AND THE RISE OF DARIUS

The greatest kings of the Persian empire were the skilled military strategists Cyrus II and Darius I. Cyrus founded the Achaemenid dynasty, whereas Darius not only challenging the might of Greece, but inaugurated a magnificent building program at Persepolis.

Cyrus II (r.559–29) was the son of Cambyses, a Persian nobleman, and Mandane, the daughter of the Median king Astyages. Legend tells us that shortly after Cyrus's birth his mother had a dream in which a great tree spread from the boy's mouth to cover the entire kingdom. This was interpreted to mean that Cyrus would usurp the throne, and the only way to avert this was to have the infant killed. The nobleman charged with this duty passed the baby to a herdsman, but he gave the child to his wife to replace the stillborn baby she had recently bore. By the age of ten, the regal bearing of Cyrus made it clear that he was not the child of a commoner. He returned to the court, where he forgave Cambyses and pardoned his life.

Cyrus the Great was driven by religious zeal to conquer the world. By 553 he had overthrown Astyages and declared himself King of the Medes and Persians. In 547–46 he captured the Lydian capital of Sardis from Croesus (r.560–46), and built his own new capital at Pasargadae. Babylon was taken in 539, in a move said to have been partly instigated by an alliance made against Persia between King Nabodinus of Babylon and Croesus of Lydia.

Cyrus claimed to be acting as the representative of the Babylonian deity Marduk, whose rituals Nabodinus had failed to observe. He stated that foreign deities who served the interests of the Zarathustrian god of good, Ahura-Mazda, should be returned to the lands from which they had been stolen by the Babylonians. Deported peoples were repatriated, and he even rebuilt the temple at Jerusalem that had been destroyed when the Jews were defeated. Although there is little evidence to suggest that Cyrus forced his religion onto

Right: Colored brick and tile wall relief of Persian archers from Persepolis.

396	386	336	334	333	332	c.331	331
Sparta fights the Corinthian War against Athens, Persia, Corinth, Thebes, and Argos	Persia gains Greek cities in Asia Minor at the end of the Corinthian War	Philip II is killed and succeeded by Alexander the Great as King of Macedon	Alexander the Great's force defeats a larger Persian army at Granicus	Alexander defeats Darius III at Isso (Issus), securing Asia Minor	Tyre is destroyed at the end of a siege by Alexander the Great	Alexander invades Egypt and founds the first of several cities named Alexandria	Alexander's army defeats the Persians at Gaugamela; Darius III flees to Bactria

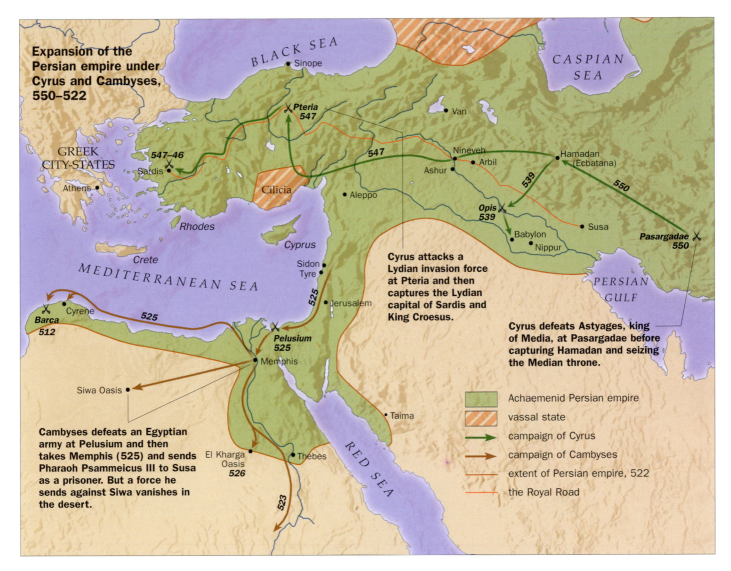

Expansion of the Persian empire under Cyrus and Cambyses, 550–522

Cyrus attacks a Lydian invasion force at Pteria and then captures the Lydian capital of Sardis and King Croesus.

Cyrus defeats Astyages, king of Media, at Pasargadae before capturing Hamadan and seizing the Median throne.

Cambyses defeats an Egyptian army at Pelusium and then takes Memphis (525) and sends Pharaoh Psammeicus III to Susa as a prisoner. But a force he sends against Siwa vanishes in the desert.

Achaemenid Persian empire
vassal state
campaign of Cyrus
campaign of Cambyses
extent of Persian empire, 522
the Royal Road

others, it is clear that the local customs and institutions he preserved were those that served his own interests.

An illustrious start

In 531 Cyrus II of Persia divided the kingdom, making his son Cambyses II the king of Babylon, while a second son, Bardiya, ruled over Persia's eastern provinces. Cyrus was killed while campaigning in 529, his body placed in a rock tomb at Pasargadae, and Cambyses duly succeeded him. Bardiya's claims to the throne made him a dangerous adversary, so Cambyses arranged for his assassination. Shortly after, in 525, Cambyses conquered Memphis and began his invasion of Egypt.

While Cambyses was campaigning in 522, a man claiming to be the resurrected Bardiya attempted to seize power in Persia. Cambyses headed home to put down the insurrection but died during the journey.

Darius, a governor of Parthia, was loyal to Cambyses and had commanded the 10,000 Immortals of the Persian army in the Egyptian campaigns. His father, Hystaspes, had given refuge to the prophet Zarathustra, and from him Darius inherited a belief in the cosmic battle of good against evil.

Feeling that Bardiya had betrayed Cambyses, Darius, with the support of seven other Persian nobles, took control of the army and had the false Bardiya executed. Thus began the rule of Darius the Great (the King of Kings). Perhaps the greatest of the Achaemenid kings, his doubtful claim to royal lineage caused unrest throughout much of the empire. Darius claimed to have fought 19 battles and captured nine kings from uprisings in Elam, Babylonia, Armenia, Parthia, and Persia during the first year of his rule.

330	330	323	312	282	281	281	c.250
Alexander the Great invades and razes Persepolis	Darius III is killed by the Bactrian governor; end of the Persian empire	Alexander dies, throwing his empire into disarray	Alexander's general Seleucus gains control of Persia and eastern territories	All of Asia Minor is under the Seleucid empire	Seleucus is assassinated by Ptolemy of Egypt and is succeeded by Antiochus I	Babylon becomes the royal city of the Seleucid empire	Bactria under Diodotus is independent of the Seleucid empire

PASARGADAE CITY

According to Roman geographer Strabo of Amasia, following an earlier account by Ctesias, Pasargadae was built on the site where Cyrus defeated the Median king Astyages. It is notable for the surviving tomb of Cyrus, maintained by Alexander, and ceremonial function.

Right: A pillar bearing a cuneiform inscription rises from the ruins of Pasargadae.

The ancient Persian city of Pasargadae lies about 50 miles northeast of Persepolis and was founded as Cyrus the Great's capital in 547, shortly after his defeat of Lydia. Strabo tells us that the Persians engaged in a desperate battle against the Medes in 553, during which they were encouraged to victory by the pleas of their women. It is said that Cyrus honored his Achaemenid Persian tribe by naming his capital after them. According to a tradition preserved

by Strabo, Pasargadae lay in the Coele Persis (the Hollow of Persia) on the River Cyrus, which Alexander called the Araxes, and from which the king took his name.

Much of Pasargadae was built by Ionian stone masons in a mixture of architectural styles; the Persians had no previous history of monumental architecture. Its remains are scattered over an area of about 500 acres, the

Tell-i-Takht (throne hill) citadel at its center overlooking a garden. To the north is a stone terrace, which forms part of a fortified area, and in the west a temple site with a fire altar dedicated to Zarathustra and a stepped platform. South is a stone tower, the Zendan-i-Suleiman (Prison of Solomon), probably a shrine or sanctuary, which modern Muslims revere as the location of Solomon's trials.

There are two main palace complexes, labeled for convenience as Palace P and Palace S. These have columned halls, columned porticos, and corner towers. The columns are of stone, whereas the walls are mud-brick. Palace P is set in a garden through which streams flow in carved limestone channels. It was probably a residential palace and has a large columned audience hall, or *apadana*, its doorways supported by massive carved stone bulls. The city is said to have had a treasury that was given to Alexander in 336 following his conquest of Persia.

Rewarding sweet success

That Pasargadae was Cyrus's capital is without doubt, since the buildings contain inscriptions in three languages, Elamite, Babylonian, and Old Persian, that state "I, Cyrus the king of the Achaemenid, have built this." About two-thirds of a mile southwest of the city is the tomb of Cyrus. This small temple about 16 feet high is set on a plinth of similar height, and was originally surrounded by gardens. The tomb was restored by Aristobulus on the instructions of Alexander the Great in January 324.

Strabo tells us that on his return from India Alexander found the tomb plundered. He punished the malefactors, and gave instructions for the tomb to be rebuilt. Prior to Alexander's restoration the tomb is said to have contained the body of Cyrus, which was laid in a golden sarcophagus on a gold couch, beside which lay a treasure-laden golden table.

Pasargadae lost its significance as a political capital when Darius built Persepolis, but nevertheless remained important as a religious center and the place where Persian kings were inaugurated. The coronation of kings was held in a sanctuary dedicated to the warrior goddess

Left: A little under a mile from the palace complex of Pasargadae stands the Tomb of Cyrus, in simple, stark isolation compared to the beautiful gardens he had created in the palace grounds. The ancient Persian word for "garden" was "paradise," a heaven on earth, and that of Pasargadae is the first known example of a monumental garden.

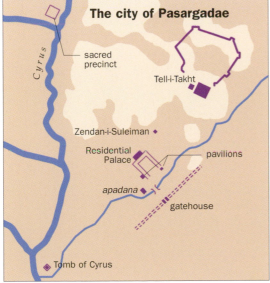

The city of Pasargadae

- sacred precinct
- Tell-i-Takht
- Zendan-i-Suleiman
- Residential Palace
- pavilions
- *apadana*
- gatehouse
- Tomb of Cyrus

Cyrus

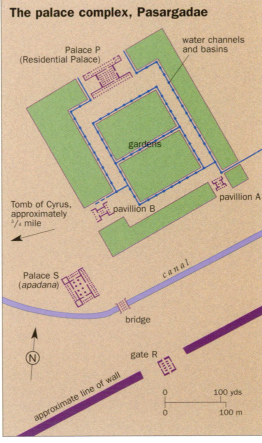

The palace complex, Pasargadae

Palace P (Residential Palace)

water channels and basins

gardens

Tomb of Cyrus, approximately 3/4 mile

pavillion B

pavillion A

Palace S (*apadana*)

canal

bridge

gate R

N

approximate line of wall

| 0 | | 100 yds |
| 0 | | 100 m |

Anaitis, where the king received a meal of figs and terebinth (a small tree from which tanning lotions and turpentine are derived), together with a cup of sour milk. Following the inauguration, the king paraded through the city and gave a gold piece to every woman in Pasargadae, in remembrance of the women who encouraged their men to defeat the Medes.

ZOROASTRIANISM AND MITHRAISM

Today a mere 200,000 followers worldwide follow the Zoroastrian ethic of "a good mind," the faith supplanted by Islam. Even in its day it was superseded by Mithraism, which found favor among the sun worshippers of the Roman empire.

A Tower of Silence stands in the desert near Yazd, Iran. To these isolated funerary monuments, Zoroastrians brought their deceased relatives and left the bodies there in state to be be picked clean to the bones by buzzards and vultures.

Zarathustra (c.628–c.551), known to the Greeks as Zoroaster, is an enigmatic figure. Little is known with certainty, but according to legend, he was born in Bactria, northwestern Afghanistan, which at that time was part of the Persian empire. He is said to have been the third of five sons of a local nobleman, Purushaspa, and a woman named Dughdhova. Unlike his brothers, who followed their father's agricultural and farming interests, Zarathustra

became a priest, founding Zoroastrianism, the religion followed by modern Parsis.

His religion stemmed from a vision of Ahura-Mazda that he recorded in a collection of hymns known as the *gâthâs*, which form part of the Avesta, the Zoroastrians' holy book. In this vision Zarathustra was told to give aid to the poor, avoid lies, and practice the cult of fire. He reformed the pantheon of Persian gods, with Ahura-Mazda as the supreme god of goodness and Ahriman as the embodiment of evil. Ahura-Mazda and Ahriman were equals, but engaged in an epic battle in which, according to Zarathustra, good would eventually prevail.

Ahura-Mazda was assisted by six Holy Immortals (Amesha Spentas), and Zarathustra did not deny the existence of a multitude of other Persian deities. He reorganized them into a complex hierarchical system of Immortals who were under the influence of either Ahura-Mazda or Ahriman, thus the Persian deities, as well as those of the nations they conquered, could be seen as opposing forces in a cosmic battle between the powers of good and evil.

The people were charged with supporting the good deities in their battle to defeat evil. Although Persian belief did not insist that any individual should follow only the powers for good, it did state that they would eventually come for judgment before Mithras (the Judger of Souls). He would conduct the righteous to the House of Best Purpose (heaven or paradise), while those who had followed the path of evil and lies would spend eternity in the Place of Worst Existence (hell).

A Roman following

The Mithras of legend was the son of Anahita, the virgin mother, who had formerly been venerated as a Babylonian fertility goddess. In Persian Mithraic worship, Mithras was the father of Ahura-Mazda and Ahriman, and acted as a mediator between the conflicting interests of his two sons. He was the patron of soldiers and armies, and introduced the handshake as a gesture of friendship, indicating that one bore no arms. The Romans, to whom Mithras was

the God of Contracts, later spread this convention throughout the Mediterranean and Europe. The Persians dedicated the seventh month and the 16th day of each month to Mithras.

Zarathustra was persecuted for his unorthodox views and forced to flee his native country. He was given sanctuary at the court of Hystaspes in Afghanistan, where he debated with the priests of Mithras and introduced his prophecies and the concept of a conflict between the forces of good and evil. He lived at Hystaspes' court until he died, aged 77, at the hands of invading nomads.

There are contradictory views as to whether Zoroastrianism was the state religion of the Persian empire. Both Darius and Xerxes seem to have embraced it, or at least taken up most of its major tenets. It is nevertheless clear that Zoroastrianism and its later offshoot, Mithraism, had a heavy influence of Persian thinking throughout the empire.

The Persians exported Mithraism to Indian and China, and the later Parthian princes of Armenia were all priests of Mithras. Even the Romans considered Mithras to be *sol invictus* (invincible sun) and the sun was the "eye of Mithras," based on the Babylonian/Persian conception of Mithras as a sun deity.

Above: Zoroastrian Fire Altars in Naqsh-e-Rustam, near the site of Persepolis, Iran.

GAMES AND PASTIMES

Zoroastrianism's struggle between the good Ahura-Mazda and evil Ahriman was easily translated to the battlefield, but Persians also associated it with their games. Their competitive nature was displayed in strategic pastimes and sporting ones that also honed their combat skills.

Under Darius and Xerxes, the Persian army went by the name of the Immortals; a term that implied they were ranked with the deities supporting Ahura-Mazda and reflecting the significance of armed might in the battles against Ahriman. It is significant that many of the Persians' games and pastimes reflect this competitive spirit, considered a trial between well matched opponents.

Among these games was polo, which received its first mention in Persian literature in 600 but was played by Iranian tribesmen well before the time of Darius I. It is the oldest known team sport, but there

Above: Bulls, horses and mythical beasts were used to top column capitals. This stone bull was originally symmetrically two-headed, a common feature at Persepolis.

In Persian belief, under the influence of Zoroastrianism, the world was engaged in a contest between good and evil under the respective leadership of Ahura-Mazda and Ahriman. Although religious doctrine permitted free will and choice, it is clear that kings believed that the good path was decreed for the Persians, whereas their enemies were inspired by evil.

were many local variants and few controls. Under Darius the rules of engagement were clarified and the sport developed as a training ground for cavalry. It was nevertheless quite different from the modern game.

With teams numbering up to a hundred on each side, Persian polo could be fast and furious, with few holds barred—fatal injuries

were not uncommon. In the later period the rules were tightened further and the sizes of teams restricted, after which it was adopted as the game of kings and emperors.

This more refined game was also played by women of the royal household; there are records of renowned female polo players and matches setting the king's team against that of the queen and her ladies-in-waiting. The Persian poet-historian Firdausi included vivid accounts of royal polo tournaments in his ninth century epic, the *Shahnamah*, in which it is clear that the game was well established long before his time.

Honing body and mind

Another game still played today, chess, is mentioned in the early Persian literature under the name of shatrang (or chatrang). Once again, it was originally used in military training. The pieces were derived from military symbols and the different moves were associated with military maneuvers and strategy. Later royal association is clear, since the name "chess" was derived from the Persian word for Shah, or ruler.

Backgammon (called *nard* in Persian), the oldest recorded game in history, was also played. The Persians used conical stones as counters

and two dice. The counters could only move along marked squares in a forward direction, with the figures of one player moving in a clockwise direction and those of the opponent anti-clockwise. The rules were phrased in typical military terminology. Each player pursued and outwitted their opponent by forcing them into a fight where his counters were outmaneuvered and "killed"—forced off the board.

Other pastimes, all with a military connection, included wrestling, weightlifting, swimming, chariot racing, horse racing, and horsemanship. Archery was practiced both as target shooting and as a feat of dexterity from horseback, during which the mounted archer displayed his ability to handle a short bow from any position on the horse.

Training in swordsmanship frequently included the use of a sword in each hand, a practical consideration for when a warrior faced two opponents. Soldiers were even trained to juggle with weights, to improve hand-eye co-ordination and develop the endurance needed on the battlefield. Falconry, originally used by desert dwellers in hunting rabbits and small game, was reserved as a sport for kings.

Above: Bas-relief of a winged monster from a wall in the Palace of darius, Susa.

DEVELOPMENTS UNDER DARIUS

Darius the Great is renowned for his military and administrative achievements. He divided the empire into lawful provinces that used standard weights, wages, and coinage in expanded trade that traveled along new roads and canals to rebuilt centers.

Above: King Darius the Great and attendants, a relief carving on the king's tomb.

After his accession in 522, one of Darius's first acts was to free Judah and rebuild the temple at Jerusalem. He restored Egyptian law, and won acclaim from Egypt as a liberator rather than a conqueror. Texts at Memphis attest to the high status that the Egyptians accorded him.

Darius was responsible for starting Persia's wars with Greece, that would ultimately lead to the conquest of Persia by Alexander the Great. The decisive point came in 490 at the battle of Marathon. A Persian fleet under the command of Darius' nephew, Artaphernes, had already captured Eretria, but was opposed near the plain of Marathon by an Athenian army under the command of Miltiades. Casualties on both sides were slight, but the Athenians claimed victory and Darius's army was forced to withdraw and relinquish any further claims to Greece.

Despite this setback, Darius is renowned for many achievements, notably his efforts in rebuilding Persia and restructuring its laws and economy. In accordance with his beliefs in Zoroastrianism, he appointed judges and made laws against those who lied or injured. He stated that his main concern was to provide security for all, so that the strong might not oppress the weak. To this end he divided the empire into 20 provinces, each with a Persian governor (or satrap) and a commander-in-chief. Governors assessed their province for tax purposes and fixed an annual tribute.

Darius brought in wage regulations that would recognize the abilities of skilled workers but provide adequately for unskilled laborers, and for women and children. To encourage fair trade and economic development, Darius standardized a system of weights and measures (in gold and silver), which were stamped with a portrait of the king as a sign of authenticity. He was also the first Persian king to mint his own coins.

Tax burden

The industrial and manufacturing bases of Persia were rebuilt and strengthened, and strict regulations governed luxury goods, household items, and their pricing. A network of trade roads was built, including the Royal Road from Susa to Sardis in Lydia. He even initiated the world's first postal system: small relay stations at regular intervals along these roads meant that messengers could obtain fresh horses and quickly carry news and letters from the provinces to the capital.

He had fruit trees transplanted from near the Euphrates into Asia Minor and Syria. Sesame was introduced to Egypt, and rice was planted

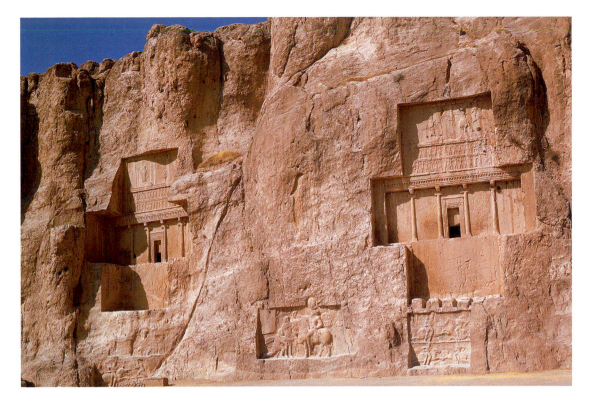

in Mesopotamia. New canals were dug, including a massive great canal, 150 feet wide, that connected the River Nile with the Gulf of Suez on the Red Sea to facilitate the Persia-Egypt trade. The building of his new capital at Persepolis was Darius's greatest project (*see the following pages*), but there was also extensive rebuilding at the old religious center of Susa and the former Mede capital at Ecbatana.

Darius had annexed Sind and the Punjab on an expedition to India. To finance his renewal projects he introduced a system of heavy taxation, from which Persian citizens were exempt. Primarily paid in gold, taxes against India and Egypt constituted almost half of the annual revenues paid into the empire. Other areas suffered from tax debts, with some rural regions forced into borrowing at 40 percent interest rate to meet the demands of the king.

Toward the end of Darius's reign tax burdens caused dissent among many regions, particularly in Egypt where it was felt that disastrous campaigns he had started against the Greeks were being funded with Egyptian wealth. Darius died in 486 and was succeeded by Xerxes, his eldest son by Queen Atossa.

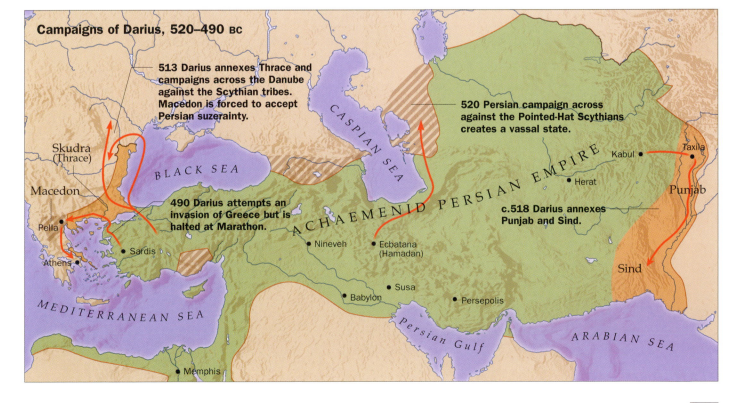

Campaigns of Darius, 520–490 BC

513 Darius annexes Thrace and campaigns across the Danube against the Scythian tribes. Macedon is forced to accept Persian suzerainty.

520 Persian campaign across against the Pointed-Hat Scythians creates a vassal state.

490 Darius attempts an invasion of Greece but is halted at Marathon.

c.518 Darius annexes Punjab and Sind.

Skudra (Thrace)

Macedon

Pella

Athens

Sardis

CASPIAN SEA

BLACK SEA

ACHAEMENID PERSIAN EMPIRE

Kabul

Herat

Taxila

Punjab

Sind

Nineveh

Ecbatana (Hamadan)

Susa

Babylon

Persepolis

MEDITERRANEAN SEA

Persian Gulf

ARABIAN SEA

Memphis

THE GLORY OF PERSEPOLIS

Less than four years into his reign, Darius began work on Persepolis, City of the Persians. Its materials, labor, and artisans came from throughout the empire, as did the finest of tributes, making Persepolis a symbol of the size and grandeur of the Persian realm.

Below: Aerial view of the archaeological site of Perspolis photographed in the 1950s by the Oriental Institute of Chicago, clearly showing the massive terrace on which the city sat.

In about 518, Darius the Great initiated his most ambitious project: the building of a new capital city at Persepolis, on the northern edge of a large fertile plain in southern Iran, about 25 miles from the old capital at Pasargadae. The scale of the task was enormous. No earlier settlement existed, and the rugged, barren, and rocky mountainside had to be cut away and leveled, holes filled with rubble, before any construction could begin. Major building work would continue at Persepolis throughout the reigns of Darius and his son Xerxes, with smaller additions made by later Achaemenid kings.

The exact purpose of Persepolis is unclear. Most of the royal treasury remained at Pasargadae and the main administrative center was at the more centrally sited city of Susa. Persepolis seems to have been planned as a spectacular statement of Persian power, possibly to declare a new era, since Darius did not come from a direct line to the throne. As such it was symbolic of the unity of the new empire, expressed through workers, materials, and carvings drawn from every corner of Darius's realm.

His records tell us that the bricks came from Babylon; the Assyrians and Ionians carried cedarwood from the mountain called Lebanon; gold was brought from Sardis and Bactria, while silver and ebony came from Egypt and ivory from Ethiopia; and lapis lazuli and cornelian were brought from Sogdiana and turquoise from Charasmia. The goldsmiths were Medes and Egyptians. Upon completion of its first phase, Persepolis was proclaimed as the new heart of the empire and the most beautiful city the world had ever seen.

Epic looting

The city was brimming with the wealth of the Persian empire. When Alexander the Great conquered Persepolis and burned it to the ground in 330—in revenge, it is said, for the burning of the Acropolis by Xerxes—he needed 20,000 mules and 5,000 camels to carry away its treasures. So complete was Alexander's destruction that Persepolis remained as an unidentified ruin until AD 1620, and it was not until 1931 that the Oriental Institute of Chicago began scientific investigation of the site.

Excavations have since allowed much of the palace complex to be accurately identified. We know where the king and his consorts lived, where he gave audiences and staged magnificent banquets, and the route of the New Year

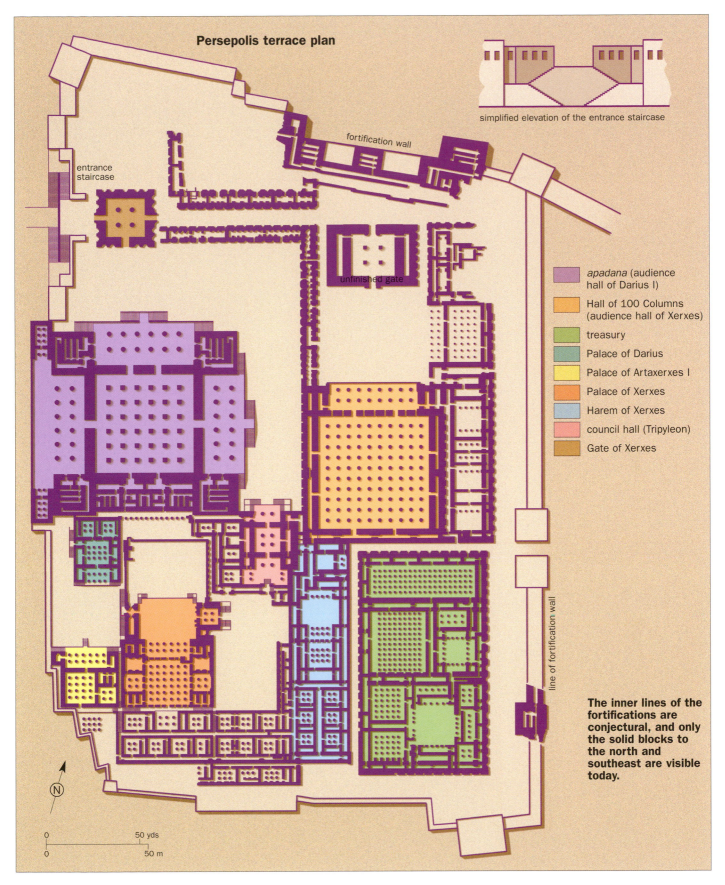

Persepolis terrace plan

simplified elevation of the entrance staircase

fortification wall

entrance
staircase

unfinished gate

line of fortification wall

apadana (audience hall of Darius I)

Hall of 100 Columns (audience hall of Xerxes)

treasury

Palace of Darius

Palace of Artaxerxes I

Palace of Xerxes

Harem of Xerxes

council hall (Tripyleon)

Gate of Xerxes

The inner lines of the fortifications are conjectural, and only the solid blocks to the north and southeast are visible today.

N

| 0 | | 50 yds |
| 0 | | 50 m |

celebrations, when delegates came to Persepolis from distant lands to pay their homage. We can even identify the locations of its drains.

The ruins that we see today have an austere presence, enhanced by the play of marble and limestone against the dull ocher of the mud-brick construction. During the time of the Achaemenid kings, however, Persepolis was a riot of color.

Above: The plan is in the same orientation as the facing photograph, allowing a direct comparison to be made.

Turquoise, lapis lazuli, and cornelian gems sparkled on columns and doors that were sheathed in silver and decorated with gold and ivory. Richly embroidered tapestries were hung between the columns, and fragments of pigment indicate that the reliefs and sculptures were painted in bright colors, as were the cedar beams that supported the ceilings and roofs.

Right: Reconstruction of Persepolis

A unfinished gate

B outbuildings and storerooms

C Hall of 100 Columns

D east gate

E tomb of Artaxerxes

F treasury

G entrance staircase

H Gate of Xerxes

J *apadana*

K council hall

L Palace of Darius I

M Palace of Xerxes

N Palace of Artaxerxes

P Harem of Xerxes

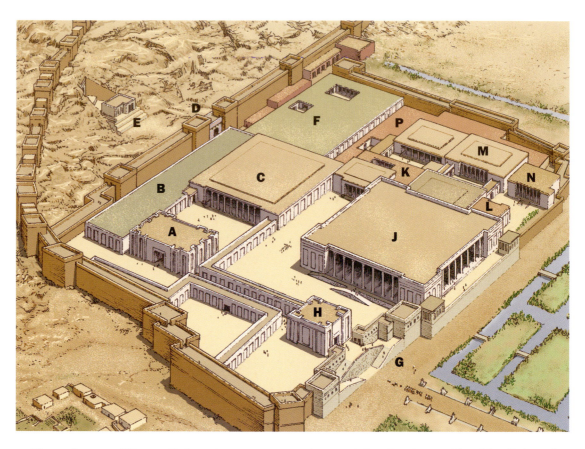

The main part of Persepolis is an immense terrace, 1,640 by 1,200 feet and about 50 feet high. It contains 12 principal structures, of which the most important public buildings were the *apadana* (audience hall), the throne hall, and Gate of Xerxes. Other buildings that were restricted to the use of the king and his entourage are the palaces of Darius and Xerxes, the royal harem, and the council hall.

Reached via two great double ceremonial staircases that converge symmetrically from the north and east sides, the *apadana* is the largest building. The great stairway is still there, wide enough for five horses to ride abreast and lined with hundreds of figures carved in low relief. These represent 23 subject nations of the Persian empire bearing tributes to the king.

Receiving royal visitors

Among the tribute-bearers are Susians offering a lioness; Babylonians, who lead a bull and carry fabrics; Lydians and Phrygians bringing gold and silver vessels engraved with ibexes, bulls, and winged horses; Indians with rare essences and precious scents; and Ionians offering goblets of wine. Mede and Persian soldiers, horses, and chariots of the Imperial Guard follow them. At the head of the stairways stand massive winged bulls, derived from Assyria but with Persian

characteristics. On the outside of the flights of steps are scenes from an old Babylonian epic depicting a lion bringing down a bull.

Next to the *apadana* is the throne room, or Hall of a Hundred Columns, built by Xerxes and his son Artaxerxes. Entrance is via the Gate of Xerxes, through which every visitor had to pass to gain audience with the king. Its east and west doorways are guarded respectively by two Assyrian man-bulls and a pair of colossal bulls, and originally had wooden double doors covered with panels of beaten metal.

The throne room was originally a reception area for visiting dignitaries, but later used as a store room and display area for tribute gifts from the royal treasury. The columns have bell-shaped bases, with their capitals shaped like pairs of animals—bulls, lions, and griffins—whose backs formed recesses for enormous cedar roof joists. There are relief carvings of throne scenes and of Xerxes engaged in combat with mythical animals.

Of the royal apartments, the most significant buildings are the palaces of Darius and Xerxes. The Palace of Darius consists of a large central hall supported on 12 columns, with three small staircases descending from this main room. Reliefs depict servants climbing the stairways from the domestic quarters and kitchens, bearing

food in covered dishes, while the door decorations show Darius leaving his palace in formal dress, followed by his personal attendants. The Palace of Xerxes is similar to that of Darius, but almost twice the size. Nearby is a small building known as the council hall. However, this appears to have served as an access chamber to the royal apartments, and contains a secret doorway that leads into the harem.

The royal harem is divided into several sections. At its center is a columned hall that faces onto a large courtyard, presumably where the queen and her retinue lived. There is a south wing containing six two- and three-roomed apartments, and a west wing with a further 16 smaller apartments that housed other female members of the royal household. Doorways lead from the apartments to enclosed gardens.

Apart from the main buildings, there are several smaller and less substantial constructions that probably served domestic purposes or were garrisons and store rooms for the Imperial Guard, while others were workrooms for artisans. A number of later buildings seem to have been constructed from the rubble of earlier Persian structures, such as the presumed, but now unidentifiable, Palace of Artaxerxes.

A massive fortified wall 33 feet thick, of which little remains, originally surrounded the entire complex, leaving only the Gate of Xerxes as a public entrance. Square mud-brick watchtowers guarded this wall at regular intervals, although only the foundations of a single tower have survived.

About three miles northwest of Persepolis is Naqsh-e-Rustam, which contains the rock-cut tombs of Darius and three of his successors, set 160 feet up a vertical cliff face (*see page 141*). Each has a façade in the form of a cross, representing the portico of a classic Persian building, bearing carvings and inscriptions. Behind each façade is a single burial chamber or vault.

Above: Alexander the Great was not the only ravager of Persepolis. The site has also suffered from earthquake damage.

Below: East staircase of the *apadana* with cravings of the tribute-bearers of Persia's 23 subject nations of the Achaemenid kings.

THE PERSIAN-GREEK WAR

Greek colonists in Ionia (Anatolia) lived under the rule of King Croesus of Lydia (r.560–46). In 546 Lydia was conquered by Cyrus of Persia and Croesus was executed, leaving Lydia under Persian control. Harsh taxes and conscription led to rebellion and war.

The oppressive rule of the Persians, which required Greek colonists to serve in the Persian army and imposed heavy taxes on Greek city-states, led to a revolt in 499 under the leadership of Aristagoras, who had been

Above: Detail of a relief carving depicting Xerxes seated on his throne receiving Mede dignitaries. This image is often confused with one virtually identical of his father Darius.

appointed by the Persians as governor of Miletus. Although Aristagoras's requests for help from Sparta were ignored, the Athenians—who considered themselves Ionian, since most of the settlers originally came from Athens—promised to send 20 ships in support of the revolution. The Athenians conquered and burned Sardis, capital of Lydia, but then returned to Athens.

Under Darius the Persians restored order over the rebellious Greek city-states in 495. In retaliation for Athenian help during the rebellion, Darius amassed a Persian army with which he intended to annex mainland Greece. Between 492 and 490 the army defeated most of the Greek city-states along the Macedonian coast and was preparing to march against Athens, when it was confronted by the much smaller Athenian army at Marathon.

Under the leadership of Miltiades, the Greeks employed new infantry techniques, sending highly mobile groups of hoplites to break through the center of the massed Persian army then regroup to attack from the rear. Miltiades had formerly been a general in the Persian army and used his knowledge of their tactics to deliver a resounding defeat: Herodotus tells us that Greek casualties amounted to only 192 men. against Persian losses of 6,400. The Persians regrouped and attempted an assault on Athens, but the athlete Pheidippides had ran ahead of the armies from Marathon and forewarned the Athenians. The Persians were driven out and Greek autonomy was restored.

A stormed fleet

These battles were decisive in history, giving Athens a revered position from which Greek culture would flourish. To the Persians, who were the greatest world power, they were merely an irritation by a troublesome border country. Darius's son, Xerxes (r.486–65), decided however that the Athenian question should be finally and irrevocable settled, and in 481 assembled the largest army Persia had ever known.

Some 150,000 men and a 600-ship navy left for Greece, encountering the Greeks at the battle of Thermopylae, where a small Spartan contingent of only 300 men led by Leonidas delayed them in a narrow pass while Athens was evacuated. Having defeated Leonidas's rearguard, the Persians marched forward to destroy Athens without meeting further resistance.

The Athenian ruler, Themistocles, had retreated to the island of Salamis where, with Spartan and Corinthian allies, he waited for the Persian fleet with a rebuilt Athenian navy of 200 ships. While Themistocles' ships sheltered in harbor, the Persian navy battled through severe storms in the Aegean Sea to reach them. Several Persian ships were lost in the storms and most of the remaining fleet was sunk when the Athenians employed new naval warfare techniques, forming their ships into attack platforms from which devastating assaults were made.

Xerxes was forced to retreat from Greece, although he left behind a considerable force under the command of one of his generals, Mardonios. Mardonios was defeated by a Greek army under the leadership of Spartan commander Pausanias at the battle of Plataea in 479. Following the battle of Salamis, the Greeks formed a new alliance, the Delian League, to protect Ionia and other Greek interests. Nominally under the control of Athens, the Delian League took its name from its treasury, based in the city of Delos.

Above: Relief of a lion attacking a bull on the east stairway of the Triplyon at Persepolis. Xerxes planned to fall on the Greek city-states like a Persian lion, sweeping all before his mighty army, but the Greeks proved to be formidable, dogged, and in the end the victors.

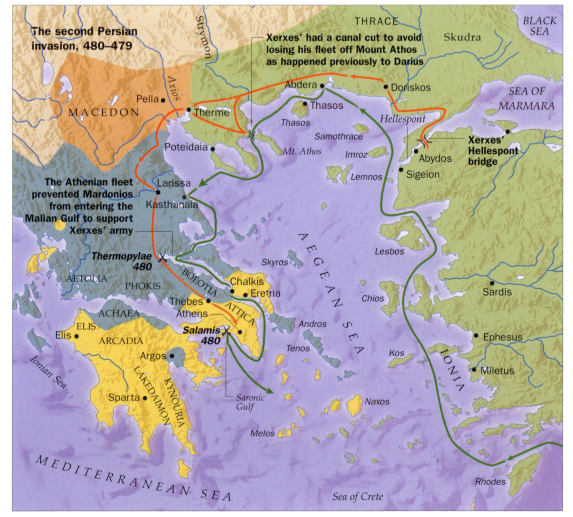

The second Persian invasion, 480–479

Xerxes' had a canal cut to avoid losing his fleet off Mount Athos as happened previously to Darius

The Athenian fleet prevented Mardonios from entering the Malian Gulf to support Xerxes' army

Thermopylae 480

Salamis 480

Xerxes' Hellespont bridge

THRACE
Skudra
BLACK SEA
SEA OF MARMARA
MACEDON
Strymon
Axios
Pella
Therme
Abdera
Doriskos
Thasos
Thasos
Samothrace
Hellespont
Poteidaia
Mt. Athos
Imroz
Abydos
Sigeion
Lemnos
Larissa
Kasthanaia
AETOLIA
PHOKIS
BOEOTIA
Chalkis
Eretria
Thebes
Athens
ATTICA
AEGEAN SEA
Skyros
Lesbos
Chios
Sardis
ACHAEA
ELIS
Elis
ARCADIA
Argos
Andros
Tenos
Kos
Ephesus
IONIA
Miletus
Ionian Sea
LAKEDAIMON
KYNOURIA
Sparta
Saronic Gulf
Naxos
Melos
MEDITERRANEAN SEA
Rhodes
Sea of Crete

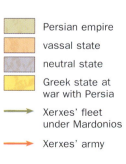

	Persian empire
	vassal state
	neutral state
	Greek state at war with Persia
→	Xerxes' fleet under Mardonios
→	Xerxes' army

PERSIAN-GREEK INFLUENCES

The survival of ancient Greek records into modern times has glorified Greece, its culture, and history at the expense of Persia. Persia was then the greatest world power with wealth and influence far in excess of that of the Greek city-states, and each admired the other nation's society.

Below: While the architraves above the doors of Xerxes' palace have an oriental look, the doorways and surrounding columns are distinctly Greek-influenced.

Popular history tends to depict the contact between Greece and Persia as one of mutual hostility. This stems in part from the fact that much of the period's contemporary history comes from Greek scholars, who glorified Greek (and particularly Athenian) aesthetics and ideals, while deriding those of their "barbarian" Persian neighbors.

Much of the contact between Persians and Greeks was maintained by the Ionians, who claimed Athenian descent but nevertheless lived within Persian-dominated Anatolia, where high-status Greeks received grants of land from the Persian kings. There were frequent intermarriages between Lydians, Greeks, and Persians, and over 300 Greeks were attached to the Achaemenid court at Persepolis.

It is also on record that Greek sculptors worked on the relief carvings at Persepolis, as well as at Susa and Pasargadae, and Persian influences are seen in sculptures from the Acropolis in Athens. There was extensive trade between Greece and Persia, and numerous diplomatic contacts and exchanges of ideas.

In addition to formal contact, conflicts between the two nations led to cultural exchange. Many Persian artifacts found their way into Greek possession as a consequence of the wars. Herodotus tells us that the spoils from the battle of Plataea alone brought goods of such splendor and wealth that they were beyond anything the Greeks could have imagined. We can assume that goods of similar magnitude must have entered Greece following other major battles.

Both the Greeks and Persians were in awe of the aesthetic qualities and intellectual abilities of

247	238	c.200	200	191	189	171–38	168
Parni chieftain Arsaces becomes ruler of Parthia	Arsaces assures Parthian rule by defeating the Seleucid governor of the region	The Parthian empire has spread along the Caspian Sea and into Seleucid territory	Antiochus III defeats the Egyptian army at Panium	Romans defeat the Seleucids at Thermopylae, driving them from Europe	Parthia becomes independent of the Seleucid empire	Parthian rule of Mithridates	Antiochus IV invades Egypt but is driven away by the Romans

the other. Darius even invited the Greek philosopher Heraclitus (c.535–475) to his court to explain some of the finer points of his theories; although it is possible this was done as much to heighten the glamor of the Persian court by asking "celebrities" to attend as it was for the pursuit of knowledge.

Shifting alliances

The battle of Plataea (479) did not end these Greek-Persian contacts and conflicts. Wars and skirmishes were to continue for another 30 years, during which large numbers of Greek mercenaries fought on both sides. The wars had become prolonged partly through the aggressive policies of the Delian League, including a virtual rout of the Persian army and navy at the River Eurymedon in 466. Problems between the Delian League and Persia diminished after Pericles (c.495–29) became leader of Athens in 462 and withdrew the Athenian contingents from fighting in the western Mediterranean, resulting in the Peace of Kallias that was signed between the league and Persia in 449.

Conflict with Sparta continued, mainly due to Sparta's refusal to recognize Athens' authority, with which it was engaged in the Peloponnesian War. In 413 Persian sympathies shifted, and Persia agreed to aid Sparta against Athens. Most of the Spartan fleet was built with Persian finance. This alliance proved fickle when the Ionian cities (to which Persia still laid claim) asked Sparta for help against Persia. To counteract this threat, Persia used its wealth to help rebuild the Athenian fleet. Persia remained hostile to Sparta until 386.

The disagreements among the Greeks and the alternating alliances made with Persia enabled the Macedonians to assert their authority under King Philip II (r.359–36).

Although the exact relationship between Greece and Macedonia is unclear—the Macedonians spoke Greek mixed with numerous oriental idioms and metaphors—Philip proclaimed a pan-Hellenic war against Persia. After Philip's murder, his son Alexander III (Alexander the Great, r.336–23) took supreme command in the wars against the Persians and was ultimately responsible for the complete destruction of the Persian empire.

Below: The Erechthion stands on the Acropolis in Athens, but the Porch of the Caryatids has columns in the form of carved figures, recalling not only Persian but also Assyrian preferences for monumental sculpture.

ALEXANDER THE GREAT

Alexander III of Macedon (356–23) was a complex character who was driven by a thirst for power and glory. A gifted commander, he led his Greek army around the known world, creating a vast empire built on conquest and stern leadership.

Alexander the Great came to prominence in 336 following the assassination of his father, Philip II. There was suspicion that Alexander had plotted the assassination, but he placed the blame on a Persian conspiracy. Backed by Philip's Macedonian army, he went to Greece, where he threatened

Right: Silver tetradrachm of Alexander depicting the conqueror wearing the ram's horn of the Egyptian god Amon.

BLACK SEA

CAUCASUS MNTS.

Danube

Thrace

Macedon

Pella

Byzantium

Granicus ✕
334

Paphlagonia

Bithynia

Gordion

Satrapy of Armenia

Satrapy of Cappadocia

Mysia

ANATOLIA

Mural

Satrapy of Atropatene

CASPIAN SEA

Zadrakarta

Epirus

Sardis

Athens

Greece

Ephesus

Miletus

Sparta

Halicarnassus

Pisidia

Tarsus

TAURUS MNTS.

Cilicia

Antioch

Issus ✕
333

Nisibis

Nineveh

Assyria

Arbil

Gaugamela 331 ✕

Tigris

Media

Ecbatana

ZAGROS MOUNTAINS

Rhagae

330

Damghan

Parthia

Darius III is murdered by his own troops

330

Rhodes

Crete

Cyprus

Syria

Thapsacus

Euphrates

MESOPOTAMIA

Seleucis

Susa

330

Persia

MEDITERRANEAN SEA

Phoenicia

Byblos

Sidon

siege Tyre
332

Damascus

Babylon

Babylonia

Alexandria Susiana

324

Cyrene

Jerusalem

Gaza

Pasargadae

Paraetonium

Alexandria

Pelusium

332

Memphis

331

Siwa

Oracle of Amon

332

Egypt

Persian Gates ✕
330

Persepolis

Carmani

PERSIAN GULF

Nile

Thebes

RED SEA

empire of Alexander, 323

Macedonian dependency, 336

Alexander's campaigns, 334–324

naval expedition of Nearchos, 325

Alexander the Great's conquest of the Persian empire, 334–324

Athens and persuaded Sparta to support his bid for power. Alexander attacked the city of Thebes, which was struggling for dominance over Athens, massacring 6,000 and selling 30,000 of its citizens into slavery. Although only 20 years old, at Corinth he

was elected supreme general of the Greek army for an invasion of Persia.

Greek support for Alexander was half-hearted. The bulk of his army was Macedonian, and he never trusted his Greek mercenaries. Even his pretext for invading Persia, based on the Persian sacking of Athens 150 years earlier, was met with derision. When Alexander finally embarked on his campaign he was so ill-equipped that he had to leave half the army behind; yet he would go on to conquer more than half the known world, from the Ionian Sea to northern India.

In 334 Alexander's tiny army crossed the Hellespont and engaged with a vastly superior Persian army at the Battle of Granicus. His military genius was immediately apparent, and the Persians were routed. The Persians who surrendered were sent back to their homes, but Alexander disregarded pleas for clemency from

Following these victories Alexander laid siege to Tyre (332), which capitulated after seven months of fighting, and then marched into Egypt. In Egypt he consulted the Oracle of Ammon and became convinced that he was one of the invincible sons of Zeus.

A traditional ruler

In an attempt to stop Alexander's rampage, the Persian king Darius III (r.336–30), offered him generous settlement terms. Under these Alexander would have had effective control of half the empire, but he rejected Darius's proposal by quoting his old tutor, Aristotle, who had said that victory came through the elimination of one's enemies, and stating that he was destined to surpass even the feats of Achilles.

Darius and Alexander met in 331 at the battle of Gaugamela, where 34,000 Persian cavalry confronted Alexander's 7,520 cavalry. By a miraculous stroke of luck, the Persian cavalry broke under a charge led by Alexander. Darius fled east toward Bactria, but he was assassinated by his cousin Bessus, who was subsequently defeated by Alexander. Alexander marched on Persepolis where, in 330, he killed its male inhabitants, enslaved its women, and burned the city to the ground.

With the entire Persian empire and much of India in his control, Alexander began to behave like the old kings and came under increasing criticism for being too "orientalized." He married a daughter of Darius III, and had 10,000 of his men marry Persian girls. Cities were founded in his name, the first in Egypt in about 331. Anyone who opposed him, including some of his own generals, was executed. Greek was adopted as the official language of the new empire and cities were built according to a Greek pattern, with market squares, schools, offices, shops, temples, theaters, and gymnasiums.

In 323 he went to Babylon to re-establish this ancient city as his capital, despite being warned that to enter Babylon would mean his death. Here Alexander suffered a sudden short but fatal illness. His empire, built on the dreams of one man, did not survive his passing: it was divided between the rule of several of his generals.

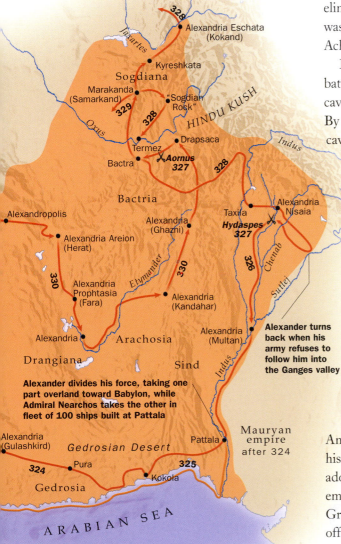

20,000 Greek mercenaries and ordered them to be slaughtered as a warning to other Greeks who might oppose his will. In the following year he defeated a second Persian army at the battle of Issus, during which 30,000 Greek mercenaries who supported the Persians were killed.

THE SELEUCID DYNASTY

Following Alexander's death in 323, his empire was divided between a number of his generals, known as the Diadochoi (successors). This caused a period of prolonged chaos during which the Diadochoi vied for control, with Seleucus I in Mesopotamia establishing a new dynasty.

When Alexander the Great's empire was divided, Ptolemy took Egypt, Lysimachos was in power in Thrace, Cassander in Macedon and Greece, Antigonos controlled Asia, and Seleucus led Babylonia. Conflict between the Diadochoi was partially resolved in 301 when Antigonos was overthrown at the battle

whom Greek language, art, and culture, especially the teachings of Aristotle, replaced Persian beliefs and ideals, leading to a division between Greek practices in the cities and Persian ones in rural areas. Seleucus established a capital at Seleucia on the Tigris, where he controlled east-west trade, and Asia Minor was added to the kingdom in 282 with the elimination of Lysimachos in Lydia. Seleucus was assassinated by Ptolemy in the following year and his son, Antiochus I, became ruler (r.281–61).

Thereafter, the Seleucid dynasty was beset by attacks from Syria and Egypt and split by internal dissent. Antiochus had his eldest son executed for leading a rebellion against him, and

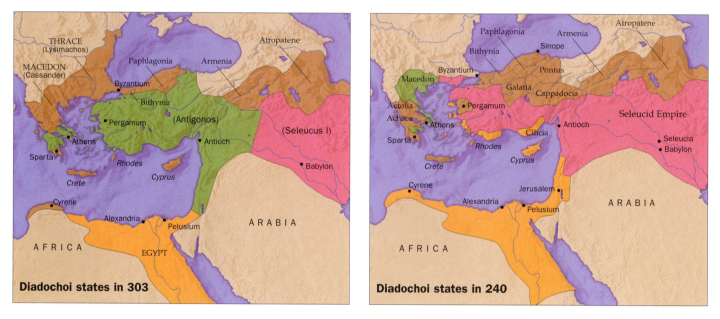

Diadochoi states in 303

Diadochoi states in 240

of Ipsus by a coalition of the other successors.

The most significant general to emerge from these struggles was Seleucus I (r.312–281), who began the process of Hellenization throughout the Mesopotamian region. He was aided by his wife Apama, the daughter of a Persian chieftain named Spitamenes, who had been educated with the family of Darius and had sound knowledge of Greek language and culture. Seleucus had difficulty consolidating his areas, since under the Persians each city operated under a separate civilian government. The emergence of the Seleucids led to partition into petty semi-independent states.

The administration was entirely in the hands of Greeks and upper-class Persians, among

his successor and younger son, Antiochus II, was poisoned by his wife, Laodice, after he deserted her for Berenice, daughter of Ptolemy. Antiochus's son Seleucus II was murdered in 225 and was succeeded by Seleucus III, who was killed by his own army.

Wars of succession

The dynasty stabilized with the succession of younger brother Antiochus III (r.223–187), who waged war against Asia Minor, besieged Palestine, defeated Achaeus at Sardis, fought with the Parthians and Bactria, and eventually defeated the Egyptians at Panium in 200. He followed these victories with excursions into Europe and an invasion of Greece; but this

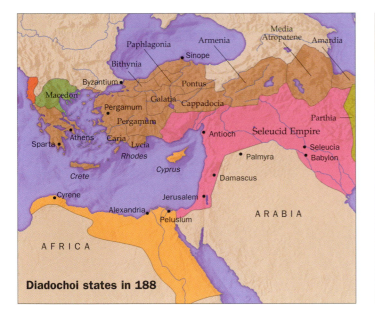

Diadochoi states in 188

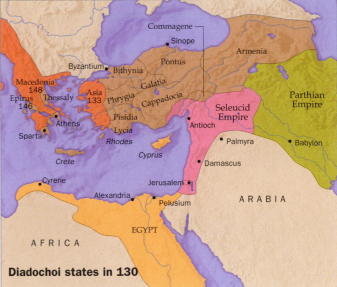

Diadochoi states in 130

angered Rome, who defeated Antiochus's forces at the battle of Thermopylae in 191, took his son prisoner, and demanded tribute and retribution. The over-reaching ambitions of Antiochus effectively broke Seleucid power and left the region vulnerable to incursions by the Parthians, who declared their independence in 189.

Antiochus III's successor, Seleucus IV, was assassinated in a court conspiracy in 175 by his minister Heliodorus, and was in turn succeeded by Antiochus IV Epiphanes (r.175–64), who had just been released from his imprisonment in Rome. Antiochus IV inherited his father's strong-headedness. He came to power as co-regent with another of Seleucus's sons, also named Antiochus, whom he had murdered.

Antiochus IV reorganized the Seleucid army along Roman lines and sent troops into Bactria. From there he assaulted Memphis in Egypt, but was forced to withdraw by a Roman army in 168. During his retreat he sacked the treasury at

Jerusalem and murdered most of its inhabitants, triggering a revolt by the Judeans. Shortly after his death Mesopotamia was lost to the Parthians under the leadership of Mithridates.

Antiochus IV left no legitimate heir and the Seleucid dynasty was split by rival factions. Corruption marked this last period of their rule. Antiochus V was murdered by Demetrius I, who was later defeated by Alexander Balas with the support of Rome. In 145 Balas died in battle with Ptolemy VI, who supported his rival, Demetrius II. Demetrius was killed at the instigation of his wife, Cleopatra Thea; but when she later tried to poison Antiochus VIII, with whom she shared the throne, he forced her to drink the chalice of wine she had prepared for him. Antiochus was in turn killed by his minister Heracleon in 96 and the dynasty degenerated into civil war, coming under the rule of Pompey the Great of Rome in 64, who eliminated it the following year.

The fate of the Diadochoi states 303–63 BC and the rise of the Parthian and Roman empires

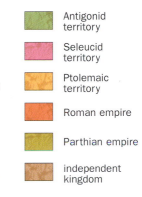

- Antigonid territory
- Seleucid territory
- Ptolemaic territory
- Roman empire
- Parthian empire
- independent kingdom

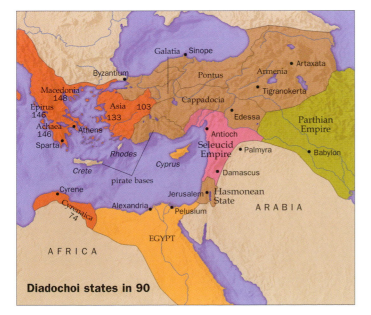

Diadochoi states in 90

Diadochoi states in 63

B.-P.	Bithynia-Pontus
Co.	Commagene
Pa.	Paphlagonia
Te.	Tectosages
To.	Tolistobogii
Tr.	Tromci

CHAPTER 10

PARTHIA, C.250 BC–AD 224

The first reference to Parthia is in an Achaemenid inscription from the time of Darius I (c.520 BC). Found at Bisitun, this inscription refers to the region as Parthava, which was then part of the Persian empire. It retained a distinctive identity as part of Hyrcania (Iran) during the period of Alexander the Great and is mentioned as a separate province during the Seleucid period.

During the reigns of the Seleucid rulers Seleucus I and Antiochus I (312–281 BC and 281–61), groups of nomadic tribesmen moved from central Asia into Parthava, where they adopted many of the local customs. These Parni nomads (called Dahai by Greek writers) left no writing or other records; little is known about them other than that they were speakers of Indo-Iranian languages.

About 247, one of the Parni chieftains began to assert his authority over the other groups to become the first Parthian ruler. His name was Arsaces (r.247–11), hence the Parthian kings are often referred to as the Arsacids. Arsaces had been a governor under Diodotus, ruler of the Bactrian Greeks, but fled westward to establish his own rule in northern Iran. He defeated Andragoras, satrap of Seleucid Parthava in 238, placing the region firmly under Parthian control.

By 200 Arsace's successors had established themselves along the southern shore of the Caspian Sea and were expanding into Seleucid territories east of Syria. They captured the city of Herat, giving them control of the Silk Road to China, and declared themselves independent of Seleucia in 189. Between 189 BC and AD 224 they were effectively masters of the entire Mesopotamian region, although war between the Seleucids and the Parthians continued for almost 30 more years. The death of Antiochus IV (r.175–64 BC) led to feuding and petty squabbling among the Seleucids that weakened the dynasty and enabled the Parthians to establish a firmer hold.

The Parthian empire, 53 BC–AD 228

Embracing various cultures

Under Mithridates (r.171–38) and Artabanus (r.127–24) all of the Iranian plateau and Tigris-Euphrates valley came under Parthian control. Mithridates called himself Philhellenos (Friend of the Greeks), although this did not prevent him from capturing the Seleucid ruler Demetrius and holding him captive for ten years.

Generally, the Parthians were tolerant of the beliefs and practices of others. Their winter capital at Ctesiphon (built in 129 BC) was established on the banks of the Tigris opposite the Seleucid capital of Seleucia, and Seleucia was allowed to preserve its own culture as well as its

independence. Greeks and Persians held important positions within Parthia, and the Parthians retained Greek methods of finance, law, and much of Greek culture.

In many senses the Parthians developed a new Greco-Iranian culture that recognized a variety of religious sects and led to a reduction in the influence of the Zoroastrian religion; although during the Parthian period this was followed by a revival of Persian ideals. Parthian policies were nevertheless liberal ones, leading to widely divergent cultural, social, and political features.

The Parthians did not develop any strong centralized

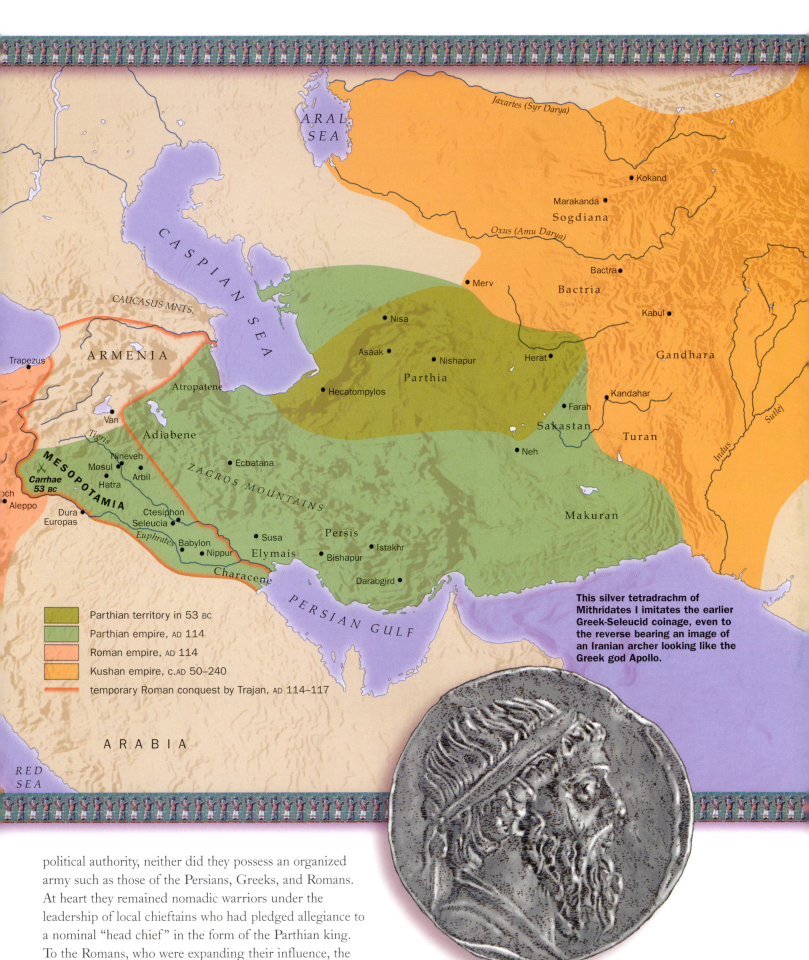

This silver tetradrachm of Mithridates I imitates the earlier Greek-Seleucid coinage, even to the reverse bearing an image of an Iranian archer looking like the Greek god Apollo.

Map legend:
- Parthian territory in 53 BC
- Parthian empire, AD 114
- Roman empire, AD 114
- Kushan empire, c.AD 50–240
- temporary Roman conquest by Trajan, AD 114–117

political authority, neither did they possess an organized army such as those of the Persians, Greeks, and Romans. At heart they remained nomadic warriors under the leadership of local chieftains who had pledged allegiance to a nominal "head chief" in the form of the Parthian king. To the Romans, who were expanding their influence, the disorganized states of the Parthians seemed easy prey; but the first Roman army to enter the region under the command of Marcus Crassus was soundly defeated in 53 BC. Thereafter the Parthians became arch-enemies of Rome, but were never defeated by a Roman army.

The Parthian period ended in AD 224 when Ardashir (r.224–41), formerly the governor of Fars, overthrew Artabanus IV (r.216–24) to establish the Sassanian dynasty, a strongly nationalistic second Persian empire.

PARTHIAN TRADE AND ADMINISTRATION

The Parthian hold over their empire was maintained through the establishment of trade and exchange contacts, rather than the massive military campaigns that had been characteristic of the earlier Achaemenid dynasties. Local freedom of beliefs and administration left it vulnerable.

Growing in importance during the Parthian empire as a Syrian Desert waystation on the trade routes between Mesopotamia and the Mediterranean, Palmyra acted as a buffer state between Parthia and Rome. The wealthy city-state was eventually absorbed into the Roman empire until its destruction in AD 272 by the emperor Aurelian after a failed Palmyrene bid for independence.

Of essential importance to the Parthian empire were the caravan trade routes to the east, which had been secured by the time of Mithridates I (r.171–38). Trade was relatively unhindered within the Parthian area, from Dura Europas in Syria to Merv in Turkmenistan, from where the caravans continued into central Asia.

Cities such as Palmyra, Hatra, and Mesene (formerly Characene), located along the trade routes, began to increase in power and wealth, and had considerable local influence. Herat, in northwestern Afghanistan, was an international meeting point for Arab traders with those of Turkmenistan and the Middle East, where grains, fruits, vegetables, and sheep were exchanged for silks and spices traded into the area by Chinese merchants.

The border town was a characteristic feature of the Parthian era, in terms of trade outlets and exchange, cultural diversity and ethnic tolerance, and the division of the region into semi-autonomous states. Roman senator and historian Pliny the Elder (AD c.23–79) wrote that the

Parthian empire consisted of 18 separate "kingdoms" and that several cities vied with each other in their national and regional importance. Among others, he named Dara in the region of Abivard, Nisaye in Parthaunisa (where the first Parthian kings were buried), and Hecatompylos in Qumes. Isidore of Charax (Charax is an unidentified site, presumed to be in or near Characene), author of *Parthian Stations* (c.26 BC), among others, recorded that each region had numerous way-stations that catered for travelers along the trade routes.

Within these regions local leaders and administrators were left unmolested by central authorities. Taxes were imposed, but these were seen to be fair and just, and there is no record that the Parthians interfered in local politics to any great extent. People were free to follow a regional leader or to honor a diverse range of local deities; the central administrative government was organized along Greek lines and essentially followed the same system as that of the Seleucids before them.

Caravan raiders

Local populations would probably have perceived little affect upon their lives. They would have noticed the introduction of a few new compound gods (a blending of Greek, Persian, and Parthian traits), as well as an influx of new beliefs brought to the regions by

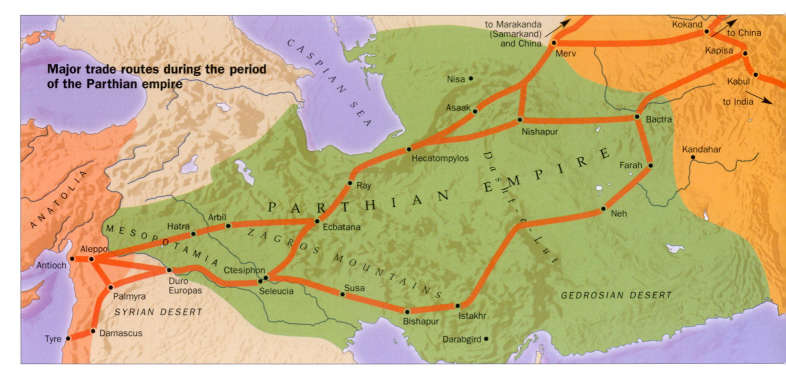

Major trade routes during the period of the Parthian empire

immigrants, and would have benefited from a greater variety of traded goods.

Although the Parthians did not attempt to expand militarily, they were nevertheless a military force of considerable strength. When forced to defend themselves from Roman incursions, they were capable of defeating highly trained legionnaires. Parthians had a history in nomadic raiding and guerilla warfare, later developed as part of their trading complex, when small units of cavalry protected trade caravans from bands of raiders. Unlike the standing armies of earlier periods that were trained in siege tactics and military discipline, these small and rather undisciplined units were under the command of local land-owners and could respond quickly and decisively when the need arose.

Inevitably, the lack of central authority and the tolerance of a diversity of religious doctrines and nationalities began to weaken the administration. Over several generations, local leaders and nobles claimed increasing power and privilege and began to challenge the Parthian dynastic families. The collapse of the Parthian empire in AD 224 was largely caused by the usurpation of power by a regional noble, Ardashir. The ruling dynasty was unable to find sufficient military support from the other regions to suppress the revolt.

MINSTRELS AND POETS

Although the courts of Parthia followed the tales set down by earlier Greeks, in outer regions and the countryside the oral tradition remained, retold and reinterpreted by the Goúsaún. Part musician, part poet, these men sang heroic tales of yore, mixed with their own topical verses.

Right: Parthian bronze figurine of the goddess Astarte. As the Phoenician predecessor to the Greek Aphrodite, and as the goddess of war and love (Morning and Evening Stars), Astarte was associated in Parthian tradition with the Assyrian/Babylonian Ishtar and the Sumerian Inanna.

Facing: Parthian limestone relief of a male deity from the 1st–2nd centuries AD. In common with many found at Hatra, this sculpture includes a military standard, here on the left. It bears a striking similarity to those eagle standards carried by the Roman legions and is often found on Parthian sculptures of eagles representing a war god.

Parthian royal courts were largely Hellenized. Greek was taught in the royal schools and much of the culture was essentially Aristotelian in nature, a trend that had been handed down from the Seleucid period, with royal princes, princesses, and their entourages well versed in the Greek epics and dramas. The feudal nature of the empire and the relatively small size of the central dynastic and administrative area meant that earlier Parthian traditions were widespread in its regions and the countryside.

Parthian traditions were largely oral ones and few contemporary references to them exist. References from later periods are sufficient for us to know that poetry and music were among the Parthians greatest pleasures. They made no distinction between the poet and the singer: the word *goúsaún* means "poet-musician-minstrel" and was adopted by several neighboring languages.

Away from the central court, there was a shift from the glorification of kings to a more populist form of the arts that has few parallels elsewhere in Mesopotamia. This reflects a heroic, chivalric, and feudal society and is apparent in a tale where Prince Rámin sings love songs to Vis (who cannot return his love, since she is the bride of his brother, King Mobad) while playing a lute; or in the story in which Bastwar, finding his father Zarér dead on the battlefield, is moved to compose a lament.

The *goúsaún* was a person of considerable social standing, and although few of their compositions were set down in writing, the existence of Parthian words in later texts attests

to the strength of the poet-minstrel tradition. *goúsaún*s were permanently attached to the courts of the noblemen, where they enjoyed privileges that extended to mocking their masters in verse. No subject was taboo—a *goúsaún* even referred to the adultery of a queen in a state performance held in the presence of both her husband and her lover.

Committing to paper

Other *goúsaún*s were itinerant minstrels, wandering from village to village for the entertainment of the general public and sometimes composing their verses in local dialects. Poet-minstrels composed verses of their own, but many of their compositions were well known renditions of folklore and fable, or of heroic deeds that had been performed in the past. Many songs dealt with deeds of valor or referred to myths that were believed to be true. Their repertoire included narrative tales, lyrical, laudatory, elegiac, and satirical verses, as well as bawdy songs and contest poems in which the *goúsaún* sang the parts of both protagonist and antagonist. These could be tales of a rejected lover, of a warrior and his enemy, or an allegorical verse describing, for example, a contest between a lion (symbolizing untamed natural forces) and a tree (immovable power).

During the latter part of the Parthian period the original tales became overlaid with Zoroastrian ideas that removed their bawdiness and banter and instilled a sense of directed purpose, rather than of simple entertainment. These tended to be more standardized and were primarily adventure tales of the gods, which had

become popular legends. In a way, this was a means of boosting national pride by recalling past glories. Topical verses were sung for the benefit of pilgrim gatherings. Semi-mythical content meant that the popular stories of warriors and heroes became less important and were replaced by tales of moral and spiritual concern. When these were written down they formed long narrative poems, or epics; a structure that was far removed from the dramatic sung short verses of the earlier period.

The role of the poet-minstrel continued well beyond the Parthian period and into Islamic times, particularly in the countryside, which was less subject to Arab influence.

Left: The ritual placing of a gold death mask over the face of the deceased is a tradition associated with the eastern regions of the Roman empire. This mask of the 2nd century, found at Nineveh, indicates cultural links between Rome and Adiabene in northern Parthia.

MITHRIDATES AND THE PARTHIAN EMPIRE

Son of Phriapathus and brother of Phraates I, Mithridates I (r.171–38 BC) used conquest to free his people from Seleucid rule and establish Parthian independence. By the time of his peaceful death Mithridates had forged a fine empire, the dynasty in the safe hands of his son, Phraates II.

Although Parthia had been established as early as 247 BC, the first Parthian kings—Arsaces I (r.247–11), Arsaces II (r.211–191), Phriapathus (r.191–76), and Phraates I (r.176–71)—recognized Seleucid dominance and paid tribute and taxes to the Seleucid kings. Parthia only became a truly independent kingdom in the reign of Mithridates I, following a war with Eucratides of Bactria, who had tried to create a Greek (Seleucid) empire in the east.

Above: The audience hall, known as the Arch of Chosroe, hints at the splendor of the palace at Ctesiphon. Although the ruined hall survived a serious earthquake in the 20th century, many other structures have had to be butressed.

Eucratides was murdered by his son in 150, leaving the path clear for Mithridates to occupy the strategic border areas of Bactria. Internal dissent among the Seleucids, fostered by Roman intrigues, weakened their hold in the Mesopotamian area and enabled Mithridates to conquer Media and then to advance into the Babylonian plain. He was able to lay absolute claim to Babylonia and Media by 141, following a successful war against the Elamites and the

capture of the Greek town of Seleucia, whose rulers became vassals of Parthia.

Saka tribe incursions into Hyrcania forced Mithridates into campaigns in southern and central Parthia. During his absence, Demetrius II, incited by the Greeks and aided by Elymais (Elam) and Persis, attempted to reassert Seleucid rule. Mithridates put down the rebellion and, in accordance with his reputation as a mild ruler who tried to conciliate his Greek subjects, had Demetrius sent into exile in Hyrcania. He was provided with a royal household and was married to Mithridates' daughter, Rhodogune. Elymais was looted in punishment for its support of Demetrius, the temples of Artemis and Athena were destroyed, and the province was added to the Parthian domains.

The name Mithridates was derived from

The Mithridatic Wars

Phraates II was succeeded for a short time by his uncle Artabanus I before his young son Mithridates II (and cousin to Phraates) came to the throne. Dating of the Parthian kings by their coinage remains uncertain, with varying authorities giving Mithridates the Great, as he came to be known, as ruling from 132–120 until either 88 or 63 BC; the later dates are those that fit with Roman history, to whom he was known as the King of Pontus. For 40 years, Mithridates II caused the Romans continual grief. Having only annexed the kingdom of Pergamum in 129 to create the province of Asia, Roman and Mithridatic interests in Anatolia clashed. At a time when Rome was coping with Teutonic invasions in the north of Italy, Mithridates extended Pontus (annexed earlier by Mithridates I) to Colchis and the Crimea.

When he next turned his attention to Paphlagonia, Cappadocia, and Galatia, Rome went to war. The future dicatator Sulla regained Cappadocia in 92, before returning to Italy to deal with an internal rebellion of allied Italian states (the Social War, 91–89 BC).

Taking advantage, Mithridates attacked the

Mithras plus *da*, meaning "given by"; at this stage in his career he added the official suffix Philhellene—"friend of the Greeks." Thus he claimed ancestry from Persian deities, while allying himself with his Seleucid subjects. When Mithridates died peacefully in 138, the Parthian empire included the heartland of Parthia, Hyrcania, Media, Babylonia, Assyria, Elymais, Persis, and the districts of Tapuria and Traxiana.

To exile and back

Mithridates was succeeded by his son, Phraates II (r.138–27). Some historians claim he was the real founder of the Parthian empire, but his role seems to have been to consolidate the kingdom that his father created. That he came to the throne when he was very young is suggested by the fact that his mother, Ri-'nu, acted as regent during the early part of his reign. His youth was spent campaigning against nomadic invaders in the east.

Faced with a Seleucid uprising in 130 led by Antiochus VII (r.137–28), Phraates released Antiochus's brother Demetrius from his exile in Hyrcania and sent him back to Babylonia to persuade Antiochus to desist. However, other Parthian dependencies joined with Antiochus and forced Phraates into the war that he had tried to avoid. Antiochus was defeated and killed, his son was sent into exile, and Demetrius's daughter was taken into Phraates' harem. Although Demetrius escaped and took refuge in Syria, Babylonia had been secured; this marked the end of Seleucid ambitions in the area.

In an attempt to follow up these victories, Phraates prepared an army to invade Syria, but the Sakas forced him into campaigning in the east. They had encroached across the Silk Road leading to Mesopotamia through Merv, Hecatompylos and Ecbatana, and were threatening the trade routes on which Parthia was dependent. The Sakae threat was eventually put down, but Phraates was killed during the campaign when Greek captives forced to serve in the Parthian army deserted.

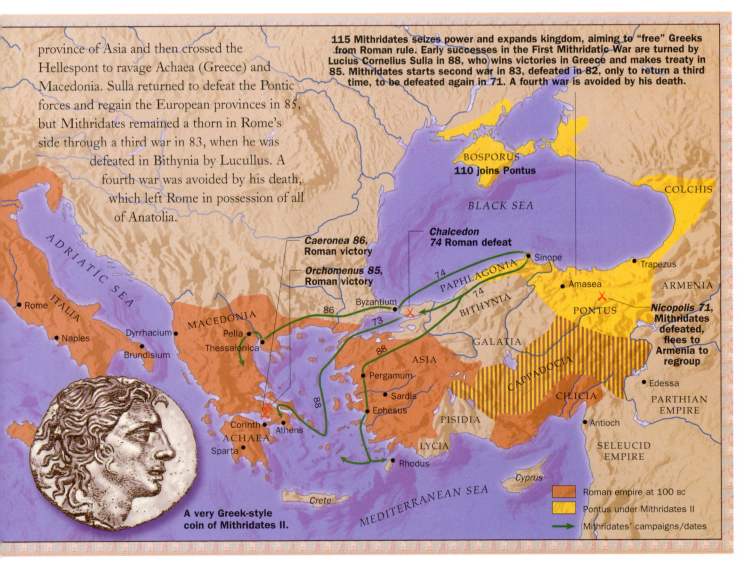

province of Asia and then crossed the Hellespont to ravage Achaea (Greece) and Macedonia. Sulla returned to defeat the Pontic forces and regain the European provinces in 85, but Mithridates remained a thorn in Rome's side through a third war in 83, when he was defeated in Bithynia by Lucullus. A fourth war was avoided by his death, which left Rome in possession of all of Anatolia.

115 Mithridates seizes power and expands kingdom, aiming to "free" Greeks from Roman rule. Early successes in the First Mithridatic War are turned by Lucius Cornelius Sulla in 88, who wins victories in Greece and makes treaty in 85. Mithridates starts second war in 83, defeated in 82, only to return a third time, to be defeated again in 71. A fourth war is avoided by his death.

BOSPORUS
110 joins Pontus

COLCHIS

BLACK SEA

Caeronea 86, Roman victory

Orchomenus 85, Roman victory

Chalcedon 74 Roman defeat

Sinope

Trapezus

ARMENIA

Byzantium

PAPHLAGONIA

BITHYNIA

Amasea

PONTUS

Nicopolis 71, Mithridates defeated, flees to Armenia to regroup

ADRIATIC SEA

ITALIA

Rome

Naples

MACEDONIA

Dyrrhacium

Pella

Thessalonica

Brundisium

GALATIA

ASIA

Pergamum

Sardis

Ephesus

CAPPADOCIA

CILICIA

Edessa

PARTHIAN EMPIRE

Antioch

Corinth

Athens

ACHAEA

Sparta

PISIDIA

LYCIA

Rhodus

Cyprus

SELEUCID EMPIRE

Crete

MEDITERRANEAN SEA

A very Greek-style coin of Mithridates II.

Roman empire at 100 BC

Pontus under Mithridates II

Mithridates' campaigns/dates

THE INDEPENDENT KINGDOMS

Much of the Parthian empire was divided into sub-kingdoms ruled by local dynasties, many of them in border areas where they could protect trade routes from outside interference. The most significant included Characene, Elymais-Susa, and Persis.

Facing: Ruins of the artisans' town at Elamite Susa (Shush), Iran.

Diversity was a strength of the Parthian empire; but it was also a weakness, since under the feudal system it could lead to internal strife. Among the most important of the sub-kingdoms were Elymais (ancient Elam), Characene, Persis, Adiabene and Atropatene, Scythia (Indo-Parthian), and Armenia.

Elymais, in the foothills of the Zagros mountains, was a major trade center with its capital at Susa. It is mentioned frequently as a supplier of arms to either support or counter insurrections, and in these reports Elymaean archers mounted on swift camels are singled out for their bravery and courage.

It is possible that the occupants of this region were originally Persian, although they were hostile to the Achaemenid kings and worshipped several local deities derived from Babylon and Assyria. They fought against the Seleucid kings Antiochus III and Antiochus IV, but supported Demetrius during his abortive attempt to oust the Parthians and restore Seleucid rule; as a punishment they were invaded by Mithridates I, who destroyed their Greek temples. After about 82 BC they were independent of Parthia and sent envoys to Rome for support against the Parthians, but by AD 1 a new line of kings bore Parthian royal names.

Characene was located at the head of the Persian Gulf, with its capital city at Charax Spasinou. Characene was founded about 180 BC by a local dynastic ruler named Hsypaosines, but seems to have enjoyed only a brief period of complete independence before it was annexed by Mithridates I. Following this it had a semi-autonomous existence, pledging to support and pay taxes to the Parthians, but able to manage its own internal affairs and issue its own coinage. Characene was an important trading city between Mesopotamia and India until the end of the Parthian period.

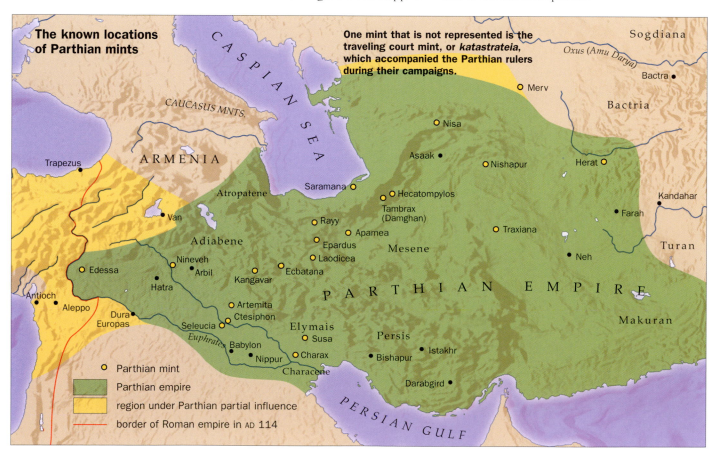

Supporting the leader

Persis has a unique position in the Parthian context. Originally the center of the Persian empire, it was a bastion of Achaemenid culture, religion, and language. Persis remained independent throughout the early years of Parthian rule, until Mithridates II claimed it as a sub-kingdom in about 80 BC. Even then it controlled its own affairs and adhered to a belief in the old religion of Zoroaster, which was to reach a climax under Ardashir I.

Little is known about the history of the sub-kingdoms of Adiabene and Atropatene, other than that they played important roles as buffer states between the various competing empires. They were used as bases by various usurpers, including Media, and seem to have changed hands frequently. Parthia, Rome, and Armenia all claimed them at different times. Their degree of independence is unknown, although their failure to issue coinage suggests that at all times they were vassal states of one of the superior powers.

The Scythians were distant relatives of the Parthians, but were responsible for many of the depredations carried out by the Sakae along the Silk Road that carried the Mesopotamia-China trade. As part of the Indo-Parthian confederation, formed in the late first century BC, they were under the leadership of several kings named Gondophares; the name of a line of Sakae chieftains, as well as a noble family name of the Suren, one of the seven royal houses of the Parthians. The Indo-Parthians controlled trade that eventually extended into Pakistan and northern India.

Armenia was really a buffer zone between the Parthians and Rome, rather than a Parthian sub-kingdom. Armenian allegiance seems to have shifted according to whichever side was in the stronger position, leading to a curious situation during the period of Nero (r.AD 54–68) when it had become expedient for the Parthians to name the candidate for Armenian kingship and for the Romans to crown him.

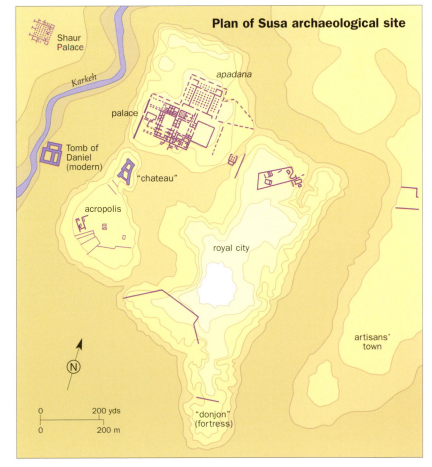

Plan of Susa archaeological site

Shaur Palace

Karkeh

apadana

palace

Tomb of Daniel (modern)

"chateau"

acropolis

royal city

artisans' town

N

0   200 yds
0   200 m

"donjon" (fortress)

ROMAN INVASIONS

The empires of Rome and Mesopotamia were separated only by a buffer zone in Armenia, and it was inevitable that these two powers would come into conflict. Although Pompey had agreed a treaty with Parthia, Roman general Marcus Licinius Crassus violated this in 53 BC, beginning a series of incursions.

Above: Marcus Licinius Crassus (115–53 BC) became the wealthiest man in Rome. As one of the triumvirs with Pompey and Julius Caesar, he craved the final battle with Mithridates, but this honor—and chance of even greater wealth—went to Pompey, leaving Crassus with the consolation prize of conquering Mesopotamia. He failed.

Above right: The emperor Marcus Aurelius Antoninus, known as Caracalla (r.AD 211–17), sought war with Parthia and mounted a powerful invasion force. But Parthia was saved when Caracalla was murdered by some of his own troops while visiting the temple of Sin at Carrhae, near to where Crassus also died.

Crassus was one of the richest men in Rome, who boasted that no man could claim to be wealthy unless he could afford a private army. He was ruthlessly ambitious, and felt that a military victory in Mesopotamia—which he viewed as a militarily weak region—would hasten his rise to political power. With seven legions comprising 30,000 men and 10,000 cavalry, he marched through Armenia and engaged the Parthians near Carrhae in 53 BC.

Despite his confidence, Crassus was inexperienced in war and the flat plains where he made his stand were ideally suited for a Parthian offensive. With 10,000 cavalry, comprised of *cataphracts* (heavy armored cavalry, *see the following page*) and lightly armed mounted bowmen, a Parthian leader known only by the family name of Suren destroyed three-quarters of Crassus's force. About 10,000 Romans were taken captive, and the legions' eagle standards fell into Parthian hands. Crassus was killed during a disorganized Roman retreat.

Following Suren's victory Armenia switched allegiance, making it necessary for Rome to instigate a second invasion to secure its border. In 36 BC a Roman army under Mark Antony, twice the size of that led by Crassus, subjugated Armenia and entered Parthian territories via Media. Antony kept to the mountain passes where the Parthians would have no advantage. A surprise attack on his siege train left 10,000 Romans dead and led to the defection of his Armenian allies.

Antony's plan was to force the Parthians into submission by besieging their cities, but the loss of his siege train made this impracticable and he was forced to retreat. Harassed by Parthian archers, Antony had lost more than half his force by the time he reached the safety of Armenia. Another 8,000 died during his retreat

from Armenia to Syria in winter conditions, making his losses far greater than those suffered by Crassus. In 32 BC Roman triumvirate rule was broken by Octavian, who defeated Antony in sea battle at Actium the following year. He and his lover Cleopatra committed suicide.

Hollow victories

Octavian, taking the name Augustus and becoming the first Roman emperor in 27, tried to resolve the Parthian-Roman deadlock with diplomacy. He placed a pro-Roman king on the Armenian throne in 20, backed up with a Roman army. Parthia and Rome, both weary of war, signed a treaty by which Armenia would remain as a neutral zone between the empires; Parthia returned the eagle standards and the Roman prisoners that it held. Augustus celebrated his "victory" in Rome and had this inscribed on his coins, even though no battle had been fought.

The peace accord remained firm until AD 114, when Emperor Trajan mounted an offensive against Parthia, on the pretext that Rome had been provoked when King Osroes I (r.109–129) deposed the pro-Roman king in Armenia. With 11 legions and auxiliary troops, Trajan conquered Armenia, captured Ctesiphon, and reached as far as the Persian Gulf. Parthia had difficulty in mounting an effective resistance and signed a peace accord. By 117, however, Parthia was in revolt. Trajan was forced to retreat and died at Selinus in Cilicia on his way back to Rome in August 117.

His successor, Hadrian, abandoned Trajan's conquests to ensure that the peace with Parthia held; but this left Parthia open to further Roman incursions. Under the joint-rule of Marcus Aurelius and Lucius Verus a Roman army sacked Ctesiphon, but Rome did not have enough power to secure the area. There were numerous Roman infringements of the Parthian-Roman accord, until a large invasion took place in 217 under Caracalla. Yet this too was indecisive, since Caracalla was murdered on his way from Edessa to Carrhae.

Unlike the Parthians, the Sassanians that replaced them after 224 had a strong centralized authority and aggressive ideas. They were not content to simply defend their lands against Roman displays of power.

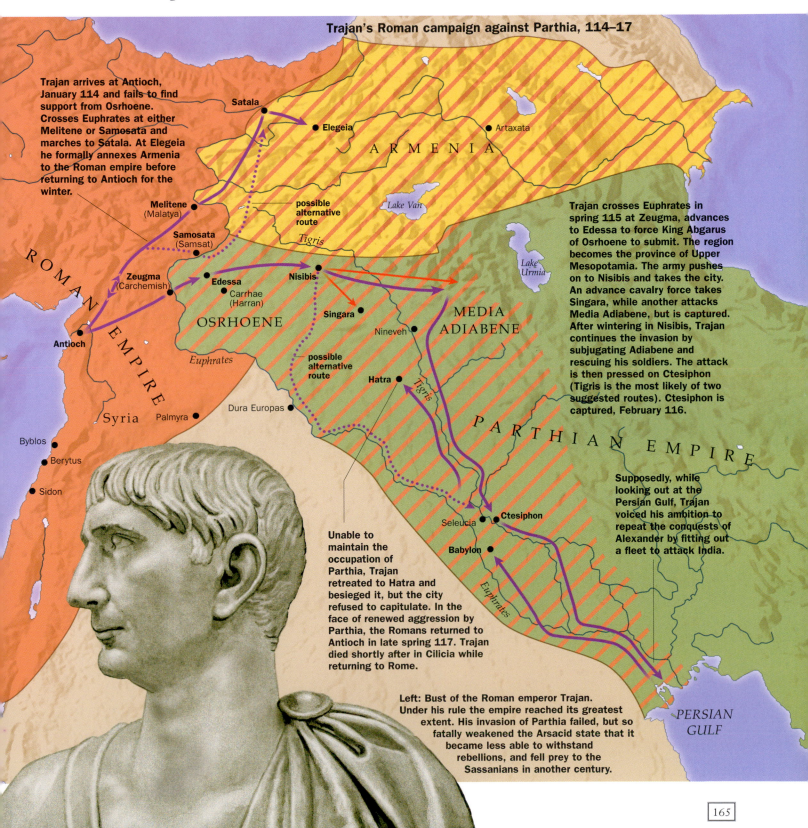

Trajan's Roman campaign against Parthia, 114–17

Trajan arrives at Antioch, January 114 and fails to find support from Osrhoene. Crosses Euphrates at either Melitene or Samosata and marches to Satala. At Elegeia he formally annexes Armenia to the Roman empire before returning to Antioch for the winter.

Satala
Elegeia
Artaxata
A R M E N I A
Lake Van
possible alternative route
Tigris
Lake Urmia

Melitene (Malatya)
Samosata (Samsat)
Zeugma (Carchemish)
Edessa
Carrhae (Harran)
Nisibis
Singara
Nineveh
MEDIA ADIABENE

R O M A N   E M P I R E
Antioch
OSRHOENE
Euphrates
possible alternative route
Hatra
Tigris
Syria
Palmyra
Dura Europas

Byblos
Berytus
Sidon

Trajan crosses Euphrates in spring 115 at Zeugma, advances to Edessa to force King Abgarus of Osrhoene to submit. The region becomes the province of Upper Mesopotamia. The army pushes on to Nisibis and takes the city. An advance cavalry force takes Singara, while another attacks Media Adiabene, but is captured. After wintering in Nisibis, Trajan continues the invasion by subjugating Adiabene and rescuing his soldiers. The attack is then pressed on Ctesiphon (Tigris is the most likely of two suggested routes). Ctesiphon is captured, February 116.

P A R T H I A N   E M P I R E

Supposedly, while looking out at the Persian Gulf, Trajan voiced his ambition to repeat the conquests of Alexander by fitting out a fleet to attack India.

Seleucia
Ctesiphon
Babylon
Euphrates

Unable to maintain the occupation of Parthia, Trajan retreated to Hatra and besieged it, but the city refused to capitulate. In the face of renewed aggression by Parthia, the Romans returned to Antioch in late spring 117. Trajan died shortly after in Cilicia while returning to Rome.

Left: Bust of the Roman emperor Trajan. Under his rule the empire reached its greatest extent. His invasion of Parthia failed, but so fatally weakened the Arsacid state that it became less able to withstand rebellions, and fell prey to the Sassanians in another century.

PERSIAN GULF

165

PARTHIAN CAVALRY

Parthian military successes were won by the efficiency of their cavalry. Light and heavy units were assigned strategic roles, riding into skirmish battles upon specially bred horses the envy of Rome. Their manning policy was notably less effective.

Parthian military concerns were largely conditioned by the feudal system in which rapid-response cavalry units were maintained by regional leaders. There was no standing army and few foot soldiers. Unlike the Seleucids, the Parthians never used elephants in war and made no use of war chariots.

The Parthians developed special breeds of horses for speed rather than endurance. These horses were renowned for their strength and agility, and have been described in Roman sources as "the most elegant riding horse in the whole world." They were sought-after in Rome, since they were superior to the Roman war horse, and were on occasion presented as gifts to Roman emperors. The Parthians also traded them into China, where they were known as "Heavenly Horses." Chinese legend has it that these horses were the offspring of dragons and that they sweated blood.

The Parthians developed both heavy and light cavalry units. The light cavalry, which usually comprised the larger part of a Parthian army, was designed for speed and therefore carried as little weight as possible. They were used for skirmishes, hit-and-run attacks, and flanking movements, but were unable to sustain close or prolonged conflict. The warriors wore no armor and were armed only with a bow and arrows.

Below: A unit of Parthian light cavalry of the 1st century BC. The rider in the foreground is turning in the saddle to execute a "Parthian shot".

Developed from the weapon used by Scythian tribesmen, the Parthian bow was quite different from the earlier Persian longbow used by footmen. These were double (recurved) composite bows that enabled arrows to pierce Roman armor. They were also short (about three feet high) and ideal for use from horseback,

36 BC	c.26 BC	20 BC	AD 53–67	AD 115–17	AD 180	AD 197–99	AD 217
Mark Antony invades Parthian territory but is ambushed and forced to retreat	Isidore of Charax writes *Parthian Stations*, describing trade between the Levant and India	A treaty between the Roman and Parthian empires makes Armenia into a buffer state	Romans fail to take control of Armenia from the Parthians, instead agreeing peace	Emperor Trajan invades Parthia but a rebellion forces Roman retreat	In Istakhr, Persis, Zoroastrian priest Sassan stirs rebellion against the Parthians	Mesopotamia is part of the Roman empire	Emperor Caracalla dies; after scrappy fighting, successor Macrinus agrees peace with Parthia

where the Parthians perfected a technique of turning in the saddle to shoot to the rear known as the "Parthian shot" (today usually coined as a "parting shot").

Bowmen were supported by the stronger horses of the *cataphract* (heavy cavalry). Both man and horse wore protective armor of steel plates sewn to a leather backing. Contemporary reports said their thick, heavy lances were capable of piercing two men at once.

A working force

The organization of the army was very loose, with a small company called a *washt*, a larger unit or *drafsh*, and a division known as a *gund*. The strength of a *drafsh* was a thousand men, under the command of a local leader, while the 10,000 soldiers of a *gund* was under a supreme commander (*spadpat*) who was chosen from a noble family.

They went into battle to the sound of kettle drums and carrying banners ornamented with dragons and the royal standard, supported by camel troops carrying spare arrows and lances. Wagons were only used for transporting females accompanying the commanders.

In battle, the light cavalry engaged first, using hit-and-run techniques in which they circled the enemy and harassed them but did not come close enough for hand-to-hand fighting. Feigning retreat, they would draw their enemy from cover then turn in the saddle to deliver the "Parthian shot," often with devastating effect. With the enemy drawn out, the *cataphract* charged in close formation to break their ranks. The light cavalry would then return to continue its harassment.

Such techniques were not suited to sustained campaigns or siege warfare. The Parthians never used the siege weapons they captured from the Roman troops, instead bringing campaigns to a close as quickly as possible. Since Parthian armies consisted of local men who had been taken away from non-military duties, it was necessary for them to return to their farms and homesteads as early as possible. This is the main reason why the Parthians did not employ expansionist policies.

AD 224	AD 238	AD 244	AD 258	AD 260	AD 267	AD 297	AD 363
Ardashir overthrows Artabanus IV; end of the Parthian empire	The Sassanians conquer Mesopotamia	Roman emperor Philip the Arabian meets Shapur near Misikhe and agrees a treaty	Hatra is sacked by Shapur I and abandoned	Shapur raids Antioch and fights the Romans at Edessa, capturing Emperor Valerian	Zenobia becomes queen of Palmyra and controls Asia Minor and Egypt	Galerius agrees peace with the Sassanians, later becoming Roman emperor	Emperor Julian fails to take Ctesiphon and is killed during the retreat

HATRA AND TRADE

At the height of its power in the first century AD, Hatra was probably the most important staging post on the Silk Road. The multi-cultural mix of merchants who would have visited this crossroads may explain the site's diverse range of architectural styles and the multitude of deities once worshipped there.

The fortress town of Hatra is in the desert area of northwest Iraq, about 60 miles southwest of Mosul on the west bank of the Wadi Tharthar. This is the most westerly point in the Mesopotamian steppe where there is a sufficient regular water supply to support a community of any size. Its prosperity was ensured through taxes it levied against the international caravan traffic between Mesopotamia, Arabia, and Persia in the east, and the Levant, Asia Minor, Europe, and North Africa in the west. Although functioning as a small independent kingdom, Hatra appears to have always been allied with larger powers.

German excavations began in 1907 and uncovered a city that was arranged within two roughly circular walls with a 1,600-foot trench between them and guarded by 163 defensive towers. Hatra shows an eclectic mix of deities

from different cultures: the gods worshipped here included the Akkadian deity Nergal (here linked with the Greek god Hermes), the Greek god Apollo, Atargatis from the Persian-Achaemenids, and the Arabian Al-Lat and Shamiyah.

At its center is a raised precinct with a temple dedicated to Shamash (the sun god) and shrines to a trinity of celestial deities identified as Maran, Martan, and Barmarin (Our Lord Father, Mother, and the Son of Our Lord). There is a pair of halls dedicated to Mithras.

The inner precinct and main temple complex also show a curious mixture of eastern and western architectural styles, with elements from Arabia, Assyria, Greece, and Rome. Its stone colonnades, arches, and classical statues give it the appearance of a Roman or Greek city, but the arches lead into open-sided pavilions reminiscent of the council tents of the Parthians and Arabs. Similar stone and brick representations of nomadic tents have been found in other Parthian cities. Old Mesopotamian building styles, similar to those at Uruk, Ashur, and Babylon, are in evidence.

Surrounding the temple precinct, but still within the inner wall, are several smaller shrines,

Below: The Ionian Greek influence is marked in this Parthian colonnade at the heart of Hatra's temple precinct.

some of which appear to be tribal sanctuaries. These originally contained statues of the kings, the royal family household, and important secular and religious officials, most of which were removed for safekeeping to the Mosul and Baghdad museums. There are a number of tower tombs and private homes, some excavated to reveal lively frescos painted in brilliant orange, black, and white depicting hunting scenes with gazelles and wild boars.

Melting pot

The exact date of Hatra's foundation is not known. It may have started life as a small trading town and oasis resting stage, perhaps with a single temple, that served as a focus for the many desert tracks that lead into the area. In the third century BC it was part of the Seleucid kingdom and then came under the authority of the Parthians; however, there are references to

indicate that it was one of the earliest settlements of Arab-speaking tribes who entered this region in about 200 BC. Inscriptions found here refer to the Parthian title King of Kings and to the King of the Arabs. It is likely that an Arabian dynasty of kings was founded here starting with Lajash (r.AD 156–67), son of the chief Nasr.

The assumption has been made that under the Parthians Hatra became the capital of a sub-kingdom that was under Arab rulers, as well as a religious center for nomadic tribes. It held a strategic position from which it could threaten Roman lines of communication and came under siege from Rome on several occasions. Both Trajan and Septimius Severus tried unsuccessfully to capture Hatra. The city was finally abandoned after being sacked by the Sassanian leader Shapur I in AD 258.

Above: Hatra's wealth derived from its position on the main trade route between Mesopotamia and the Mediterranean is evident from the lavish public buildings, which rivaled any in the neighboring Roman empire.

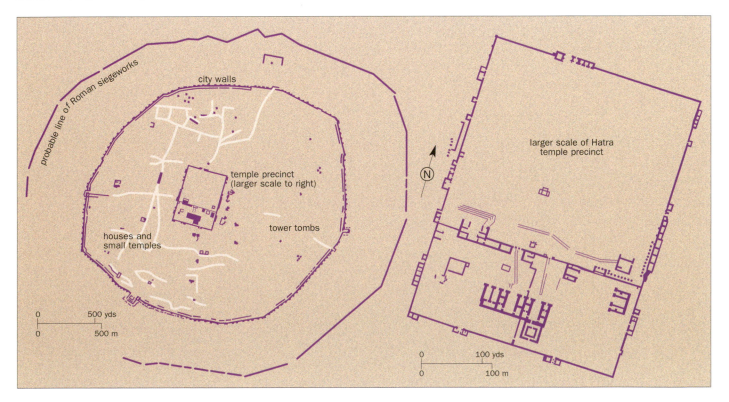

probable line of Roman siegeworks

city walls

temple precinct (larger scale to right)

houses and small temples

tower tombs

larger scale of Hatra temple precinct

N

0   500 yds
0   500 m

0   100 yds
0   100 m

CHRISTIAN IMMIGRATION

By AD 200 Christianity had spread throughout Asia and Syria. Driven to Mesopotamia as a result of Roman persecution elsewhere, it remained a marginal faith, at odds with the multiple-god beliefs that surrounded it. Its fate in the region was at the whim of greater forces.

Above: The Armenian church of St. Thaddeus (the Ghara Kilissa, or "Black Church") near Maku in Iranian Azerbaijan. Many Christians fleeing from Roman persecution in Syria found new homes in Armenia and Azerbaijan, as well as throughout Mesopotamia.

Roman and Parthian attitudes were completely opposite. Whereas the Romans adopted an aggressive expansionist policy supported by a highly centralized authority with a well-disciplined army, the Parthians were content to rely on trading and amicable relationships with their neighbors. Although they could respond effectively when threatened, Parthians tended to be tolerant.

This difference in attitude meant that many religious sects that were oppressed by the Romans were present within Parthian territories; thus the early centuries of Parthian rule were marked by a generally liberal policy that enabled

Jewish and other minority communities to flourish. Christian missionaries from Syria were actively working in Mesopotamia from about the first century AD.

At first, Christianity was seen as a fragmentary incident of Jewish history; early Christian centers were established in cities that already had a strong Jewish presence. The most important of these was Arbela, a small Parthian border town in the region of Adiabene about 50 miles east of the Tigris, which had a sizeable Jewish-Christian community after AD 36. Nearby Nisibis, which had a Jewish academy, also had an active Christian faith. Christianity spread to Edessa in the Osrhoene region, which became an important missionary center.

By AD 200 there were about 150 Christian churches in Mesopotamia, all of which regarded Antioch in Syria as the focus of their faith and the seat of authority. By the third century the number of Christian churches in Persia had increased to 360. Undoubtedly many of the Christians were driven toward Parthia by their persecution in Rome. There was a tendency for Persia to see Christians as friends simply because Rome saw them as enemies.

Closed communities

The liberality of the Christian faith, which asked adherence to a set of beliefs rather than lengthy training and slavish following of ritual dogma, was particularly appealing to Parthian women. Under the male-dominated feudal systems of Parthia, women had relatively few rights, whereas Christianity offered a basis of some equality. The early Christian Church was most important to rural areas and had a largely female congregation; once established, it found adherents among men and at royal and noble courts.

Compared to other faiths, however, Christianity was more tolerated than actively supported. Christian saints were not brought into the pantheon of Parthian deities in the same way as those of the Greeks had been, as in the composite god Nergal-Hermes, for example. This was not necessarily because most were unwilling to accept Christian ideals, but stemmed from the fact that Christian communities saw other religious expressions as pagan and could not contemplate duality in their beliefs. Parthian Christian communities have frequently been described as "closed communities" but this segregation was largely at the instigation of the Christians themselves.

During the latter part of the Parthian era there was a revival of old Persian beliefs and a return to Zoroastrianism. Even though Christianity and Zoroastrianism had much in common, particularly the belief in a struggle between good and evil and the concept of heaven and hell, Christianity became increasingly isolated. There was never an outright ban, but under the Sassanians there was active discouragement of any religion that did not adhere to the teachings of Zoroaster.

Due in large part to their self-imposed separation from the state, Christians came under increasing pressure. Following the conversion of the Roman emperor Constantine and the adoption of Christianity as Rome's state religion in 312, Christians were seen as allies of the Persian enemy. Sassanian persecution included the imposition of heavy taxes on Christians (twice those levied against other religions), the loss of some property and civil rights, and even the execution of a number of bishops.

Above: Christian communities have survived in Mesopotamia until today. This Iraqi Christian woman is seen praying during Christmas Eve services at the Al Aela Almukdsa church, Baghdad, in 2003. Due to the fraught conditions, an imposed curfew meant that the midnight mass had to be held at midday instead.

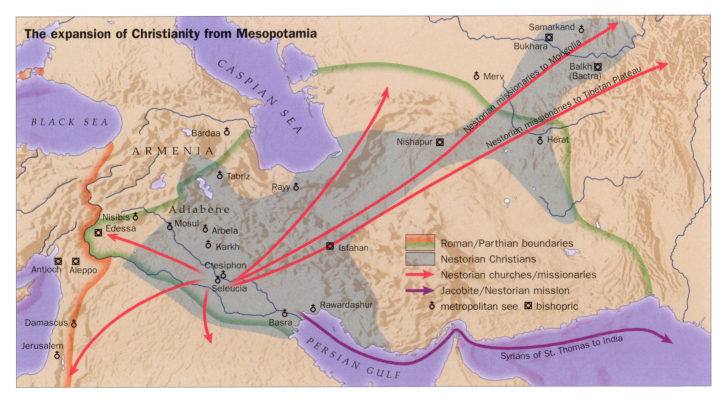

The expansion of Christianity from Mesopotamia

BLACK SEA

CASPIAN SEA

ARMENIA

Bardaa ♂

Tabriz ♂

Rayy ♂

Nishapur ◙

Merv ♂

Samarkand ♂

Bukhara ◙

Balkh ◙ (Bactra)

Herat ♂

Nestorian missionaries to Mongolia

Nestorian missionaries to Tibetan Plateau

Nisibis ♂
◙ Edessa

Adiabene

Mosul ♂

Arbela ♂

Karkh ♂

Isfahan ◙

Antioch ◙ ◙ Aleppo

Ctesiphon

Seleucia

Damascus ♂

Jerusalem ♂

Rawardashur ♂

Basra ♂

PERSIAN GULF

Syrians of St. Thomas to India

Roman/Parthian boundaries
Nestorian Christians
Nestorian churches/missionaries
Jacobite/Nestorian mission
♂ metropolitan see ◙ bishopric

THE SASSANIAN REVOLT

The Parthian empire's flexibility led to its downfall. With no state religion and a weak administration surrounded by independent kingdoms, new ideas, movements, and even armies were allowed to develop. In the province of Persis, a Zoroastrian priest began to preach against Parthian rule.

The lack of central authority during the Parthian period enabled numerous self-governed kingdoms and religious cults to grow. Many of these were modernizing movements that introduced new artistic and architectural forms and incorporated new ideas from Greece and Rome, as well as from beliefs held by the Arabs, Jews, and Christians. At the same time, the absence of an authoritarian line or doctrine allowed more conservative factions to decry these innovations as a sign of decadence and loss of faith, and they called for a return to earlier ways.

Part of the conservative reproach was that the dynastic family lived in splendid luxury from the proceeds of taxes that were imposed upon trade. However, the collection of taxes was largely in the hands of the border towns, and many local leaders were reluctant to share this wealth in support of a decadent lifestyle from which they derived little personal benefit.

In the early Parthian period, the ruling dynasty had commanded sufficient loyalty to be able to put down these insurrections; but the Parthian-Roman wars weakened the central dynasty's hold on the resources and manpower they needed to maintain their position. Some provincial governors started to build powerful armies of their own, strong enough to threaten the dynasty.

Matters were particularly volatile in the border areas and towns that were on the caravan routes, and it was in one of these, Istakhr in the province of Persis (Fars), that a Zoroastrian priest named Sassan began preaching for the overthrow of the Parthian "foreigners" in about AD 180. Little remains of the town of Istakhr, although it is clear that it was a stronghold of the Zoroastrian faith, since it had a fire sanctuary dedicated to Anahita, the old Persian goddess of women, fertility, and war.

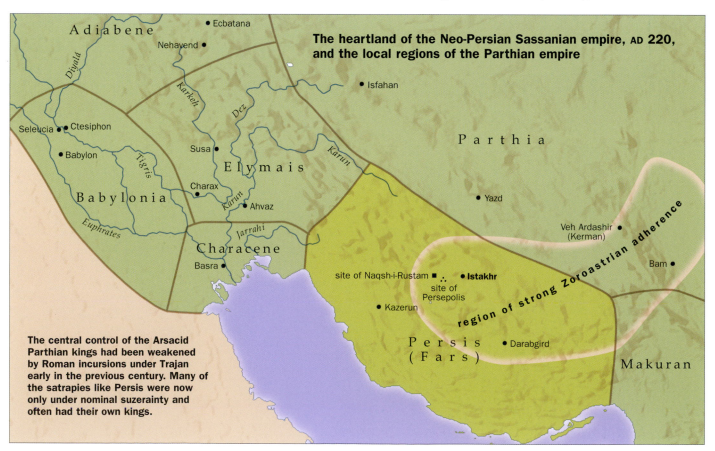

The heartland of the Neo-Persian Sassanian empire, AD 220, and the local regions of the Parthian empire

The central control of the Arsacid Parthian kings had been weakened by Roman incursions under Trajan early in the previous century. Many of the satrapies like Persis were now only under nominal suzerainty and often had their own kings.

Sassanian legends

Sassan's background is in doubt. The most plausible theory is that he was a rebel leader who spent much of his life in exile, when he is said to have "wandered with Kurdish shepherds." He gained influence through marriage to Rodak, who was the daughter of Gochihr, ruler of the province of Persis (Fars), which enabled Sassan to obtain the position of high priest at the fire sanctuary in the capital town of Istakhr.

Although Sassan's lineage is now disputed, it was widely believed at the time that he was a direct descendant of the Achaemenid king Darius III; thus lending legitimacy to his claims for the restoration of Zoroastrian beliefs and a return to Achaemenid ideals. He collaborated with his son Papak in assassinating Gochihr and

seizing the throne, following which they declared Persis independent from Parthia and built a royal palace at Firuzabad to rival that of the Parthian dynasts.

There is, however, a more romantic legend in which Sassan is shown as a humble priest without a temple appointment, whom Papak took pity on and employed as a shepherd. Papak had a dream in which he saw Sassan riding a white elephant (a symbol of kingship) with white light radiating from his head. Papak's sages and dream interpreters told him that this meant a son of Sassan would become a great emperor, who would overthrow the Parthians. Papak's response to these auguries was to marry his own daughter to Sassan. The son of this union was Ardashir, whom Papak adopted to give him a legitimate claim to the throne.

Above: Carved into the rockface at Naqsh-e-Rustam, burial place of the Achaemenid kings Darius I and Artazerxes I near to the ruins of Persepolis, Ardashir I on the right is invested by the Zoroastrian god of goo, Ahura Mazda.

CHAPTER 11
THE SASSANIAN EMPIRE,
AD 224–651

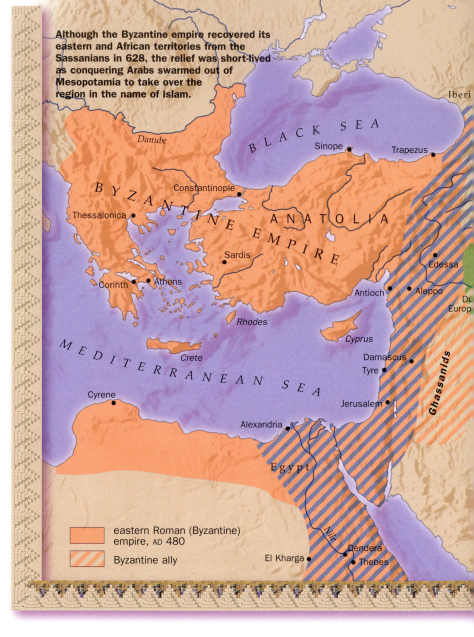

The Sassanian empire, AD 224–637

Although the Byzantine empire recovered its eastern and African territories from the Sassanians in 628, the relief was short-lived as conquering Arabs swarmed out of Mesopotamia to take over the region in the name of Islam.

eastern Roman (Byzantine) empire, AD 480

Byzantine ally

The Sassanian period, or second Persian empire, began with the overthrow of Parthian King Artabanus IV (r.AD 216–24) by Ardashir I (r.224–39), and was to last until the domination of the Islamic state in 651. Ardashir, grandson of Sassan, was educated at the royal court in Persis (Fars) and became an envoy to Parthia, where he was ordered to accompany Artabanus's sons. He soon proved himself superior to them in the chase, at war, polo, chess (chatrang), and in intellectual skills.

Artabanus's sons claimed credit for Ardashir's deeds. Legend states that when he expressed his anger Ardashir was stripped of his honors and set to work as a stable-boy, where he fell in love with a favorite maid of Artabanus. One day, Artabanus called his sages and astrologers to predict what the future held, and was told that if anyone ran away from his kingdom within the next three days, that person would attain greatness and take his place. When the maid told Ardashir this, he saddled two horses and they fled toward Persis.

Artabanus hastened in pursuit with 4,000 men. Each time he asked people if they had seen Ardashir and the maid, he was told they "flew like a violent wind, pursued by a powerful eagle." Eventually some travelers told him that the eagle was now perched on Ardashir's horse. Informed by sages that the eagle represented the kingship of the Achaemenids that had come to Ardashir, Artabanus returned home to assemble an army large enough to invade Persis.

Ardashir was afraid he would be unable to withstand this army, but Banak, the chief of Sparhan, sent his sons and soldiers to his aid, as did the chiefs of many different provinces in Persis. The army of Artabanus was defeated in the battle that followed, putting the Parthian overlord into such a rage that he called together all the soldiers of Rai, Demavand, Delman, and Patash-Khvargar with the intention of killing Ardashir and destroying Persis. But the power of the Achaemenid kings was with Ardashir; Artabanus was killed and all the riches of Parthia fell into Ardashir's hands.

Enemies on all sides

Madig, king of the Kurds, attacked Ardashir's battle-weary troops and defeated them, leaving Ardashir to find his way back alone. Two shepherds gave him rest for the night, telling of a nearby fertile valley with many soldiers who would support him. With this force, Ardashir mounted a surprise attack against Madig and claimed the Kurdish territories as his own.

Now the army of Haftan-Bokht, leader of the Worms, overwhelmed Ardashir's cavalry, carrying the Kurdish treasures to his own kingdom and defeating the army that

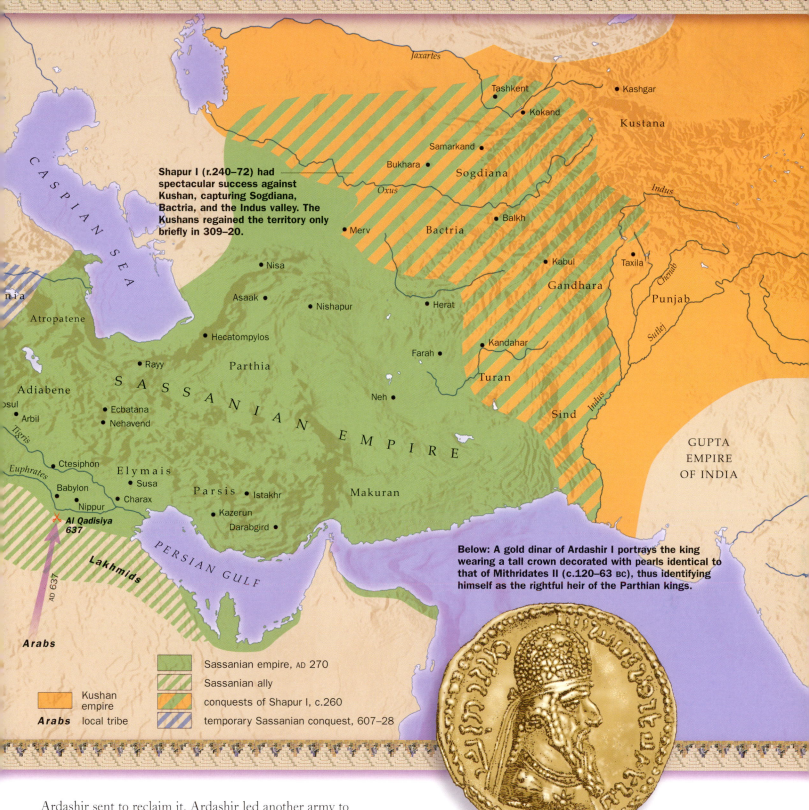

Shapur I (r.240–72) had spectacular success against Kushan, capturing Sogdiana, Bactria, and the Indus valley. The Kushans regained the territory only briefly in 309–20.

Below: A gold dinar of Ardashir I portrays the king wearing a tall crown decorated with pearls identical to that of Mithridates II (c.120–63 BC), thus identifying himself as the rightful heir of the Parthian kings.

CASPIAN SEA

Jaxartes

Kashgar

Tashkent

Kokand

Kustana

Samarkand

Bukhara

Sogdiana

Oxus

Merv

Bactria

Balkh

Indus

Nisa

Atropatene

Asaak

Nishapur

Herat

Kabul

Gandhara

Taxila

Punjab

nia

Hecatompylos

Parthia

Rayy

Chenab

Kandahar

Adiabene

S A S S A N I A N   E M P I R E

Farah

Turan

Sutlej

osul

Ecbatana

Nehavend

Neh

Sind

Indus

Arbil

Tigris

GUPTA
EMPIRE
OF INDIA

Euphrates

Ctesiphon

Elymais

Susa

Parsis

Istakhr

Makuran

Babylon

Charax

Nippur

Kazerun

Al Qadisiya
637

Darabgird

PERSIAN GULF

Lakhmids

AD 637

Arabs

Sassanian empire, AD 270

Sassanian ally

Kushan empire

conquests of Shapur I, c.260

Arabs local tribe

temporary Sassanian conquest, 607–28

Ardashir sent to reclaim it. Ardashir led another army to besiege Haftan-Bokht's capital, but Arabs assisted the Worms and hemmed him in.

Meanwhile Mitrok, a chief of Zarham in Persis, had raided Ardashir's capital. Again, Ardashir traveled back alone and was counseled by two brothers, who advised him to kill Mitrok and go in disguise to Haftan-Bokht. So he feigned friendship until such time as they dined together, when he seized Haftan-Bokht and poured molten brass down his throat.

Ardashir fought many victorious battles, but one day his wife, a daughter of Artabanus, tried to poison him. As he lifted the glass of poisoned wine, a red hawk flew into the room and smashed it to the floor. Realizing that treachery had been attempted, Ardashir ordered his wife to be killed; however, she pleaded leniency from the executioner since she was seven months pregnant with Ardashir's child. The boy she bore was the second great leader of the Sassanian empire, Shapur I.

SHAPUR'S VICTORIES

Shapur I (r.241–72), son and successor of Ardashir I, was a warrior king who extended the Sassanian empire and proclaimed himself "King of the World." His greatest victory came at Edessa against the forces of Emperor Valerian, later celebrated graphically in skin and stone.

Although at its greatest extent his empire barely exceeded that of Ardashir, Shapur conquered Nisibis (Nusaybin) and Carrhae and began advancing into Syria, where he presented the Sassanian army as a serious threat to the security of Rome's eastern borders. In an attempt to minimize the threat posed by Shapur, Roman Emperor Gordian III (r.238–44) moved troops to the area under the command of his *praefectus praetorio* (a commander of the praetorian guard), Timesitheus. Timesitheus, a wise and experienced politician and military commander, was Gordian's father-in-law, and under the

emperor he enjoyed the respect and popularity of the legions. Shapur was defeated, but in 244 Timesitheus died of illness and his brother Philip the Arab was appointed in his place.

Philip conspired to have Gordian murdered after stirring up dissent among the Roman troops, and signed a treaty with Shapur that guaranteed Sassanian dominance in Armenia and Mesopotamia. When Roman attention was diverted to its western borders by an invasion of the Goths, Shapur grasped this opportunity to invade Syria and plunder Antioch.

The Roman response to Shapur's expansionism came in 260, when Valerian (r.253–60) relieved Antioch and engaged Shapur's forces at the battle of Edessa. Historical sources referring to this battle are unclear. They generally agree that Valerian was defeated; however there is evidence to suggest that the fight was won by Valerian's troops who then found themselves short of supplies and

Right: However dubious Shapur's triumph over the Roman emperor Philip the Arab in 244 (*see caption facing*) may be—no Roman records exist of the event—his victory over the emperor Valerian in 260 is not in doubt. This rock-carving commemorates the battle, showing Shapur's troops fighting Roman legionaries.

were forced to take refuge in Edessa, where they were stricken by plague.

Estimates suggest that 70,000 of the Roman troops were killed or captured. With his forces so severely reduced or incapacitated, Valerian had no choice but to seek a treaty with Shapur to gain safe conduct from the country. At the council meeting Shapur seized Valerian and carried him off to imprisonment and execution, later displaying his flailed skin outside Ctesiphon as a warning to the Romans.

Palmyra and Zenobia

Meanwhile, Septimius Odaenathus, leader of the powerful Septimii family of Palmyra and a former general under Valerian, began to claim parts of Shapur's territories as his own. The Septimii, although nominally Roman citizens, had always maintained a degree of autonomy and did not feel bound to decisions made by the Roman senate. Shapur's expansion had begun to threaten Palmyra's control of the eastern trade, and Odaenathus allied himself with the new emperor, Gallienus (r.253–68) and began to threaten Ctesiphon. Their combined forces defeated Shapur's army, but shortly after in 267 Odaenathus and his eldest son were murdered, leaving the Palmyrene throne in the hands of his wife Zenobia.

Zenobia was renowned for her beauty and

heartless cruelty—rumors persisted it was she who plotted the murders. She soon lost the trust of Gallienus, who sent an army under Heraclius against Palmyra. Heraclius was defeated, and again Shapur used the dissent within Rome and its allies to his advantage. He reconquered Nisibis and Carrhae and captured the royal harem, although he too failed to destroy the power of Palmyra, which only fell in 272 after Emperor Aurelian (r.270–75) led a siege.

In addition to military conquests, Shapur tried to control religious expression. There were no decrees against the practice of "foreign" religions, yet it is clear that these were not encouraged. Mani (c.216–c.276), the founder of Manichaeism, was officially placed under his protection; yet widespread rumors suggest that Mani was a prisoner of Shapur.

Persian power was maintained under Shapur and the economy was rebuilt, but he also promoted a program of public works and did much to enhance intellectual activity among the Sassanian elite, including commissioning the translation of Greek and Indian writings. His death, however, was a commemoration of his role as the warrior king. His rock-cut tomb is in the valley of Istakhr near Persepolis, where carvings depict Shapur on horseback in royal armor. Before him Valerian kneels in supplication.

Above: This rock-carving sited between the tombs of Darius I and Artaxerxes (*see also picture on page 141*) at Naqsh-e-Rustam, celebrates the victory of Shapur I over the Romans in 260. The captured emperor Valerian is seen kneeling before the mounted king, while behind him stands the emperor Philip the Arab (r.244–49), who had just succeeded Gordian III. According to the Sassanian version of events, the Romans had marched down the Euphrates early in 244 and met the Sassanid army near Misikhe (Fallujah, to the west of Baghdad), where Shapur was victorious. However, Roman histories disagree, and certainly Philip was not defeated in this battle.

SASSANIAN-ROMAN WARS

The change from Parthian to Sassanian domination of Mesopotamia and its environs altered the relationship between Persia and Rome in profound ways. A weakened Roman empire was faced with a series of aggressive Sassanian leaders, finding itself forced to seek peace with a superior adversary.

Below: Close to old Persepolis, the crumbling domes and walls of the Sassanian palace near Sarvestan, Iran face the erosion of the dry desert air of the Shiraz region.

Unlike the Parthians, who had been content to defend their borders and maintain only a loosely organized feudal state, the Sassanians attempted to restore the glory of the Persian empire as it had been under Cyrus the Great. Under the able control of leaders such as Ardashir I (r.224–39), Shapur I (r.240–72), and Shapur II (r.309–79), the Sassanian army was reorganized and given a highly efficient central command. Neighboring kingdoms were conquered and invasion forces sent into India, Armenia, Bactria, and Gandhara. Ctesiphon was restored into a magnificent capital city to rival those built by the Sassanians' Achaemenid

predecessors at Persepolis and Susa.

While the Sassanians were growing in strength, the power and influence of Rome's eastern provinces were waning while it dealt with more immediate problems from the Germanic tribes in its western domains. In 257 Emperor Valerian (r.253–60) rescued Antioch from Syrian dominance, leaving his son Gallienus (r.253–68) to defend western territories. But in 260 Shapur I plundered Antioch and withstood the army that Valerian sent against him at the battle of Edessa.

Divisions between the eastern and western Roman empires led the pro-Christian Constantine I (r.312–37) to establish a new eastern Roman capital at Constantinople (formerly Byzantium) in 330, during the reign of Shapur II. This marked the beginning of a period of Sassanian intolerance toward other cults and religions, partly because it now placed the Christians within the sphere of Roman rather than Persian influence.

Favorable treaties

In 363 Emperor Julian (r.361–63), fresh from successes on the western front, marched on Ctesiphon. Julian's forces secured the surrender of a number of Sassanian provinces, but found Ctesiphon too stoutly defended to be taken other than by an extended siege. Unprepared and running short on provisions, Julian acceded to his generals' demands for a retreat; but was hit in the abdomen by a Sassanian spear in a minor skirmish during the withdrawal along the Tigris to Nisibis and died from his wound. His successor, Jovian (r.363–64), was forced to agree a peace treaty with Shapur II, by which Rome surrendered all claims to territories in the Upper Tigris and east of Singara and Nisibis, in return for the safe conduct of the Roman armies.

The eastern Roman empire slowly evolved into the Greek-speaking Byzantine state. Contemporary reports claim that the splendor of the Sassanian court surpassed all the glories of Byzantium. Despite this surface rivalry, an uneasy peace was maintained between the Sassanians and Byzantium, until the Sassanians reopened hostilities during the reigns of Kavad (488–531) and his son Khosrow I (531–79).

Khosrow invaded Syria and laid siege to Roman centers. Emperor Justinian (r.527–65) attempted to reconquer lost territories in Italy,

Spain, and northern Africa; but this forced him
to reduce Roman defenses in the east, and
Khosrow took advantage. Antioch fell in 540.
The terms of the 562 peace treaty left Byzantium
paying a vast annual subsidy to Persia.

Under Khosrow II (r.590–628) the
Sassanians became legendary for their splendor.
They had an efficient administration and
remarkably productive cities, with superb skills
in metalwork, architecture, sculpture, and
textiles. In the belief that the Sassanian empire

was indestructible, Khosrow reopened hostilities
with Byzantium in 602.

His forces were initially successful. Egypt,
Syria, and Palestine were conquered and by 612
Sassanian forces had penetrated as far as the
Bosphorus and were in sight of Constantinople.
Byzantine emperor Heraclius (r.610–41)
retaliated and invaded Persia, sacking Ctesiphon
in 627; Khosrow II was deposed and murdered
by his own followers. Ten years later, Islamic
Arabs brought down the Sassanian empire.

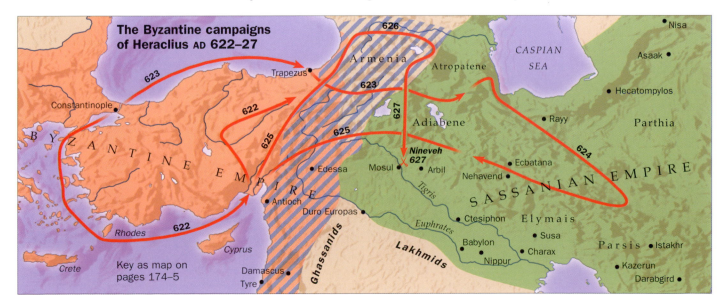

The Byzantine campaigns
of Heraclius AD 622–27

Key as map on
pages 174–5

THE SASSANIAN ARMY

The Sassanian military was based on the cataphract that had been developed by the Parthians, evolved to use better arms and armor, supported by the archers and footmen of the infantry. Under a strict hierarchy and answerable to the monarchy, this standing force would not repeat Parthian mistakes.

Ardashir removed control of the cavalry from the control of the satraps (governors) and feudal princes and placed it under his personal command as a professional standing army with a distinct warrior class (*artestda*). Once the military commander at Darabgerd,

Right: Sassanian heavy cavalryman in action, depicted in a 3rd-century relief of an equestrian battle carved at Naqsh-e-Rustam, Iran.

Ardashir drew on his extensive knowledge of tactics and history when he restored the Achaemenid military organization with a reformed *cataphract* (heavy cavalry), using lighter forms of armor and supported by siege machines adopted from the Romans. Although Sassanians did not use war chariots, they employed defensive weapons, including catapults, boiling liquid, and firebrands.

The *cataphract* formed the core of the standing army (*spah*) and was drawn from the ranks of the nobility. They underwent "hard service," which included military training and discipline, as well as exercises in warfare and military tactics.

Heavy cavalry units wore armor consisting of a leather backing covered with plates of iron that completely protected the rider and the forequarters of his horse. They were supplied with a helmet, hauberk (chainmail coat), breastplate, gauntlets, girdle, thigh guards, lance, sword, battle-axe, mace, bowcase with two bows and two bowstrings, and a quiver holding 30 arrows. They did not use stirrups, but had a cantled war saddle with guard clamps across the top of the rider's thighs that kept him seated in shock combat.

Among the cavalry was an elite corps of 10,000 men known as the Immortals who had sworn never to retreat in battle. A distinguished

| **485** The White Huns or Hepthalites of central Asia conquer parts of Sassanian empire | **527** Under Justinian, the eastern Roman empire becomes the Byzantine empire | **540** Sassanians under Khosrow I sack Antioch | **c.562** Sassanians and Turks defeat the Hepthalites (White Huns) | **562** The Byzantine empire agrees an unfavorable peace with Sassanians | **602** Khosrow II breaks the treaty and begins expansion by conquest | **610** Mohammed has his first vision of the Archangel Gabriel | **627** Emperor Heraclius invades Persia and sacks Ctesiphon; Khosrow II is deposed |

horseman could achieve a position equivalent to that of the knight in medieval Europe. He then became a trusted bodyguard to the king and had status next to that of the royal family.

The Sassanians did not have a permanent light cavalry, instead employing allies or mercenaries from warlike tribes who fought under their own chiefs and had their own specialty. Dailamites, for instance, were skilled with the sword and dagger, whereas Arab mercenaries were efficient in desert warfare.

Earning glory

The larger part of the army was its infantry, comprised of archers and ordinary footmen armed with a spear and shield. Footmen were conscripted from the peasantry and received no pay, acting as pages to the *cataphract* and engaged in duties such as digging tunnels to undermine enemy fortifications.

The more highly ranked archers had composite bows and a rectangular shield covered with wickerwork and rawhide that were supplied to them by the state. It was their duty to advance in close formation, showering enemies with arrows and opening a gap in their ranks through which the cavalry could launch

an assault. By the sixth and seventh centuries AD both the cavalry and archers were recognized as state officials and were entitled to receive pay and subsidies. Border areas continued to be defended by resettled war-like tribes.

In battle formation, the imperial banner was carried in the center of the Sassanian forces, where the king or his commander-in-chief overlooked the battlefield from an elevated throne on the back of a white war elephant. Surrounding him was a protective force of a hundred royal archers.

The strength of one division of the standing army was set at 10,000 men, with a total number of enlisted soldiers in excess of 70,000. These were divided into several *gunds* (companies), each consisting of a number of separate *draff* units. In overall command was the *arghed*, the highest military title, who was always a member of the Sassanian royal family. Beneath him was the *eran-spahbed*, or supreme commander and king's counsel, empowered to act as a spokesman in peace negotiations. During the latter part of Sassanian rule the *eran-spahbed* was replaced by four *spahbed*s, each of whom had military authority over a quarter of the empire.

Below: Bahram (Vahram) II fighting an enemy. Bahram (r.277–94) suffered a reign of continual internal strife, which made him unable to counter a Roman invasion under the emperor Carus, who accomplished much in his one-year reign (282–3). The Romans encountered little resistance from Sassanian border guards on the Euphrates, and Seleucia was captured, once again returning Mesopotamia to Roman sovereignty. Carus then marched down the Tigris unopposed and reached Ctesiphon. Bahram's throne was only saved by the sudden and mysterious death of Carus, which led to a short civil war. Within a year Diocletian (r.284–311) was Rome's sole ruler, and he made a long-lasting peace with the Sassanian empire.

628	630	632–34	634	636	638	642	651
Peace between the Byzantine and Sassanian empires	Muslims take control of Mecca	Abu Bakr succeeds Mohammed; starts campaigns against the Sassanians and Byzantium	A Muslim army defeats the Sassanians at the Battle of Chains	Rustam of Persia is defeated by Arab Muslims at the Battle of Al-Qadisiyah	The muslims control Syria, Jerusalem, and Damascus	Sassanian empire falls at the battle of Nehavend and the Arabs invade Persia	Muslims have conquered all Sassanian territory

SASSANIAN ART

Trade and warfare brought immense wealth to the Sassanian empire, which financed programs of irrigation and town building on a previously unknown scale. This activity peaked during the reign of Khosrow II (590–628), but clearly identifiable Sassanian art was apparent as early as Ardashir's rule.

Below: A 6th-century Sassanian silver salver decorated with a raised relief depicting a griffon.

Firuzabad, Ardashir's capital, used architecture as a statement of independence from Parthia. Its buildings were constructed as fortresses, as were those of the later Sassanians,

but there was also an insistence that they should be richly decorated. Much of this was applied decoration, in the form of wall-paintings or plaster relief, of which little has survived. We

frequently have only remnants of the bare mud-brick construction that underlay the decoration, but there are clues from archaeology and the reports of contemporary Arab traders/historians that enable us to reconstruct these buildings at the height of their splendor.

They had characteristic barrel-vaulting, supported on pillars with bulls' heads capitals, in the Achaemenid tradition. Fragments of mosaic glass cubes covered with gold have been found from the upper parts of walls, while the lower parts were covered with multi-colored slabs of marble. Both the inside and outside of the buildings had stucco decoration, consisting of animals, human figures, and geometric and floral motifs. Niches in the walls were decorated with meandering linear patterns and acanthus leaves, all painted in vivid red, yellow, and black.

At Ctesiphon the floor of the state chamber was covered with a silk carpet embroidered with gold threads and sewn with pearls and other precious stones. Other floors suggest Graeco-Roman prototypes in their elaborate mosaic patterning depicting women weaving garlands, dancing, holding bouquets, playing the harp, or reclining on cushions. Roman prisoners captured by Shapur after his defeat of Valerian included architects, engineers, and technicians, who were employed in the building of dams, bridges, and roads. Also characteristic of this period, in stark contrast to the elaborate royal residences, were the simple and restrained forms of Zoroastrian fire temples, often consisting of little more than a vaulted chapel.

Deduced identities

Sassanian art developed in sophistication from Ardashir's time through to that of Khosrow, but it is difficult to establish a chronological sequence other than in coinage. On coins it is possible to identify the different kings through the specific crown that each wears, even when there is no identifying inscription. There was little attempt at realistic portraiture in Sassanian art, unlike that of Rome during the same period.

There are no surviving wall-paintings or textiles, but we know from Arab reports that silk weaving had been introduced into Persia and that there were heavily embroidered royal fabrics, studded with pearls and precious stones. The minor arts are best represented by metalwork, for which we have a large number of metal vessels, plates, and gold and silver vases decorated with ibexes, flora, people, and hunting scenes. These vessels have a variety of forms, but uniformly share a high technical skill in the application of hammering, beating, engraving, casting, and enameling.

Sassanian rock carvings, of which about 30 well-preserved examples are known from Persis (Fars), are in relief, although often deeply undercut to give the impression of being in the round. All appear to have been made for the glorification of a king, again identified from their characteristic headgear. Most contain historical or religious elements, with figures gradated in size according to their importance, and again there is a tendency to emphasize decorative detail. Thus we can discern details such as the long beards of men pulled through a ring or ribbon, or the folds on loose capes worn over a long sleeved shirt, even though the depiction of realistic poses may be absent. Compositions were generally symmetrical and arranged to create a triangular effect.

Above: Crafted at some point between the 5th and 6th centuries, this silver plate shows a Sassanian king hunting. It also proves the point that the royal sport of lion-hunting had survived for more than two millennia. He is depicted firing over his shoulder in the manner of the Parthian shot.

THE RISE OF ISLAM

The Sassanian army had proven effective in ousting the Parthians and had withstood the incursions of Rome and Byzantium; but it became too inflexible to counter the new threat posed by Arab raiders, united under the new religion of Islam.

Above: Sadly destroyed by the earthquake of early 2004, with massive loss of life, the ancient city of Arg-e-Bam dates back to the Sassanian period, including the citadel on its hill, photographed here in 1997. The lower fortification walls and some of the structures in the center are from later periods, between the 16th and 18th centuries.

Ironically, it was the Arabs' equestrian skills that were to overwhelm the highly acclaimed Sassanian cavalry. The Sassanians had tended to dismiss the poorly organized tribal Arabs as an irrelevant military force, but Arab power came to the forefront during the reign of the last Sassanian king, Yazdgird III (r.633–51). He had come to the throne as a boy and was at the mercy of self-serving advisers. Through their ill-conceived plans, Yazdgird let the Sassanian empire decay and fall back into feudalism. With Rome no longer a threat and an uneasy neutrality with Byzantium, they had become complacent.

A new movement was emerging in Mecca among the Arab Quraysh tribe. A boy known as al-Amin (The Faithful) was born in 571. His father died before his birth and at the age of six he lost his mother, his grandfather and a slave woman called Umm Ayman helping to raise him. At the age of 25 he married Khadijah, a well-to-do merchant's widow who had financed a trading expedition to Syria he embarked upon with his uncle.

Unsatisfied with his now-privileged lifestyle, he would go into the desert to think, where he received a series of visions of the Angel Gabriel, whose words formed the basis of Islam and the Koran. Persecuted in Mecca, the Prophet is said to have undertaken a miraculous journey to Jerusalem before going to Medina (his mother's native city), where he preached the Islamic doctrine of a single deity, Allah, and changed his name to Mohammed. Mohammed gradually gained converts to his beliefs, and promoted a non-aggression pact between Muslim Arabs.

The rift between Mecca and Medina came to a head when 300 Muslims from Medina intercepted a caravan from Mecca and defeated a thousand pagan "non-believers." The economic and military struggle was settled with a treaty in 628, and in 630–31 (the Year of Delegations) many leading tribes lent their allegiance to the Prophet.

Mohammed died 632 and was succeeded by the first Caliph, Abu Bakr (Mohammed's father-in-law). Abu Bakr began campaigns against the Sassanians and Byzantium, and was succeeded by Umar (r.634–44, another father-in-law), who introduced an administration and a standing army to the Islamic state.

A lighter touch

In 634 Arab armies under Khalid Ibn al-Walid, who had been a companion of Mohammed, invaded Sassanian areas and were victorious at the Battle of the Chains (Sassanian soldiers were said to be chained together to prevent them fleeing the battlefield). The Muslim Arabs then imposed a tax known as the *jizya* on all non-Muslims. Many wealthy Sassanians avoided this punitive tax by converting to Islam, which required a simple declaration of faith, which also enabled them to benefit from trade opportunities within the Islamic world. Mohammed's ideals were now being disseminated both by militaristic exploits and through trading advantages.

There was a brief rallying of the Sassanians under Rustam of Persia, but these forces were defeated in 636 at the battle of Al-Qadisiyah, despite the fact that Sassanians outnumbered Arabs by six to one. The Arab forces pushed on

to the Sassanian capital at Ctesiphon, and under Umar's leadership seized Syria, Jerusalem, and Damascus by 638 after defeating the Byzantine emperor Heraclius (r.610–41).

The rapid overthrow of the Sassanians by the Arabs was due, in part, to the fact that the Muslim warriors were fighting a *jihad* (holy war) that forbade rape or the killing of women, children, religious leaders, and non-combatants. Often the occupying Arab forces were welcomed as being less oppressive than the Sassanian warlords they were replacing.

Another factor was that the Sassanian heavy cavalry succumbed readily to Arab warriors mounted on fleet ponies. The outcome might have been different had the Sassanians employed light cavalry; however, this had been run down after earlier battles against Rome and Byzantium had been won by the *cataphract*.

In 642 the Sassanians were defeated at Nehavend and the Arabs overran Persia. By 651 Muslim armies had conquered all Sassanian domains, Islam had been adopted as the state religion, and Arabic had replaced Persian as the official language.

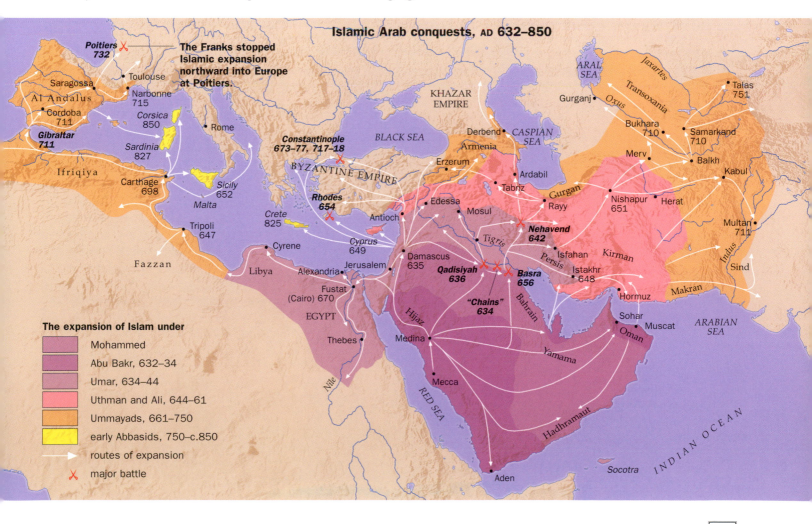

A MESOPOTAMIAN LEGACY

In Western culture, a great deal of emphasis is placed on heritage derived from the ancient Greek and Roman worlds, while comparatively little attention is given to that of the pre-Islamic Near East. Many cultural elements that we take for granted today, including much that descends from Greco-Roman heritage, have an origin within Mesopotamia.

Mesopotamia is sometimes referred to as the "cradle of civilization." This region, between the Euphrates and Tigris, was a difficult but nevertheless extremely fertile area. Between 12,000 and 10,000 years ago, its people began to practice agriculture and animal husbandry. These two innovations enabled them to form settled communities and led to the invention of agricultural tools such as the hoe, plow, and multi-bladed sickle (the world's first composite tool), as well as to the domestication of further animal species. By 5000 BC the wild ass, or onager, had been domesticated as a draft animal, with subsequent improvements in systems of transportation and communication.

So efficient were they that there was a food surplus, which enabled them to develop the earliest known permanent settlements. By 3600 (the earliest date for which we have accurate records) Warka had a population of between 20,000 and 30,000 and occupied an area of about two square miles: double the size of classical Athens. Urban communities, supported by outlying farms, led to new social, political, literary, and philosophical advances.

Among the many innovations from Mesopotamia is the first evidence of counting in about 5000, using marked tokens. As the token system became more complex, it evolved into both applied mathematics and writing, and led to the invention of the alphabet about 2500, later exported to Greece, and from there to Rome. Agricultural development and refined irrigation enabled the expansion of urban communities, the growth of organized states, and the institution of a kingship that exercised distinct political leadership, leading to the establishment of the world's first empire by the Akkadians in 2340.

Influencing future empires

Other Mesopotamian accomplishments include metal-working (7000), smelting (5000), and bronze alloys (3000); the first use of glass (2500) and discovery of glass-blowing; and the invention of the wheeled chariot (3000), the spoked wheel (2000), and the potter's wheel (2000). They built the world's first monumental architecture, which necessitated the invention of the rod, plumb line, and measuring line for surveying, and the development of heavy lifting techniques.

As early as the Bronze Age they had established long-distance trade, which extended from the Baltic to the Mediterranean and led to the further development and dissemination of Mesopotamian technical skills and ideas. The first codes of law were written by them, and they were the first to establish courts that would protect the interests of weaker members of the community. In religion, they influenced the Greeks, Romans, Christians, Egyptians, and Islam, and the colonial expansion of Mesopotamia in the first millennium rivaled that of Greece and Rome.

Although different civilizations flourished and waned throughout the long period of Mesopotamian history, from the first cities until the overthrow of the Sassanians by Muslim Arabs in AD 651, there had been a continuity in cultural identity. There remains a legacy in the Mesopotamian inventions that enabled the growth of both the West and the Orient, in the Greco-Oriental culture that heavily influenced medieval Europe as well as the Arab world, and the incorporation of Mesopotamian beliefs in both Christian and Muslim theology.

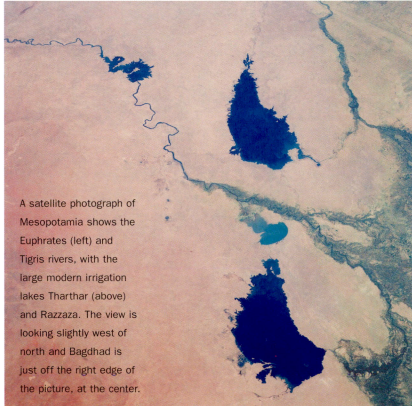

A satellite photograph of Mesopotamia shows the Euphrates (left) and Tigris rivers, with the large modern irrigation lakes Tharthar (above) and Razzaza. The view is looking slightly west of north and Bagdhad is just off the right edge of the picture, at the center.

GLOSSARY

ACHAEMENID: A dynasty of ancient Persia, also known as the Persian empire. It was founded in 539 by Cyrus the Great, son of a minor ruler in Iran named Achaemenes, and is noted for its developments in art and architecture, literature, and for the spread of the Zoroastrian religion. The dynasty ended when its last king, Darius III, was defeated by Alexander the Great in 330.

AHRIMAN: In Zoroastrian religion, the Persian deity of darkness, who is in opposition to his brother Ahura-Mazda. He is a destructive spirit, responsible for introducing death to the world.

AHURA-MAZDA: In Zoroastrian religion, the Persian deity of goodness and knowledge, who is in opposition to his brother Ahriman. He is a creator god, sometimes referred to as Lord Wisdom.

AKKADIAN: Dynasty founded by Sargon of Agade, who combined Sumer and Akkad to form an early empire. It was overthrown by the Gutians. The name also refers to an ancient branch of the Semitic languages.

ALEXANDER III: Also known as Alexander the Great, r.336–23. Macedonian general who defeated the Achaemenid Persian empire. Son of Philip II of Macedon and educated by Aristotle, he was responsible for the spread of Greek civilization in the Mediterranean and western Asia.

AMELU: Babylonian aristocratic group. They were land-owners who enjoyed full citizenship.

AMORITE: Old Testament name for the Elamites, an ancient people living in Mesopotamia, Syria, and Palestine in the third millennium BC.

AN: Sumerian god of the sky; the personification of heaven. In Sumerian myth he is depicted as the father of Enlil.

ANTIOCHUS I: Seleucid ruler 281–61 who succeeded Seleucus I.

ANTIOCHUS III: Seleucid ruler 223–187, sometimes known as Antiochus the Great. He restored and expanded the Seleucid kingdom.

ANTIOCHUS IV: Seleucid ruler 175–64 whose death left the region open to Parthian domination. He attempted to Hellenize the Jews, leading to a revival of Jewish nationalism.

ANU: In the Assyrian-Babylonian pantheon, the equivalent of the Sumerian god An, though he now becomes the god of kingship as well as that of heaven.

ANUNNAKI: The four creator gods in Sumerian mythology.

ARAMAIC: A Semitic language closely related to Hebrew, also known as Aramaean. It was used as a *lingua franca* in the Near East from 700 and is still spoken in some communities.

ARDASHIR: Formerly the governor of Fars (Persis). He overthrew the last Parthian ruler, Artabanus V, to reunite Persia and establish the Sassanian empire (r.AD 224–41). Founded a new capital city at Ctesiphon and introduced Zoroastrianism as the state religion.

ARDU: Babylonian, generally translated as "slaves." These were captives or free citizens who had been sold into slavery through indebtedness. They had the right to own property, but any proceeds from this went to the master to whom they were indebted.

ARGHED: A Sassanian military commander in charge of a company of troops. The highest military title.

ARSACES I: Early Parthian king under the domination of Seleucia, r.247–11. The early Parthian period is sometimes referred to as the Arsacid era. Arsaces was originally a governor under Diodotus, the ruler of the Bactrian Greeks.

ARSACES II: Early Parthian king under the domination of Seleucia, r.211–191.

ARTABANUS IV: The last of the Parthian kings, r. AD 216–44. His overthrow by Ardashir led to the establishment of the Sassanian empire.

ARTAXERXES I: Persian king 465–25. He is mentioned in Ezra 4:7 as appointing Nehemiah as governor in Jerusalem.

ARTAXERXES II: Persian king 404–359, he crushed the rebellion of his brother Cyrus the Younger and defeated the Spartans.

ARTAXERXES III: Persian king c.358–38, son of Artaxerxes II. He killed his brothers and brought Egypt back into the Persian empire, but his reign was a despotic one. He was murdered by his minister Bagoas in 338.

ARTESTDAR: A professional soldier during the Sassanian period.

ASHUR: Principal deity of the Assyrians; Assyria translates as the lands of Ashur. He combined the qualities of Marduk and Enlil, and was a god of war. He is portrayed as a winged disc enclosing a drawn bow. His consort was Ishtar.

ASHURBANIPAL: Assyrian king 669–27, son and successor of Esarhaddon, grandson of Sennacherib. Last of the Assyrian kings, renowned for the library he established at Nineveh, which contained 20,000–30,000 clay tablets recording Assyrian literature. He was trained as a scribe and was fluent in both Sumerian and Akkadian.

ASNAPPEER: Biblical name for Ashurbanipal.

ASSYRIAN: Located in what is now northern Iraq and centered on the city-state of Ashur on the west bank of the Tigris. Established as an empire c.1400 but reached its zenith as the Neo-Assyrian empire in 1100–612.

BABIL: Old name for Babylon. Babylon is a Greek rendition of Babil or Bab-ili, meaning the Gate of the God.

BABYLONIA: Region in southern Mesopotamia, referred to in the early period as Sumer. Babylonia was a political entity 1900–1100, when Sumer and Akkad were united by the Amorites. The name is sometimes used to refer to the Neo-Babylonian, or Chaldean, empire of 612–539.

CATAPHRACT: Heavy armored cavalry used by the Parthians and Sassanians.

CHALDEAN: Also referred to as Neo or New Babylonian, 612–539. In the southern part of Babylon, formed by Semitic peoples originating from Arabia who settled in the region c.800.

CODE OF HAMMURABI: Set of laws compiled by Hammurabi consisting of 282 provisions and setting out judgments and punishments. The code is the origin of "an eye for an eye, a tooth for a tooth".

CRADLE OF CIVILIZATION: Term for Mesopotamia, corresponding roughly to the area of modern Iraq, which contains the earliest evidence for agriculture, urban communities, and for the formation of empires.

CROESUS: King of Lydia 560–46. Expanded his domains to include all the Greek cities on the coast of Asia Minor, but was conquered by Cyrus the Great in 546. Croesus was executed and Lydia became part of the Achaemenid empire, leading to the Persian-Greek wars.

CUNEIFORM: Wedge-shaped form of writing, widespread in Mesopotamia and Persia, made with a stylus in wet clay and characterized by its straight-edged, block-like form.

CYRUS II: Persian king 559–29, follower of Zarathustra and high priest of Marduk. Also known as Cyrus the Great, he was the son of Cambyses of the Achaemenid family, and founder of the Achaemenid Persian empire. He built a new capital city at Pasargadae.

DAGON: Sumerian god of storms. Dagon was the state deity of Ur under the Third Dynasty.

DAHAI: Greek name for the Parni, ancestors of the Parthians.

DARIUS I: Persian king 522–486, also known as Darius the Great. He restored order in Persia and improved commerce and transportation. He divided the region into 20 semi-autonomous provinces, and was the first Persian king to mint his own coins. He built Persepolis as the new Persian capital and invited the Greek philosopher Heraclitus to his court; but he was also responsible for initiating Persia's wars with Greece.

DARIUS III: Persian king 336–30. He underestimated Alexander the Great and brought about the demise of the Achaemenid dynasty in Persia.

DELIAN LEAGUE: Greek alliance of city-states founded in 477 under Athenian leadership following losses incurred in the Greek-Persian wars. Its name is from its treasury on the Greek island of Delos, although it was later moved to Athens by Pericles.

DIADOCHOI: Alexander the Great's five senior commanders, who divided the Macedonian empire on his death. Ptolemy controlled Egypt, Lysimachos Thrace, Cassander Macedon and Greece, Antigonos Asia, and Seleucus led Babylonia.

DRAFSH: A unit of the Parthian army consisting of a thousand men; Sassanian units used the spelling *draff*.

EANNA: Sumerian goddess of love.

EANNATUM: Grandson of Ur-Nina of Lagash, r. 2454–25. Engaged in a war of conquest against Ur, Uruk, and Kish.

EARLY DYNASTIC: Period of the first kingdoms in Sumeria, c.2900–2400, and of

the first urbanized city-states in Mesopotamia.

EDUBBA: A Sumerian master-scribe, often occupying a position as a temple administrator and as a member of the royal household. The edubba was a scholar, responsible for developing new theories in mathematics, medicine, and law.

ELAMITE: Inhabitant of ancient Elam, now southwest Iran.

ENKI: Lord Earth, god of water and god of wisdom. The patron deity of writing during the Sumerian era. He controlled the flow of the Euphrates and Tigris, on which the agricultural pursuits of the Sumerians were dependent.

ENLIL: God of wind and principal deity of the Sumerians. He was the son of An (Sky) and Ki (Earth), and was believed to be in possession of the Tablet of Destiny that controlled the fate of people.

ENSI: Sumerian title for provincial governor appointed by the royal court, but earlier it was sometimes applied to the king, since he was the governor of all Sumer or was seen as governor of deities' wishes on earth.

EPIC OF GILGAMESH: The oldest surviving epic poem, in which Gilgamesh and Enkidu take a fantastic journey in search of the secret of immortality and during which the principles of Sumerian kingship are defined.

ERAN-SPAHBED: Supreme military commander of the Sassanian army. The title refers to his role as king's counsel and has military and political implications.

ERIDU GENESIS: Mythical account of Sumerian origin. Adapan, the first man, is credited with the creation of the world and with giving humans the power of speech.

ESARHADDON: Assyrian king 681–69. The younger son of Sennacherib, Esarhaddon exacted tribute from Israel and Judah in order to secure funds for the rebuilding of Babylon.

FERTILE CRESCENT: An area from the Mediterranean coast of Syria, Lebanon, and Israel to the valley of the Tigris and Euphrates rivers, to the Persian Gulf, in which the early civilizations of the Sumerians, Assyrians, Babylonians, Hittites, and Hebrews were formed.

GILGAMESH: Semi-legendary king of Uruk and hero of an Akkadian epic story.

GOÚSÁUN: Parthian term referring to a poet-musician-minstrel. Goúsáun were attached to the royal court, but also traveled the regions as itinerant poets.

GUDEA: King of Lagash 2141–22 who attempted to restore Sumerian sovereignty but was ultimately under the sway of the Gutians.

GUND: A company of the Parthian army consisting of 10,000 men.

GUTIAN: A warrior tribe from the Zagros mountains on the Iran-Iraq border. They invaded the Akkadian empire, leading to a period of strife and civil war.

HAMMURABI: King of Babylon 1792–50 who reorganized the Babylonian empire and designed its capital city. He was responsible for publishing a code of law that protected citizens' rights.

HITTITE: A major power in Asia Minor (Turkey), 1700–1200. They conquered northern and central Syria and most of Lebanon, but were eventually absorbed into the Assyrian and Babylonian empires.

HOPLITE: Heavily armed Greek foot soldier.

HYRCANIA: Early name for Iran.

IMMORTALS: Elite Sassanian cavalry troop, inspired by the god Ahura-Mazda. They swore never to retreat in battle and formed a royal guard for the king.

INANNA: The Lady of Heaven. Sumerian fertility goddess and patron of store-houses.

ISHHAKU: An early Assyrian ruler; a priest-prince or governor rather than a king, since Assyrian states were vassals or possibly allies of greater nations.

ISHTAR: Principal goddess in Assyro-Babylonian mythology, daughter of the sky god, Anu, and the moon goddess, Sin. She was a mother goddess and goddess of fertility, but is notoriously and inaccurately described by Herodotus as a goddess of sex and sinful behavior.

KAMAMIK-I-ARDASHIR: Literally, the "Records of Ardashir." Semi-mythological tale describing the rise to power of the Sassanian king Ardashir I.

KASSITE: One of the Hurrian tribes from the Zagros mountains. They overran Babylon in 1595 and formed a loose kingdom c.1570 BC–c.1160, for a brief period of which Assyria was a vassal state.

LAND OF OMRI: The Assyrian name for Israel.

LUGAL: Sumerian "great man." Originally the name given to a titled landowner, but as their power increased the title became associated with that of the *ensi* (provincial governor) and eventually with that of the king himself.

MANISHTUSHU: Akkadian king 2269–55, twin or elder brother of Rimush. His succession to the throne was opposed by a coalition of 32 rebel Sumerian kings.

MARDUK: The principal Babylonian deity, said to be the child of the Sumerian god Enlil. He is sometimes called Bel, or Bel-Marduk, and is said to have been a god of magic and incantations. His status derives from his role as patron deity of Babylon, where he is represented as a double-headed sun god.

MARYANNU: The elite of the Mitanni's feudal hierarchy, the maryannu bred horses and sheep on country estates and lived in homes that rivaled palaces.

MASHKIM: An official at the Sumerian court. His role appears to have been similar to that of court clerk.

MEDE: Indo-European groups who inhabited the ancient region of Media in modern Azerbaijan, northwest Iran, and northeast Iraq. Between the seventh and sixth centuries BC they controlled an empire that included most of Iran.

MESANNEPADDA: King of Ur 2560–25 BC, one of the first Sumerian monarchs to claim sovereignty over all of Sumer.

MESOPOTAMIA: An ancient region of southwest Asia, corresponding roughly to the modern area of Iraq, that lay between the Euphrates and the Tigris. It was the location of the early civilizations of Sumer, Akkad, Babylonia, and Assyria.

MITANNI: One of the Hurrian states that had control over a loose empire c.1550–1335 BC, and which probably acted as an intermediary between Mesopotamia and Egypt.

MITHRAISM: Later offshoot of Zoroastrianism, based on the cult of Mithras, the god of light, truth, and honor. It was the state religion of Persia, and was exported to India and China. Mithraism was adopted by the Romans as Sol Invictus (invincible sun), and the Mithraic festival of Natalis Solis Invicti on December 25 was taken over by Christians in the fourth century AD.

MITHRAS: Persian sun god, the son of Anahita, the virgin mother, and a Babylonian fertility goddess. Patron of soldiers and armies and the Judger of Souls who conducted the righteous to the House of Best Purpose. In Roman law he was known as the God of Contracts. Principal deity during the Achaemenid period.

MITHRIDATES I: Parthian ruler 171–38 BC, gaining independence from the Seleucids. Called himself Philhellenos to express friendship for the Greeks.

MURSILIS: Hittite king 1620–590 BC who expanded the Hittite empire in 1595. He defeated Babylonia and Syria, but was unable to consolidate the empire.

MUSHLALU: A semi-circular watchtower, part of Assyrian fortifications.

MUSKINU: The modern rendition of this term is "beggars," but during the Babylonian period it referred to citizens who had no claims to land ownership.

NABOPOLASSAR: Babylonian king 630–05 BC. Allied with the Medes to defeat Assyria and its Egyptian allies and declared Babylon independent. Succeeded by Nebuchadnezzar II.

NABU: The Assyrian god of writing and son of Marduk. He has a temple erected in his honor at Nimrud.

NAMMU: Sumerian goddess who is said to have given birth to the other deities.

NANNA: Sumerian moon god, and the son of Enlil and his wife Ninlil. He was in control of the months and seasons.

NARAM-SIN: Akkadian king 2254–17 BC, son of Manishtushu and grandson of Sargon, who led campaigns to maintain the empire.

NARD: Persian game similar to modern backgammon. It is the oldest recorded game in history.

NEBUCHADNEZZAR II: Chaldean king 605–562 BC who defeated Assyria and Egypt. Son of Nabopolassar, he was a high priest of Marduk and Nabu, and rebuilt Babylon in their honor.

NEO-BABYLONIAN: The Chaldean period in Mesopotamia preceding the Hittite invasions in 1595.

NINTUR: Sumerian deity. The Lady of the Stony Ground and mother of wildlife.

NINURTA: Sumerian war god who protected agriculture and had mastery over storms. Ninurta was the patron deity of the Assyrian capital at Nimrud.

PARNI: Indo-Iranian nomadic tribesmen who moved from central Asia into Parthia during the early Seleucid period. Ancestors of the Parthians.

PARTHIAN: Iranian groups of Scythian origin. They built an empire that lasted from 247 BC until AD 224, which at the height of its power extended from the Euphrates to the Indus. They fought several successful campaigns against the Romans.

PATHAVA: Achaemenid spelling for Parthia, originally part of the Persian empire.

PERSIA: Old name for Iran, but also refers to the empire established by the Achaemenid dynasty that included parts of Greece and extended into India. The empire was destroyed by Alexander the Great in 330.

PERSIS: Old name for Persia.

PHILIP II: King of Macedon 359–36 BC and father of Alexander the Great. He is believed to have been assassinated by his son.

PHRAATES II: He succeeded his father Mithridates to the Parthian throne, r.138–27 BC; some claim he was the true founder of the Parthian empire.

PTOLEMY I: One of the Diadochoi, Ptolemy established a dynasty that ruled Egypt from 323 to 30 BC. He was king 305–284, during which he created a library at Alexandria and Egypt grew to dominate eastern Mediterranean trade.

RIMUSH: Akkadian king 2278–70, successor to and son of Sargon, who struggled to suppress a rebellion of city-states led by Lagash and Ur.

ROYAL TOMBS: The series of royal burials discovered at Ur in 1927 by Leonard Woolley, which revealed hitherto unknown information about Sumerian social status, manufacture, and arts.

SARDANAPALUS: Greek name for Ashurbanipal.

SARGON: Akkadian king 2335–279 BC who overthrew Ur and created the combined state of Sumer and Akkad; recorded as the world's first empire builder. He conquered southern Mesopotamia, as well as parts of Anatolia, Syria, and Iran.

SARGON II: Assyrian king 722–05 BC, seizing power from Shalmaneser V. He was responsible for the relocation of the Hebrews after his conquest of Israel, and built a new Assyrian capital, Dur-Sharrukin (Sargon's Fortress).

SASSAN: Zoroastrian priest who preached against Parthian rule and restored the old Achaemenid ideals during the late Parthian period and was instrumental in the establishment of the Sassanian throne.

SASSANIAN: A nationalistic second Persian empire, AD 224–651, marked by a return to Zoroastrian beliefs and practices.

SATRAP: Persian name for the governor of a province; a satrapy was a self-governing province of Mesopotamia.

GLOSSARY

SCYTHIAN: Distant relatives of the Parthians. They were responsible for many of the depredations carried out along the Silk Road during the first century BC.

SEALAND: Tribal groups leade by feudal warlords who occupied southern Mesopotamia in the 16th century BC.

SELEUCID: Dynasty founded by Seleucus, who established a capital at Seleucia that controlled the Greek-Persian trade.

SELEUCUS I: Seleucid ruler 312–281 who inherited part of Alexander the Great's empire. He added Asia Minor to his kingdom with the death of rival Diadochoi Lysimachos, but was assassinated by Ptolemy.

SENNACHERIB: Assyrian king 704–681 BC who destroyed Babylon in 689. Son of Sargon, he was killed by a court assassin, leading to a dynastic revolt.

SHALMANESER I: Assyrian king 1274–45 BC. He conquered the Mitanni and extended the empire into western Mesopotamia and northern Syria. Founded the city of Nimrud, recorded in the Old Testament under the name of Calah.

SHAMASH: Sun god of the Sumerians during the revival period following the demise of the Akkadian empire. Later adopted as the Parthian sun god.

SHAPUR I: Sassanian king AD 240–72 who defeated the Roman emperor Valerian who attempted to half the empire's expansion at Edessa. Son of Ardashir, he instituted extensive economic, building, and educational programs.

SHATRANG: Also called chatrang. Persian game similar to modern chess.

SIN: The Assyrian moon god.

SPADPAT: Supreme commander of the Parthian army, generally chosen from a noble family and trained in military strategy.

SPAH: The Sassanian standing army.

SPAHBED: Military commander of one of the four regions during the late Sassanian period.

SUMERIAN: Indigenous non-Semitic peoples of ancient Sumer. The word is also used in reference to their language, the oldest known in written form.

TIGLATH-PILESER III: Assyrian king 745–27 BC, he made fundamental changes to the Assyrian empire and organized it into provinces that paid tribute to the state. He is mentioned in the Bible under the name of Pul.

TOWER OF BABEL: The Etemenanki Ziggurat at Babylon that was dedicated to the god Marduk, but which became enshrined in myth as the basis for the Tower of Babel.

UR-NAMMU: Sumerian king 2113–95 BC, founder of the Third Dynasty of Ur and brother of Utuhegal. His code of law is the first known to be committed to writing.

UTU: The Sumerian sun god. He governed the days and was the dispenser of justice.

UTUHEGAL: Sumerian king of Uruk 2133–13 BC, who seized power to enable him to dominate Sumer. He initiated a long campaign against the Gutians.

XERXES I: Persian king 486–65 BC. Defeated a Spartan army at Thermopylae and invaded Athens but was murdered in a palace intrigue.

YAZDGIRD III: Last of the Sassanian kings. During his reign, AD 633–51, the Sassanian empire fell into decay and was overthrown by Arabs united under Islam.

ZARATHUSTRA: Persian prophet, known to the Greeks as Zoroaster. The founder of the Zoroastrian religion.

ZIGGURAT: A stepped pyramid, usually constructed as the principal building in a Mesopotamian city and dedicated to its patron deity.

ZIUSUDRA: In Sumerian myth, a pious man who built a boat to save the animals from a great flood and was granted immortality as a reward. He is equivalent to, but predates, Noah in Christian theology.

ZOROASTER: Greek spelling of Zarathustra, who established Zoroastrianism, which become the state religion of the Persian empire.

Further reading

Averbeck, Richard E., Mark W. Chavalas, David B. Weisberg & Penelope B. Hunter-Stiebel, *Life and Culture in the Ancient Near East* (CDL Press 2003);

Caubet, Annie & Patrick Pouyssegur, *The Ancient Near East* (Éditions Pierre Terrail 1998);

Dalley, Stephanie & C.J. Fordyce, *Myths from Mesopotamia: Creation, The Flood, Gilgamesh, and Others* (Oxford University Press 1998);

Finegan, Jack, *Archaeological History of the Ancient Middle East* (Dorset Press 1986);

Goldschmidt, Arthur Jr., *A Concise History of the Middle East* (7th edition, Westview Press 2001);

Kramer, Samuel Noah, *Cradle of Civilization* (Little Brown & Co. 1969);

Kramer, Samuel Noah, *The Sumerians: Their History, Culture, and Character* (University of Chicago Press 1963);

Moberly, F.J., *Military Operations in Mesopotamia* (Imperial War Museum 1997);

Postgate, Nicholas & J.N. Postgate, *Early Mesopotamia: Society and Economy at the Dawn of History* (Routledge 1994);

Roaf, Michael, *The Cultural Atlas of Mesopotamia and the Ancient Near East* (Checkmark Books 1990);

Roux, Georges, *Ancient Iraq* (Penguin USA 1993);

Saggs, H.W.F., *Babylonians* (British Museum Press 1995);

Saggs, H.W.F., *Everyday Life in Babylonia and Assyria* (Assyrian International 1965);

Saggs, H.W.F., *The Might That Was Assyria* (Sidgwick & Jackson 1984);

Sicker, Martin, *The Pre-Islamic Middle East* (Praeger Publishers 2000);

Snell, Daniel C., *Life in the Ancient Near East: 3100–332 BCE* (Yale University Press 1998);

Woolley, Sir Leonard, *Ur of the Chaldees* (Herbert Press 1982).

INDEX